The World of International Financial Centres

The World of International Financial Centres

Opportunities, Concerns, and Regulations

Peter Yeoh

Wolters Kluwer

Published by:
Kluwer Law International B.V.
PO Box 316
2400 AH Alphen aan den Rijn
The Netherlands
E-mail: international-sales@wolterskluwer.com
Website: lrus.wolterskluwer.com

Sold and distributed by:
Wolters Kluwer Legal & Regulatory U.S.
7201 McKinney Circle
Frederick, MD 21704
United States of America
E-mail: customer.service@wolterskluwer.com

ISBN 978-94-035-3554-8

e-Book: ISBN 978-94-035-3555-5
web-PDF: ISBN 978-94-035-3560-9

About the Author

Peter Yeoh is a Research Fellow at the School of Law, Social Sciences and Communications at the University of Wolverhampton. He has also previously served at senior level in the manufacturing and financial services sectors. He has degrees in economics, management and law, master's degrees in the same disciplines and a doctorate in corporate and financial services law. Yeoh is a reviewer in several business and financial services law journals. He has also published more than forty papers in various corporate and financial services peer-review law journals, several book chapters, and two books related to crypto assets and digital financial services or financial technology entities, otherwise known as Fintechs.

Table of Contents

Acknowledgements

I truly enjoyed writing this book. I hope readers would get as much out of reading it, as I did, writing it. I hope too to give adequate credit to those researchers before me, and to also highlight enough the key controversies of particular corporate governance (CG) themes that they deserve.

I am also particularly grateful to the exceptional behind-the-scenes contributions and guidance from Lisa Zoltowska, the Editor cum Taxation Section Head of Business Law Review (BLR). There are of course various others too who gave the needed support to ensure the timely completion of the book.

I would also like to thank my immediate family members for their patience and understanding as I isolated myself from the usual family outings and other regular family engagements. They gave emotional support when needed and positive encouragement when things stood in my way.

Peter Yeoh
April 2021

Preface

New era International Financial Centres (IFCs) have been around since the 1980s. Significant portions of all international banking assets and liabilities are said to be transmitted via IFCs or offshore financial centres (OFCs), while significant amounts of multinational corporations' foreign direct investments (FDIs) are suspected to have been routed through these tax havens as they are sometimes known. The latter does not necessarily imply that tax avoidance and tax evasion have occurred. Still, the International Consortium of Investigative Journalists (ICIJ) released its preliminary findings in May 2016 suggesting how the world's rich and powerful used the Panama offshore financial centre and other far-flung jurisdictions to hide assets and avoid regulatory oversight by setting up anonymous shell companies. The more than one million leaked files examined by the ICIJ further suggests how some senior politicians and some financial elites of the world employ offshore companies to facilitate drug trafficking, financial fraud, arms deal, and tax evasion.

More revelations came from revelations at Appleby, a big offshore global law firm serving big clients like commodities giant Glencore, oil major Shell, and Goldman Sachs. These revelations a sequel to the Panama Papers (PP) came to be known as the Paradise Papers (PRP), also released by the ICIJ on 5 November 2017. The PRP disclosed in particular the secret practices of the UK's tax haven and the suspected criminality of Glencore's Congo deals. This exerted tremendous pressure on the EU to act on its general failures to respond effectively on corporate secrecy, corruption and money laundering revealed in the PP, some eighteen months earlier. Global Witness called upon the EU to shine the light on anonymous companies and trusts that facilitated corruption, money laundering, tax evasion, terrorism, and human trafficking. This was something stressed upon much earlier by an eminent US judge when he argued that sunlight was the best disinfectant for business wrongdoers hiding behind walls of secrecies.

IFCs have in the modern era been a subject of general controversies though not all are of the same stripes. There are those which are run with the intention of raising their global profiles for a bigger stake of global financial capitalism. Here, financial services accounted for increasing share of their national incomes relative to other economic sectors. More and more modern economies are pursuing these. Others are said to camouflage under this banner, while promoting enabling facilities and mechanisms for tax avoidance, which are not legally wrong, and tax evasion which are legally wrong.

The PP and PRP revelations are not the first time and unlikely to be the last time that illicit activities are uncovered in IFCs. They, or at least some, have been flagged up in the past for allowing illegal financial activities to take place in their jurisdictions without proper oversight. The Organisation for Economic Co-operation and Development (OECD), the global forum for thirty-five countries cooperating for the promotion of policies to improve economic and social well-being of people around the world, has previously recognized various issues posed by IFCs, and in particular tax havens.

Investopedia defines tax havens as countries offering foreign individuals and businesses a minimal tax liability in a politically and economically stable environment, with little or no financial information shared with foreign tax authorities. This had led various jurisdictions to engage in tax competition using unfair tax incentives, including little cooperation in international efforts to curb tax avoidance. This, in general, raises general fears of race to the bottom thereby depriving some countries of much capital needed to combat poverty and inequality. Tax havens have also been increasingly tagged as secrecy jurisdictions where transactions are undertaken in opaque manners. Responding to global criticisms, and in particular from global civil society organizations (CSOs), many tax havens perceived as uncooperative or lacking in transparency have undertaken to increase financial transparency.

The OECD in 2000 had used its own criteria to categorize a number of jurisdictions as tax havens, with negative connotations for those not making formal commitments to implement the OECD's standards of transparency and exchange of information. Those jurisdictions without formal OECD commitments are tagged as uncooperative tax havens. In May 2009, the OECD extinguished the list of uncooperative tax havens. The OECD categorization for tax havens have excluded low-tax jurisdictions some of which are perceived as tax havens and this courted global controversies.

As alluded to earlier, the OECD blacklisted thirty-five countries from the forty-seven jurisdictions it examined, but all these have been removed since 2009 as they progressively undertake to share information. In reality though, the initiatives to rein in on tax havens were not entirely successful. The spotlight on tax havens intensified subsequent to the 2007-2008 global financial crisis (GFC). This led to various high-profile problems of financial services operations in various tax havens. In general, no countries want to be blacklisted as uncooperative tax havens. This is because this carries legal implications, as generally, disciplinary laws and sanctions are imposed for those tagged as such.

The OECD most recently launched the Base Erosion and Profit Shifting (BEPS) initiative. This, among other things, incorporated guidance from the Global Forum on Transparency and Exchange of Information for Tax Purposes (GFTEITP). Countries were rated on the basis of this as compliant, largely compliant, partially compliant, or non-compliant. Of the 105 reviews undertaken in 2014, forty-two were rated as non-compliant. The 2016 OECD review suggests general improvements. This listing aside, increasing criticisms have been made that some notable tax havens and those with large aspects of tax haven practices have been excluded. So, the controversies over tax havens continue and are now receiving even greater global attention as a consequence of the revelations by the PP and PRP mentioned earlier.

This book is written to provide a clearer picture of how IFCs or OFCs grew into prominence and global controversies, as well as the likely direction they would take in the future. I hope big companies, fast-growing small companies, individuals with significant assets to spare, policymakers, and financial professionals could find something of relevance to their interests in various portions of this book.

CHAPTER 1
Overview

§1.01 INTRODUCTION

For many years, there were occasional snippets of revelations of corporate secrecies. On 9 May 2016, the world woke up to the stunning reality of analysed leaked documents, known as the Panama Papers (PP). The PP comprised over 11.5 million leaked files exposing a cast of senior politicians, financial elites, and business corporations using offshore companies to facilitate drug trafficking, financial fraud, tax evasion, arms deals, and bribery. The International Consortium of Investigative Journalists (ICIJ) contributed the analysed documents. The revelation though stunning is not altogether unsurprising given that earlier in 2013 the ICIJ had disclosed some 100,000 offshore entities in its offshore leaked investigations.[1]

The ICIJ searchable database unveiled the secrecy of some 214,000 offshore entities in twenty-one jurisdictions extending from Nevada to Hong Kong and the British Virgin Islands (BVI). The ICIJ claims this to be largest ever disclosure of public information about offshore companies and the actors behind them, in other words the identifications of the beneficial owners behind the opaque structures. The world was probably stunned by the sheer scale and extensiveness of the PP more than the general prevailing perceptions that most offshore financial centres (OFCs) operate as tax or secrecy havens to attract business in the highly competitive global financial services landscape.

OFCs, IFCs, or tax havens in the modern era grew from the 1980s as the world became increasingly globalized. Almost every jurisdiction has some tax havens or OFC features, but a small number could be just tax havens, or just OFCs. Jurisdictions are used generally in this book to refer to any territory with its own legal system, regardless of whether it is an independent or sovereign state. They could be a part of a federal or

1. M.W. Guevara. 2016. 'ICIJ releases database revealing thousands of offshore companies', *ICIJ 9/5/16*.

confederal state like Dubai; a dependent, associated or overseas territory like the Cayman Island and the Isle of Man; or an internal zone to which a special legal regime is been applied like Hong Kong or Labuan.[2] Many OFC centres have been blamed for serving as receptacles for surplus cash, surplus capital, or unexplained wealth of multinationals, financial elites, celebrities, senior political leaders, and others seeking to avoid the attention of the world at large; but in particular the watchful eyes of financial or tax regulators. This book, however, argues that the OFCs could not be entirely blamed for concealments of all these surpluses, as a combination of factors; like multinationals' (MNCs') business tax strategies, competing national tax and investment policies, globalization, financialization, and unintentional flaws of Western capitalism sewn together gave rise to these surpluses that are now in some ways tainted with negativity.

§1.02 GLOBALIZATION AND FINANCIALIZATION

Chapter 2, following this chapter, will address global finance and the financialization process and their significance in global economy. All countries are integrated in the world economy in varying degrees. Globalization in its modern phase was promoted by the US, UK, and other advanced Western economies. Inspired by the arguments of Adam Smith, these countries adhered to the idea that countries would benefit economically when goods and services flow freely across the world, with each specializing in economic activities where they enjoy comparative advantage. Globalization involves international integration brought about by the interchange of world views, ideas, products and other aspects of national cultures. From the business standpoint, globalization, in general, is understood to be the process by which businesses start operating on an international scale using international business strategies.

This is to differentiate it from the globalization of law, culture, and politics. Globalization where this book is concerned is viewed from the international finance perspective. This, to be more precise, concerns the notion of financialization. This has to do with the transformation of economies worldwide over the last three decades, with the retreat of governments and the expansion of markets. With the growth of economic transactions globally, domestic and international financial transactions have also expanded by leaps and bounds. The altering global economic landscape is marked by the rise of neoliberalism, globalization, and financialization. The financialization phenomenon is looked upon differently, but broadly it could be taken to mean the increasing role of financial motives, financial markets, financial actors, and financial institutions in the running of domestic and international economies.[3]

2. N. Fowler. 2019. 'The corporate tax haven index: Solving the world's broken tax system in out monthly podcast', the Taxcast, *Tax Justice Network (TJN) 26/6/19*; L. Booijink & F. Weyzig. 2016. 'Identifying tax havens and offshore financial centres', *Tax Justice Network (TJN)*.
3. G.A. Epstein. 2005. *Financialization and the world economy*, Cheltenham: Edward Elgar.

§1.03 TAX HAVENS

Discussions in Chapter 2 provide the setting for in-depth discussions on the growing significance of international financial centres (IFCs), OFCs, or tax havens in Chapter 3. For the purpose of this book, on most occasions, the three terms would be employed interchangeably from here onwards. OFCs came about in the 1980s and are deemed as small low-tax jurisdictions specializing in the delivery of corporate and commercial services to non-resident offshore companies and for the investment of offshore funds.[4] They became attractive to even small economies as they could be launched with relatively low start-up costs. OFCs attracted the attention of global development agencies because they have captured a significant proportion of global financial flows. There are now growing concerns over potential risks posed by OFCs to the international financial systems, especially in the light of these being the preferred destinations of criminals for storage of their ill-gotten crypto assets, like Bitcoin.

OFCs across the world, are in reality, competing for greater chunks of the fast-growing global financial services market. They compete by differentiating in terms of lower tax, financial efficiencies, macroeconomic stability, and so on. Since the 2007 Global Financial Crisis (GFC) originated from the US and radiated mostly across the UK, before impacting other jurisdictions, the causes and consequences of the GFC are commonly discussed by focusing on the 'New York-London axis'. The implication of this perspective is that the debate on global financial reform has to take seriously the reality of global financial centres, and in particular, the New York-London axis. This has to change if global finance needs to change.[5] The severe impact of the crisis on the public finances of the significantly impacted economies led to accelerated efforts to increase revenue and the strengthening of the global financial systems. Tax havens became the low-hanging fruit for global initiatives that target them and the tax and regulatory environments from which OFCs operate. This is understandable given the magnitude and scale of illicit financial flows (IFFs) as would be analysed in Chapter 4.

§1.04 GLOBAL FINANCIAL FLOWS AND IFFS

Despite the severe impacts of the GFC particularly on advanced economies like the US and the EU, their financial markets continue to provide some three-quarters of global financial services. This is achieved, however, with substantially lower overall levels of market activities in other economic segments.[6] Against this, emerging financial markets, particularly in Asia, grew strongly accelerating the catching-up process between developed and developing economies. Some research insights nevertheless suggest that the role of OFCs in the discredited international financial systems tends to be exaggerated or misconstrued. This led G20 leaders agreeing to take actions only

4. A. Zorome. 2007. 'Concept of offshore financial centres: In search for an operational definition', *IMF Working Paper WP/07/087.*
5. D. Wojcik. 2012. 'The dark side of NY-LON: Financial centres and the global financial crisis', *Urban Studies*, Vol. 50(13): 2736-2752.
6. S. Kern. 2010. 'Global financial centres after the crisis', *Deutsche Bank Research Paper 2/8/16.*

against non-cooperative OFCs and in particular tax havens. Controversially, this left out some notable OFCs in developed economies with reputations as tax or secrecy haves.[7]

Revamping the global financial system included global efforts to look for financial activities that undermine the system, meaning illicit capital flows. Such efforts are being accelerated in response to revelations of huge IFFs that could have strengthened the public finances of all economies, but in particular those from emerging economies (EMEs).[8] Asia accounting for 61.2% of cumulative outflows represented the main driver of such flows from developing economies. This is mainly accounted for by five Asian economies. This was followed by those in the Western hemisphere, the Middle East, North Africa and parts of Eastern and Central Europe. IFFs in general refer to money illegally earned, transferred, or employed that crosses borders.[9] IFFs are said to lessen resources for development, but are also symptomatic of other issues that work against poverty reduction and shared prosperity, including vested interests and weak transparency and accountability. IFFs are also said to be facilitated by the use of legal structures, such as corporate veils, to hide stolen assets.[10] Corruption alone is estimated at some USD 40 billion annually. All these issues are therefore discussed in Chapter 4 providing the contextual background for the stunning revelations of the scale of the problem as analysed in Chapter 5.

§1.05 PANAMA AND PARADISE PAPERS

Continuing global efforts to curb IFFs witnessed further challenges, when the PP were released giving confirmation that current efforts do not appear to be working that well. The May 2016 exposures of senior politicians and financial elites hiding their wealth in secretive OFCs, like the Panama refocused attention on the contributions of tax havens to IFFs. The implications of history's largest leak had only commenced to unfold. The leak comprised 2.6 terabytes of data from Panamanian law firm Mossack Fonseca linking one hundred and forty world leaders from more than fifty countries to secret offshore accounts in twenty-one different OFCs. Offshore accounts have long courted controversies. The usual modus operandi is the employment of legal shell companies that are known to be linked to illegal activities linked to the underground economy.

At least three major implications arise from this phenomenal leak, said to be larger than that of the 2010 WikiLeaks and the 2013 Snowden's NSA leak combined.[11] These have to do with the lost credibility of some political leaders across the world, the evidence that corruption is more widespread than believed, and mounting public

7. G. Loomer & G. Maffini. 2009. 'Tax havens and the financial crisis', *Eureka April 2009*.
8. D. Kar & S. Freitas. 2012. *Illicit financial flows from developing countries: 2001-2010*, Washington DC: Global Financial Integrity.
9. E.V.D.D. De Willebois. 2016. 'Illicit financial flows (IFFs)', *World Bank Paper 14/4/16*.
10. E.V.D.D. De Willebois, E.M. Halter, R.A. Harrison, J.W. Park & J.C. Sharman. 2011. *The puppet masters: How the corrupt use legal structures to hide stolen assets and what to do about it*, Washington DC: International Bank for Reconstruction and Development (IBRD).
11. B. Golodryga. 2016. '3 major implications of the Panama Papers leak', *The Huffington Post 21/4/16*.

pressures to curb these practices via serious crackdowns on evasions, enhanced international cooperation, and global tax reforms.[12] The PP revelations in particular raised important questions about the role of tax havens.[13] The unintended consequences are equally telling, as the PP revelations eroded further the credibility and reputations of the political establishments, especially with regard to their ability to govern from the centre. This is already being tested in the US, UK, Germany, and large tracts of Europe.[14] These and other matters taken up together in Chapter 5 accelerated calls for global tax reforms.

§1.06 GLOBAL TAX REFORMS

Topping the lists of financial responses to the PP leaks are the enhanced pressures for global tax reforms. This matter is discussed in Chapter 6. The 2013 ICJN revelation alluded to initiatives implemented much earlier. These included regulatory reforms initiated, since the 2001 Enron saga and in the immediate aftermaths of the 2007-2008 GFC. These have been continuing with the G20 economies and the Organization for Economic Co-operation and Development (OECD) taking the lead, and with the US and UK taking isolated bigger efforts of their own. In an immediate response, the US called for international tax reforms.[15] The US was concerned over the scale of tax avoidance involving Fortune 500 companies to the magnitude of trillion dollars worldwide. This is because such perfectly legal structures as employed in these suspected tax haven jurisdictions use tax avoidance practices to deprive governments of lost revenue that has to be made up somewhere.

The US led the way with its Justice Department confirming its examination of possible US links to leaked documents from the PP. But, left unsaid is the use of ultra-light regulatory enclaves found in parts of the country. Indeed, the PP revelations accelerated the global tax reform agenda triggered at the G8 meeting at Lough Erne in 2013. Here, represented leaders reached consensus to work towards a common framework for multinationals to report to tax authorities where they achieve their profits and pay their taxes across the world. This involved country-by-country (CbC) reporting by multinationals, rather than simply lumping these in global or regional narratives. For various reasons, countries differ in their stands over this kind of reporting. The PP and PRP have exerted pressures globally for the universal adoption of this approach.[16] The current US Biden administration has taken the lead on this matter with the G7 economies said to be reaching consensus on this and other matters.

12. *Supra* note [11]. Golodryga. 2016.
13. P. Huttle & A. Leandro. 2016. 'The implications of the Panama Papers: What's at stake: The Panama Papers leaked last week raised important questions about the role of tax havens. We explain the mechanics of tax evasion and review the most important lessons to take away from the leaks', *Bruegel 18/4/16*.
14. M.A. Erian. 2016. 'Unintended consequences of the Panama Papers', *Bloomberg View 11/4/16*.
15. R. Neate & D. Smith. 2016. 'Obama calls for international tax reform amid Panama Papers revelations: Unscripted remarks come as Justice Department confirms it is examining US links to leaked documents from Panama-based tax firm Mossack Fonseca', *The Guardian 5/4/16*.
16. L. Seabrooke & D. Wigan. 2016. 'The Panama Papers and corporate tax reform: How leaks created a window of opportunity', *Foreign Affairs 6/5/16*.

This apparent global-like solution for a more equitable and fairer way for dealing with taxation dilemma that the world has been trying for years to resolve provides a good setting for ending this book.

§1.07 CONCLUDING REMARKS

This book concludes in Chapter 7. Here, the various themes teased out in the text are sewn together to draw integrated insights on the emergence of tax havens in the modern era, why they persist despite gradual tightening of the rules regarding tax and financial transparencies led by the OECD and others, and why the PP could accelerate global tax reforms in a world increasingly troubled by persistent IFFs. The momentum generated by the PP revelations for global tax reforms, as well as reforms of financial reporting systems in OFCs, was further reinforced by revelations in the Paradise Papers (PRP), with more tantalizing revelations of opaque investments of more MNCs, celebrities, and other dignitaries. These revelations prove how collaborations between journalists in highly digitalized network communities can contribute to hitherto difficult to access global financial information.[17]

17. P. Berglez & A. Gearning. 2018. 'The Panama and Paradise Papers: The rise of a global fourth estate', *International Journal of Communications*, Vol. 12(2018): 4573-4592.

CHAPTER 2
Globalization and Financialization

§2.01 INTRODUCTION

This chapter introduces the concept and meaning of financialization, one of the main contributing factors to the rise and accelerated growths of OFCs and, in particular, tax haven. The financialization process is also explained to provide better understanding of how it played its role in nurturing the wellbeing of tax haven. This chapter would also show how and why good lessons could be drawn as financialization evolved across the world, from emerging to advanced economies. The two-way interactions between national economic policies and financialization are also brought up in the chapter to show their mutual connecting impacts. The main economic impacts of financialization would also be discussed using country case analysis. Attention is also given in this chapter to the more modern forms of financialization products and services emerging from the digital era, like crypto assets that are increasingly popular in tax havens because of their treasured confidentiality characteristics.

§2.02 MEANING OF FINANCIALIZATION

There appears to be no common understanding of financialization and even less about its significance and implications to national economies and the world economy. There are those using the term to imply the ascendancy of shareholder value as a form of corporate governance (CG), and by extension, suggesting the growing dominance of capital market financial systems over bank-based financial systems; those suggesting the increasing power of political and financial elites; those suggesting the explosive growth of financial trading through many new financial or exotic instruments; or by others referring to it as a pattern of accumulation in which profit-making occurs increasingly through financial channels, rather than through trade and commodity production.[18]

A broader but relative widely followed definition of financialization suggests that it means the expanding role of financial motives, financial markets, financial actors and financial institutions in the operation of the domestic and international economies.[19] This perspective reflects the multifaceted nature of the financialization process. It unveils the interconnectedness of the global political economy and suggests the unprecedented influence that financial intermediaries and technologies exert over people's daily lives. It involves changes within the financial sector itself, within productive industry, and within the average household. With the US currency as the anchor global currency and with financialization's global integrated feature, this means that developments in the US could impact much of the rest of the world as clearly shown by the 2008 GFC.

§2.03 FINANCIALIZATION PROCESS

Financialization is also the process whereby financial markets, financial institutions, and financial elites exert influence over economic policy and economic outcomes.[20] It transforms the operation of economic systems at the micro- and macro-dimensions with shrinking regulations of its rules. Deregulations, while accelerating growth of financial services, brought with them enhanced risks and surge of highly speculative financial transactions. Hence, financialization as a process that transforms the fundamental aspects of capitalist micro- and macro-dynamics is currently generally the mainstream view,[21] especially following a class-based analysis[22] of a new phase of capitalist accumulation associated with centralization and concentration of capital leading to the power rise of cohorts of finance capitalists and financial markets exerting overwhelming influence over outcomes and policies in the neoliberal era. Political economy financialization research analysed the macroeconomic impact of financialization on real capital accumulation, rising inequity, macro instability, economic crisis, financial squeeze of industrial capital, finance-led accumulation regime;[23] and the micro-level transformations in CG and firm behaviour, particularly on how the shareholder value movement has impacted the way businesses are managed and led.[24]

18. G. Krippner. 2005. 'The financialization of the American economy', *Socio-Economic Review*, Vol. 3(2):173-208.
19. G. Epstein. 2005. *Financialization and the world economy.* Cheltenham: Edward Elgar.
20. T.I. Palley. 2007. 'Financialization: What it is and why it matters', *The Levy Economics Institute Working Paper No. 525 December 2007.*
21. J.P. Goldstein. 2009. 'The political economy of financialization', *Review of Radical Political Economics*, Vol. 41(4):453-457.
22. R. Hilferding. 1981. *Finance capital.* London: Routledge.
23. R.W. Parentau. 2005. 'The late 1990s' US bubble: Financialization in the extreme' in G. Epstein (ed.), *Financialization and the world economy,* Cheltenham: Edward Elgar.
24. *Supra* note [21]. Goldstein. 2009.

§2.04 FINANCIALIZATION EVOLUTION

The financial sector, given the economic stance especially in the US, UK, and Europe, grew steadily since the 1970s and into the 2020s. This has set a new direction, especially in the US and UK from making things to making money from money.[25] With this, inevitably financial services swelled as the rest of the economy weakens. This helped to divert income from labour to capital as substantiated by the rise in profits in the capital markets from less than 10% in 1982 to 40% of all corporate profits by 2003.[26]

Indeed, since the 1980s, financial services stimulated by short-term financial returns overwhelmed long-term goals like technology and product development investments leading to the dwindling of manufacturing in both the US and the UK. Manufacturing became dominant in China, India, and much of the Asian region, where this still holds sway. Indeed, this became the 2016 Presidential campaign fodder where it has been suggested that these and other economies 'stole' US jobs, or hollowed jobs in the US working middle-class heartland. This suggestion attracted widespread support from the working middle class even though evidence suggests more loss of jobs from automation and robotics and the financialization of the US economy where investments and jobs in the financial sector grew.[27]

Financialization therefore enables financial services to upstage the real sector, transfers income from the real sector to the financial services sector, but has the unintended consequence of income inequality because of greater returns to financial elites but wage stagnation for the working middle class.[28] Research, for instance, suggests that since the 1980s, compensations in financial services now returned 70% more on average.[29] Also, of the 400 Americans on Forbes's first rich people list in 1982, only just 4.4% derived their wealth from finance. This increased to 20% by 2011.[30] Forbes's 2014 list of the 400 richest Americans showed some 26% deriving their wealth from investing, hedge funds, and private equity.[31]

§2.05 FINANCIALIZATION AND NATIONAL ECONOMIC POLICIES

Financialization did not just happen. Political decisions and non-decisions facilitated the process of financialization to take off and gather momentum.[32] Though deregulation responded in part to regulatory arbitrage and loopholes that some corporations

25. M. Collins. 2015. 'Wall Street and the financialization of the economy', *Forbes 4/2/15.*
26. *Supra* note [25]. Collins. 2015.
27. B. Heater. 2017. 'Technology is killing jobs, and only technology can save them', *Tech Crunch 27/3/17.*
28. B. Bartlett. 2013. 'Financialization as a cause of economic malaise', *The New York Times 11/6/13.*
29. *Supra* note [28]. Bartlett. 2013.
30. S.N. Kaplan & J.D. Rauh. 2013. 'Family, education and sources of wealth among the richest Americans, 1982-2012', *American Economic Review,* Vol. 103(3): 158-162.
31. B. Walsh. 2015. 'Forbes 500 list reveals a disturbing truth about our economy', *Huffington Post 3/2/15.*
32. F. Thomson & S. Dutta. 2016. 'Financialisation: A primer', *Transnational Institute (TNI) 6/1/16.*

were already exploiting, policies at national and international levels also actively encouraged activities and changes that buttressed financialization. Further, non-actions, like the refusals to intervene in financial activities that could be potentially destabilizing, have been just as responsible as active policy reforms. Example of these could include the slowness of many national policies, or regulations of not responding decisively to serious risks posed to not so well-informed investors posed by various crypto assets, and in particular, bitcoin.[33]

Neoliberal policy, to some extent, also bolstered financialization.[34] The past few decades of maintaining low inflation, in contrast to the post-war Keynesian era macroeconomic goal of maintaining full employment, has particularly benefited the financial sector, as inflation erodes the value of financial assets. The priority given to inflation skewed benefits to the financial sector. A rise in interest rates could, for instance, worsen debt loads for homes, businesses, and governments alike, as this could contribute to the stifling of growth, as a consequence of increasing credit costs.

Simultaneously, high interest rates tend to benefit the financial sector and could encourage investors to flock to financial assets against the better goal of long-term productive investments in the real economy. Nevertheless, the relation between financial gains and interest rates is not straightforward. Indeed, it was extremely low interest rates that initially fuelled the financial bubble in the US. Financial institutions exploited low Federal Fund Rates by leveraging their investments. This is shown in the high levels of debt taken on by them during the boom.

With little options on the matter, some governments have continued to succumb to such economic policies. The moment financial liberalization has taken hold, and capital is unshackled from its chains, national policy autonomy is to an extent limited. On the one hand, the ability to access private financial sources depended on credit-worthiness, as assessed by international institutions and rating agencies, on the other, countries that do not comply with investor interests are punished by capital flight where investors moved their money out of a country towards greater returns elsewhere.

This 'golden straitjacket' or capital mobility, as referred to by Thomas Friedman served as a disciplinary instrument that compelled governments to employ the appropriate monetary and fiscal policies, like balanced budgets that could require harsh austerity measures, low inflation, generous tax codes, and deregulated financial markets.[35] Such austerity rules though do not apply in the event of a financial crisis, where governments are expected to bail out private investors and institutions.

Therefore, market discipline dictates not the desired level of government spending, but the desired forms.[36] Budgets, for instance, that include funds for health, education, or social security are viewed as objectionable, whereas in the case of a financial crisis, governments are expected to empty their coffers. Financial institutions'

33. D.J. Cumming, S. Johan & A. Pant. 2019. 'Regulation of the crypto-economy: Managing risk, challenges, and regulatory uncertainty', *Risk and Financial Management*, Vol. 12 (2019): 126-139.
34. *Supra* note [32]. Thomson & Dutta. 2016.
35. *Supra* note [32]. Thomson & Dutta. 2016.
36. *Supra* note [32]. Thomson & Dutta. 2016.

bailouts by the US and various European governments subsequent to the 2008 GFC are good examples. Despite such injections of cash, financial systems remained reluctant to lend, and the credit crunch persisted during and in the immediate years of the 2007 GFC. Simultaneously, but conversely, financial institutions recovered profitability relatively much faster, and were indeed, not hesitant in paying out large rewards to their senior management and dividends to their affluent shareholders. This led, for instance, to the UK government calling for CG reforms to restrain excessive risk-taking and excessive remunerations in the banking industry.[37]

Taking aside those situations where regulators' options were apparently constrained, other cases in other parts of the world suggested clearly, political and economic interests, as the ultimate determinants in financially biased policymaking. In the case of countries with aging populations, with imminent risks of pension crises, there could be various possible solutions to deal with the problem. Coincidentally, most governments tilted in the same directions involving a closer integration of their pension systems with the global financial markets, that is to say, more people's retirement savings are now invested in capital markets than ever. This stance benefited foremost the financial services industry with new income and profit channels.[38] Second, the rising demand for financial assets encourages asset price inflation propping up finance-led accumulation.

Third, and importantly, growing numbers of individuals with stakes in the financial markets facilitate support policies that end up benefiting large financial firms. Financialized pension schemes therefore help to cultivate a culture of finance among the population. The US exemplifies an economy where politicians pander to the interests of the financial sector. These are demonstrated by extensive congressional lobbying by big banks, huge political donations by big banks, and the revolving door between Wall Street and Washington lawmakers, where individuals rotate between positions as policymakers and regulators and high-paying jobs in the financial sector. The recent appointments of former heads of US regulatory entities into large Fintech firms as CEOs or senior board members give good credence to this observation.

A poll conducted by the Harvard Institute of Politics in April 2016 to gauge public feelings of the US capitalist system suggests increasing numbers of Americans uncomfortable with their economic system's foundation. The 2016 Presidential campaign turned on the questions of who, precisely, the system is working for and against, as well as why eight years and several trillions of dollars of stimulus on from the GFC, the economy is still growing relatively slowly.[39] Too-big-to-fail (TBTF) financial institutions, hedge-fund billionaires, offshore tax avoidance, and other outrages are symptomatic of US market capitalism benefiting the few with many deprived of the American dream. The campaign process reflected the crisis of faith in the US capitalist system, where the financialization of its economy is highly significant.

37. R. McCormick & A. Minto. 2014. 'Governance of banks in an era of regulatory change and declining public confidence'.
38. *Supra* note [32]. Thomson & Dutta. 2016.
39. R. Foroohar. 2016. 'American capitalism's great crisis', *Time 12/5/16*.

§2.06 FINANCIALIZATION ECONOMIC IMPACTS AND COUNTRY CASE ANALYSIS

The hitherto relationship between the financial system and businesses where finance essentially served businesses in all advanced economies and in particular the US and the UK has switched to now where capital markets and the banking sector are funding less new investments but more against existing assets like housing, stocks and bonds. Interestingly, current data suggests finance accounting for some 7% of the US economy, up from 4% in 1980. It also accounts up to around 25% of all corporate profits, but creates a mere 4% of all jobs.[40] The financialization process might, however, put advanced economies, like the US and UK, at risks of debt deflation and prolonged recession, as happened in the immediate subsequent years of the 2007 GFC.

This phenomenon is not confined to the US and the UK, as the world's other market-based economies are also coping with elements of the same issue. Greece, EU's poster child for excessive debts is argued to have its financial crisis roots from the mid-1990s onwards when the economy transited to financialization under the modernizing cabinet of Costas Simitis.[41] This contention is further reinforced by the global fault-lines perspective that claims that geographies, cultures, politics, and security along national, regional and global dimensions need also to be factored into the argument.

Financialization is therefore an economic illness associated with the growth in size and scope of finance and financial activity and the ascendancy of shareholder value as the preferred model for CG. It includes links to the rise of risky, selfish thinking in private and public sectors, to the increasing political power of financiers and the CEOs they enrich, and to the markets know best mantra. The costs of social or public absorption of private debts, inclusive of fiscal incentives, tax havens, and fiscal evasion, together with cuts in essential social spending and infrastructure investments constrained the ability of the state to pursue wider economic and social policies. This contributed to the undermining of the economic and social process of reproduction and accumulation of capital.[42]

At its peak, Greek total debt was estimated at USD 360 billion. In tangent with global trends, real estate bubbles and securitization formed the bulk of the debt portfolio. Tax havens, fiscal evasion, and fiscal incentives further contributed to the state's fiscal fragility. There were fundamental structural changes in public sector exposure of debts that grew from 27% to 77%, while at the same time the exposure of the private sector and of households to debts fell from 43% and 30% to 5% and 18% respectively.[43] This suggests that the public absorbed more than half of the private

40. R. Foroohar. 2016. *Makers and takers: The rise of finance and the fall of American business*, New York, Crown Publishing Group.
41. V.K. Fouskas & C. Dimoulas. 2013. *Greece, financialization and the economy: The political economy of debt and financial destruction*, Basingstoke: Palgrave Macmillan.
42. C.N. Castel-Branco. 2016. 'Debt, global financialization and the periphery: Comparing and contrasting Mozambique', *Financialization of Land and Ecology Short Course*, Dar es Salaam, 21-25 November 2016.
43. *Supra* note [42]. Castel-Branco. 2016.

sector and household debts. The rescued financial packages enabled banks to capitalize on the Greek debt. This contributed to the trapping of the Greek economy into a vicious cycle of debt.

Hence, the absorption of the private debt by the public together with the European rescue packages for the Greek public debt quadrupled the weight of the Greek debt owed to the Euro Zone. This further meant that around 90% of the lending to Greece was expended on debt repayments suggesting further that it did not support the accumulation of real, but only fictitious capital.[44] Also, finance from the Euro bank was transmitted to Greece via commercial banks with spreads of around 5%-6% points. This suggests that commercial banks' returns on financial operations sourced by European taxpayers' money came to around 300%-400%. Greece was required to respond to the crisis through massive privatization and painful social austerity. These together supported accumulation of fictitious capital and undermined social and economic generation of employment and real capital.

To put in context, however, rescue packages for the twenty largest banks that caved under the GFC crisis exceeded USD 14 trillion. This is forty times Greek public debt and 1,000 times the public debt of Mozambique.[45] Further, four of these twenty largest banks had a total debt of USD 7.7 trillion, and with eleven of this same cohort having debts larger than that for Greece. Financialization indeed matters to EU periphery states, because excessive capital flows can damage the structures of small open economies, as well as amplify boom-bust cycles with large distortionary and distributional effects.

Large gross capital flows from the rest of the world to Ireland and Iceland, for instance, acted to destabilize their economies in the run up to the 2008 crisis. Empirical insights reinforced the argument that financial liberalization promoted financialization in such economies.[46] Hence, foreign rentiers' income share in the form of interest and dividends is positively linked to financialization. Such enormous profit outflows to non-residents asserted a negative pressure on the current account balance. As demonstrated in small economies, like Ireland and Ireland, this accentuated financial fragility and impacted the autonomy of their macroeconomic policies.

Insights from these two small open economies suggest, first, that speculative capital flows create financial instability, and this suggests the need for macroprudential policies that limit the size of such inflows to prevent a sudden stop of the inflow from creating unmanageable financial and macroeconomic disturbances. Second, small open economies should not have large banking sectors even if they have a lender of last resort like in the Eurozone, because the sovereign has to be able to recapitalize the banks if they suffer losses. In the absence of a lender of last resort, as in the case of Iceland, a large banking system is inherently fragile since a suspicion about liquidity problems could easily cause a bank run. This means a well-diversified

44. *Supra* note [42]. Castel-Branco. 2016.
45. *Supra* note [42]. Castel-Branco. 2016.
46. H. Raza, B.R. Gudmundsson, S. Kinsella & G. Zoega. 2016. 'Two thorns of experience: Financialisation in Iceland and Ireland', *International Review of Applied Economics*, Vol. 30(6): 771-789.

economy is needed to support a large banking system. As a comparative note, tax havens have capital accumulation of some USD 7 trillion, and in the case of the UK, some GBP 500 billion in tax incentives were awarded to large corporations from 2010 to 2015, while social spending cuts for the same period came to about GBP 150 billion.[47]

Financialization research initially focused on the US and UK experiences, but the concept is increasingly now applied to EMEs. Empirical research insights suggest considerable variations in financialization experiences of EMEs.[48] Asset price volatility is found across continents. Asia has been more exposed to capital inflows. Here, stock markets have gained prominence and private sector debts have climbed. For emerging Europe, financial deregulation has been more pronounced with lower levels but strong increases in household debts. The situation is similar in South Africa. This African EME representative in the study showed comparatively high household debts. Financialization is weaker in Latin America. Overall, EMEs mostly rank lower than the US or the UK on the proxy financialization indicators, other than the important exception of house price volatility.

Here, EMEs across geographic regions sometimes experienced stronger and frequently more persistent volatility than the Anglo-Saxon economies. This is of serious concerns, given the more limited resources of EMEs to deal with the adverse effects resulting from asset price bubbles.

Financialization is premised on creative financial innovations supporting economic development and contributing to global market efficiency. Instead, the outcome was the massive 2007 GFC bubble inflated by high leverage and a collapse requiring massive public sector bailouts from which the world has yet to totally unwind.[49] Hence, the heart of the problem of financialization has been the growing inequality of income and wealth as succinctly argued by Nobel Laureate Stiglitz and Piketty. Owing to financialization, the global financial system is turning over faster and still confronted with an increasing maturity mismatch.

Trading in foreign exchange markets averaged USD 5.3 trillion daily in April 2013. This was 60.6% higher than the USD 3.3 trillion in April 2007, with most of these conducted between financial institutions. The data also suggests that with every USD 1 FX trade with a non-financial counterparty, there was USD 10 equivalent of trades between financial institutions.[50] Also, concentration in the financial sector was expanding. The Financial Stability Board's (FSB's) data on the top twenty-eight globally systemically significant financial institutions suggests that their assets climb to USD 5.4 trillion or 63.3% of 2011 world gross domestic product (GDP), compared to 47.7% in 2002.[51] Financial theory suggests that risk is best diversified, but geographical diversification via globalization hides the fact that everything was interconnected and

47. *Supra* note [42]. Castel-Branco. 2016.
48. E. Karwowski & E. Stockhammer. 2016. 'Financialisation in emerging economies: A systematic overview and comparison with Anglo-Saxon economies', *Post Keynesian Economics Study Group (PKSG) Working Paper 1616.*
49. A. Sheng. 2013. 'The end of financialization', *The China Post 15/9/13.*
50. *Supra* note [49]. Sheng. 2013.
51. *Supra* note [49]. Sheng. 2013.

became more and more co-related with each other. Borderless finance implies global integration and global interconnectedness. Failures in one hub like Lehman in 2007 radiates from the US to much of the rest of the world.[52]

Few take seriously the massive credit being generated below-the-line, netted out, moved off-balance sheet to special investment vehicles or totally offshore, thus failing to spot the shell game where someone had taken the shell.[53] Large parts of the world responded to the ill effects of financialization with more financialization via quantitative easing (QE) and fighting complexity with more complexity, or new rules. QE is a monetary policy where central banks purchase long-term bonds from private investors like pension funds or insurance firms using newly created digital money.[54] Its purpose is to inject liquidity into financial markets to keep interest rates low. The idea is to encourage borrowing and jump-start demand in the economy. Instead, as shown in the US, UK and elsewhere, the gains flowed mainly to the financial elites.[55]

Five years into QE in big economies like the US, UK and Japan, strong global recovery remains elusive.[56] This occurred with huge increases in public expenditures blowing up sovereign debts of advanced economies to 100% of GDP, while central bank balances ballooned massively with interest rates close to zero. Though QE was a tool of last resort, the printing of more central bank debts to prevent bubble deflation was to use more debt to cure debt. This is sustainable only under lower and lower interest rates. The threats of tapering suggests that if real interest rates rise, the current asset bubbles and value of sovereign debts would deflate inducing huge losses to recur and forcing central banks to print more money. Real interest rates rose, despite QE holding the risk-free rate low, because the market perceived those risks and uncertainties were rising.

Policymakers in the context of the liquidity trap tide had generally responded with monetary policies, fiscal policies, macro-prudential policies, but too few with structural reforms.[57] Emerging markets now faced the prospects of returning to recession because of the threats of withdrawal of monetary policies. Financialization with grand designs for global economic efficiency instead generated the unintended impact of increased inequality, slowing down investments in real production, inflicted pressures on indebted households and individuals leading to a decline in democratic accountability.[58]

Crisis of faith in the US capitalism model which is now said to be divorced from the real economy is, however, not cast in stone, and general expectations are that it can

52. G.L. Kaminsky, M.C. Reinhart & C.A. Vegh. 2003. 'The unholy trinity of financial contagion', *Journal of Economic Perspectives*, Vol. 17(4): 51-74.
53. D. Wighton. 2017. 'What we have learned 10 years after Chick Prince told Wall St to keep dancing', *Financial News 14/7/17.*
54. L.R. Ricketts. 2011. 'Quantitative easing explained', *Federal Reserve Bank of St. Louis Economic Information Newsletter April 2011.*
55. J.J. Chung. 2017. 'Wealth inequality as explained by quantitative easing and law's inertia', *UMKC Law Review*, Vol. 85(2017): 275-310.
56. *Supra* note [49]. Sheng. 2013.
57. OECD. 2009. 'Structural reform at a time of financial crisis' in OECD, *Economic policy reforms going for growth*, Paris: OECD.
58. *Supra* note [49]. Sheng. 2013.

be fixed.[59] Since the core of the problem is the asset side of central banks' balance sheet, this needs to be resolved via structural reforms, suggesting dealing with the quality of assets, and not the quantity of liability. There is the urgent need to deleverage by increasing the quality of equity, and not by inflating debt.

But QE is corroding the long-term income of insurance and pension funds which have the capacity to invest in long-term equity and assets as their incomes have been curtailed by lower interest rates. Therefore, the answer to unsustainable financialization is not more debt, but more equity of or the real net worth of real sectors, meaning households, businesses, and the government sectors. These have to be generated via real sector reforms. Insights from the 2008 GFC suggest the need for rebalancing or the moving away from short-termism towards long-term financing of the real economy to promote the quality, but not the quantity of assets that could contribute to GDP growth; addressing social inequality by enhancing access to financing or financial inclusion; and funding of infrastructure developments to sustain long-term growth.[60]

Financialization works through changes in the structure and operation of financial markets, changes in the behaviour of non-financial businesses, and economic policy changes. Given the disruptions and problems posed by financialization as vividly seen in the immediate years before and subsequent to the GFC, suggestions have been made to counter its undesired impacts. This involves using a multifaceted agenda. It incorporates restoration of policy control over financial markets. This further entails challenging the neoliberal economic policy paradigms fostered by financialization, getting businesses to incorporate other stakeholders' interests rather than merely the financial elites, and initiating reforms in the political process to lessen the dominance of big corporations and the affluent financial elites.[61]

Indeed, over the past three decades, financial markets have permeated the geographic and social spaces.[62] Capital markets altered the manner businesses are structured and operated, while generating a new class of entrepreneurs enriched by Initial Public Offerings (IPOs). Public policies grew more accommodating to both domestic and foreign investments. Many and more kinds of assets have been securitized, while domains not considered to be assets were all transformed into tradable financial products. It became increasingly common for all kinds of cash flows to be securitized and transformed into financial instruments.

These are said to have generated pervasive social impacts that included the transformation of the corporate sector and increases in inequality. This led to new avenues and targets of social movement activisms. In short, every domain of social life was impacted by financialization, from inequality and social mobility to local politics and urban planning to social movements and state power. These upgraded financial

59. *Supra* note [40]. Foroohar. 2016.
60. *Supra* note [49]. Sheng. 2013.
61. T.I. Palley. 2007. 'Financialization: What it is and why it matters', *The Levy Economics Institute Working Paper No. 525 December 2007.*
62. G.F. Davis & S. Kim. 2015. 'Financialization of the economy', *Annual Review of Sociology*, Vol. 41(August 2015): 203-221.

markets and the logic of finance as the primary force that shapes the future of economies and societies.[63]

It has been alluded to earlier that financialization contributed to the 2007-2008 GFC. One study argues that, while there were other contributing factors to the GFC, among the most important were rising inequality and stagnant incomes for most US workers, growing private sector debts, deregulation, rise of shadow unregulated financial institutions, and the complex financialization of the global economy.[64] Gradual transformation of advanced economies, like the US and the UK, subsequent to the post-war period generated the conditions that led to the GFC. The US Government played a role, but the US Treasury and the Federal Reserve took much of the responsibility for the bailouts. The Fed's unprecedented extension of the Government's safety net to the TBTF financial and non-financial institutions validated questionable, risky, and in some cases, illegal activities of the top brass on Wall Street. Thus, financialization with its domestic and international effects has interacted with the polarization of income distribution to generate the structural imbalances that led to the GFC.[65]

It has been further argued that the bailouts accentuated the distribution of income and wealth to the top one-tenth of 1%. They kept the same management in charge, while paying record bonuses to the top echelon associated with CG failures.[66] The immediate aftermaths of the GFC saw fraudulent activities exposed with leading global banks paying huge fines for bad behaviours, but the lack or absence of prosecutions of criminal behaviours by top management riled the general public. It is further argued that TBTF institutions should have been required to submit to Fed oversight and top management removed as conditions for bailouts. The Attorney General's office could have been called in to examine cases for prosecution, and financial services reined in. Such and more related actions could have left the financial system healthier and smaller and avoided the moral hazard problems that have grown over the past three decades while bringing down the influence that the big banks have over policymaking in the US.[67]

A cross-country study suggests that a debt-led private demand boom regime was observed in the US, UK, Span, Estonia, Greece and South Africa, while an export-led mercantilist kind was observed in Germany, Japan, and Sweden.[68] These two regimes possessed internal contradictions, with regard to household debts and with regard to foreign debts of the counterpart current account deficit economies. Such features could undermine the sustainability of these regimes and lead to financial and economic crises. In contrast, France, Hungary, Portugal, and Turkey all show indicators of a

63. *Supra* note [62]. Davis & Kim. 2015.
64. L.R. Wray. 2012. 'Global financial crisis: A Minskyan interpretation of the causes, the Fed's bailout, and the future', *Levy Economics Institute Working Paper No. 711 March 2012.*
65. E. Stockhammer. 2012. 'Financialization and the global economy' in G. Epstein (ed.), *The political economy of financial crises*, Oxford: Oxford University Press.
66. *Supra* note [64]. Wray. 2012.
67. *Supra* note [64]. Wray. 2012.
68. N. Dodig, E. Hein & D. Detzer. 2015. 'Financialisation and the financial and economic crises: Theoretical framework and empirical analysis for 15 countries', *Institute for International Political Economy Berlin Working Paper No. 54/2015.*

domestic demand kind of development. The same study examined the immediate aftermath of the GFC, by examining transmission mechanisms and the main barriers to recovery. It found that the export-led cluster and in particular Germany and Sweden recovered quickly, because their domestic balance sheets were generally in order, and the crisis was contained by immediate state responses, besides benefitting from the recovery of the world economy.

By comparison, debt-led private demand boom and domestic-led economies with monetary policy autonomy found success in stabilizing the financial sector and the economy through government deficits.[69] In debt-led private demand boom countries like the US, UK, and South Africa, there were emerging signs of shifts towards domestic demand-led growth accompanied by improvements of their private sectors' financial balances. The catching-up domestic demand-led economies in the group comprising Turkey, Hungary and Poland, showed rather quick recovery of financial flows. On the other hand, for debt-led private demand boom and domestic demand-led economies without monetary policy autonomies, such as the six EMU economies of Estonia, France, Greece, Italy, Portugal and Spain, macroeconomic stabilization was terminated first by financial market pressure and then by fiscal austerity.

§2.07 FINANCIALIZATION PRODUCTS AND SERVICES AND TAX HAVENS

It could next be useful then to extend further from the insights of financialization on economies to look at its particular impact on tax havens. The IMF recognized that half the international financial flows went through tax havens,[70] and the situation today is probably similar, if not worse. In general, financiers used these OFCs, because they could employ, misapply, and abuse situations in which there are practically no controls over regulations. They strategically employed many of these OFCs, despite a full understanding that tax havens have become a pivotal part of global financial stability. It appears that the role played by tax havens in the global economy is much too important to allow nation states to launch anything but symbolic attacks on the system. Since the 1950s, tax havens have developed tremendously, along with offshore finance, as an element of the financialization of the global economy.[71]

The first indication of the global economy's financialization was the Eurodollar market. The international monetary system set up in Bretton Woods in 1944 led to the US dollar becoming the reference for international trade.[72] As international exchanges developed, more and more dollars landed in the hands of corporate managers or foreign states outside the US. The Bank of England (BOE) together with the City of London created the Eurodollar market. They allowed financial transactions between non-residents to be transacted in London in a different currency than the British pound, without any control and any regulation by any official authority.

69. *Supra* note [68]. Dodig, Hein & Detzer. 2015.
70. IMF. 2000. 'Offshore financial centres: IMF background paper', *IMF 23/6/00*.
71. The Spark. 2013. 'Tax havens: Outpost for the world of finance', *The Spark 26/7/13*.
72. *Supra* note [71]. The Spark. 2013.

Within this framework, multinational banks engaged speculative attacks on different currencies, purchasing without difficulties, and without any limits all the necessary dollars to do it. Simultaneously, international finance corporations began to use many British Commonwealth Islands exempted from any taxes, as bases for their headquarters or operations. New financial centres emerged in areas more or less remote from London, but permanently connected to the City's Eurodollar market. The US big banks followed suit in the mid-1960s, as they could be treated like any other banks by the UK, when they set themselves in former British colonies of the Caribbean. However, in 1973 when the Bretton Woods system collapsed, the follow-through permanently changing exchange rates, generated suitable conditions for speculations without any limitations and a generalized monetary inflation.[73] A deep recession followed together with massive unemployment.

For better or for worse, financialization has transformed the global financial markets. The demise of the Bretton Woods monetary system and extinctions of gold-backed dollars as the international currency, fixed exchange rates, and limited capital mobility in the early 1970s accelerated growths in global liquidity prompting a surge of financial liberalization and deregulation. Floating exchange rates and unregulated capital flows presented hazards for some, but immense opportunities for financial innovations like derivatives emerged to address these risks and for speculative profit-making.

Financial markets consequently grew in absolute and relative terms. The value of foreign exchange transactions to global trade for instance went from 2:1 in 1973 to 90:1 in 2004.[74] Technologies played a part too. Computerized trading rose to about 70% of financial market activity in the US, with Europe only just under 40%. Shares held for average four years in the 1960s now could be held for twenty seconds. Financialization involves radical transformation within the financial sector, but altered also, entire economies, and indeed the global economy. This extended from households and businesses to the functioning of monetary systems and commodity markets.

Banking transformed too, from the business model of savings and lending, to loans being repackaged, sold, and traded and speculated in global markets. Financialization also contributed to the emergence of shadow banking or new kinds of financial institutions and practices like securitization that were subjected to lesser regulatory oversights, than conventional commercial banks. Despite initiatives to rein in some of their activities, it now occupied more than a quarter of the entire financial system, and much bigger than before the 2008 GFC.[75] It is now perceived to be of huge systemic or contagion risks in China, now the world's second largest economy with significant global impact.[76] This was aptly demonstrated in 2016 when China's capital market came under severe pressures.

73. *Supra* note [71]. The Spark. 2013.
74. F. Thomson & S. Dutta. 2016. 'Financialisation: A primer', *Transnational Institute (TNI) 6/1/16.*
75. *Supra* note [74]. Thomson & Dutta. 2016.
76. G. Wildau. 2017. 'China launches fresh attack on shadow banking risk: Previous efforts have failed to curb growth in non-bank credit', *Financial Times 22/2/17.*

Conventional banking to make up for its eroding income sources now turned more and more to a blend of financialized personal income and higher investment banking practices that eventually contributed to the origins of the 2008 GFC. The combination of shadow banking, new directions in conventional commercial banking and investments, and the rising participation of institutional investors in the capital and financial markets led to a growing business culture with enhanced focus on short-term profit-making. The concern is now about which financial assets gave better returns, and less to do with the growth of the real economy.

Liberalized capital flows and the emergence of foreign exchange activities as the biggest market in the world are supposed to benefit both advanced economies and EMEs. In theory, investors would be motivated to go to capital-scarce emerging markets where returns are likely to be higher. Instead, free capital movements led to unprecedented volatility of exchange rates, stock market values, and interest rates and subsequently greater instability with enhanced financial crisis risk. In the 2000s, capital flowed instead from developing to developed economies in search of better security and return. Earlier, a middle-income economy, like Malaysia, in the midst of the 1997 Asian Financial Crisis (AFC) turned to capital controls to halt financial instability and falling confidence, while the adjacent economies of Thailand and Indonesia opted for IMF supervision. Both approaches eventually succeeded but with Malaysia not having to endure IMF's painful adjustment process. This led to the IMF conceding to the use of capital controls under particular circumstances.

The 1997 AFC also led to reserve accumulation as an insurance plan against speculative currency attacks and sudden capital flows in many Asian economies, with China leading the pack. The unintentional consequence is one, where many of these economies escalated their short-term external debts to fund government spending and private investments, with rates determined commercially that were often high not counting currency fluctuation risks, while their reserves largely invested in US Government securities earning relatively lower returns.[77] Also, to sterilize the potential inflation impacts of reserve accumulation, these economies issued higher-rate government bonds thereby increasing domestic public debts to absorb liquidity, or remove money from circulation. The difference in interest rates meant further losses for developing economies.

Thus, free capital flows associated with much of the financialization process could create unintentional problems that could limit national policy choices. The global financial markets in their present forms were being compared to risks in ordinary casinos. In the latter, however, people could choose whether or not to take risks at the card tables, but the former or casino capitalism drags everyone into the game involuntarily.[78] An important financial innovation driving contemporary finance is securitization. This is the transformation of streams of future income into a financial

77. J.P. Paincera. 2009. 'Developing countries in the era of financialisation: From deficit accumulation to reserve accumulation' *Research on Money and Finance Discussion Paper, School of Oriental and African Studies (SOAS) 4/2/09.*

78. P. Gowan. 1999. *The global gamble*, London: Verso; S. Strange. 1997. *Casino capitalism*, Manchester: Manchester University Press.

security ready for sale straightaway.[79] The late David Bowie, for instance, sold Bowie Bonds that investors could buy. He got money straightaway from the royalties on his record, while investors get royalties yearly. Securitization could be applied to anything with regular flows of incomes, like mortgages, student loans, water services, road tolls, telephone bills, export earning, sports and movie stars' incomes, tax revenues or even sustainable forest management.[80]

The quest is to seek ventures or situations with steady and predictable income flows, and the quest for banking is to repackage loans for onward sale, rather than holding on to these, as in the past. This could add much more liquidity to the economy, higher financial leverage, and higher risks, not only for businesses and households but also for the public sector. Future-flow securitizations enable both private and public entities access to low-cost credit in global capital markets isolated from official credit ratings and national economic performance criterion. But, as witnessed in the events leading to the GFC and its immediate aftermaths, when these sold future income flows did not come about, market participants were impacted variously, with some more serious than the others. Taken as whole, this led to the 2007 GFC. Recall, earlier in 2000, Enron and other Wall Street giants fell largely because of excessive financial leveraging made possible by securitization.[81] For this occasion, however, it was the banks that indulged massively in this. Other structural causes of course also contributed to the 2007 GFC.[82]

The next big thing that financialization help brought about is derivatives. These are financial contracts that derive value from the performance of selected underlying factors.[83] These do not have to be tangible things. Weather derivatives, for instance, allow farmers and others to hedge against hurricanes, floods, snowfalls, or the level of sulphur in the air. Instead of claims on future streams of incomes, as in securitization, derivatives constitute an exchange of performance exposures, where gains and losses are articulated simply in the changing price of the derivative itself. Officially, derivatives are viewed as risk management or hedging instruments, but in various instances, derivatives used to hedge against volatility has itself become a source of volatility, as speculation on derivatives markets rely on volatility to achieve profits.[84]

Given the volatility and high risks implications, computerized risk modelling that appear seemingly rigorous and scientific are employed to mitigate risks. However, the inferences applied in these models using past prices might not hold in unprecedented times of crisis, where prices of different assets move in tandem. These risk management techniques in practice induce financial market participants to act *en masse* in the

79. T. Hale. 2015. 'Securitisation: The chicken and egg version', *Financial Times 3/11/15*.
80. *Supra* note [74]. Thomson & Dutta. 2016.
81. P. Dembinski, C. Lager & A. Cornford. 2006. *Enron and world fiancé: A case study in ethics*, Basingstoke: Palgrave Macmillan.
82. Crotty. 2008. 'Structural causes of the global financial crisis: A critical assessment of the new financial architecture', *University of Massachusetts Economics Department Working Paper Series 16*.
83. IMF. 1998. 'Financial derivatives', *IMF Paper Presented at the 11th Meeting of the IMF Committee of Balance of Payment Statistics*, Washington D.C., 21-23 October 1998.
84. S. Jeanneau & M. Micu. 2003. 'Volatility and derivatives turnover: A tenuous relationship', *BIS Quarterly Review*, March 2003: 57-65.

same directions, thereby accentuating instability, and the probability of large price swings. The system at the same time has built-in incentives, that in reality enhanced risk levels and instability to contribute to the 2008 GFC.[85]

Conventional commercial banks were incentivized to ignore risks levels in the original mortgage loans, when they switched to the originate-to-distribute model, while global credit ratings agencies (CRAs), who were paid by them, tend to rate in positive terms. Volatility in real markets heightened and the potential for risk management undermined, especially when financial speculators participated in the commodities derivatives' markets. Nevertheless, evidence suggests that derivatives and in particular credit default swaps might have amplified the 2007 GFC, but the crisis was driven largely more by the boom and bust in property markets.[86]

Early beginnings of the twenty-first century saw financial market participants looking towards commodity derivatives, as the alternative for declining returns on equities, especially subsequent to the Dotcom crash.[87] Past patterns show commodity prices generally changed in line with inflation and moving against the direction of bonds and equities, other than between 2005 and 2008 when commodity and equity prices were positively correlated. This made commodities powerfully attractive to those seeking to protect against losses in other investments. The surge in demand for commodity derivatives upped their prices to render them even more appealing to financial investors.

US commodity futures indices, for example, rose from an estimated USD 13 billion in 2003 to USD 260 billion in 2008, while the notional value outstanding on over-the-counter (OTC) commodity derivatives contracts grew to around USD 13 trillion in mid-2008, or around fourteen-times from 2002.[88] Deregulation resulting from lobbying by large financial enterprises, via legislations like the 2000 Commodity Futures Modernization Act, combined with other decisions from the US Commodity Futures Trading Commission, like the reductions in and exemptions from position limits, weakened regulations applied to the capital markets.

This led to unregulated OTC speculative trading without supervision driving tremendous growths in commodity derivatives trading. These developments delink commodity markets from physical market conditions. Speculators do not commonly invest according to supply and demand conditions in particular physical markets, but instead in connection with the performance of other financial assets. This probably contributed to the simultaneous rise and fall of different commodity prices, not easily understood by supply and demand factors, and with speculators not having interests in the commodities themselves. The Food and Agriculture Organization (FAO) estimated

85. *Supra* note [74]. Thomson & Dutta. 2016.
86. H. Colon. 2016. 'The role of derivatives in the financial crisis', *National Center for Policy Analysis (NCPA), Issue Brief No. 187,* January 2016: 1-14.
87. *Supra* note [74]. Thomson & Dutta. 2016.
88. N. Colbran. 2011. 'The financialisation of agricultural commodity futures trading and its impact on the 2006-2008 global food crisis', *University of New South Wales (UNSW) Law Research Paper No. 2011-14:1-13.*

that around 2% of commodity futures contracts ended with delivery of the physical product.[89]

External financial market participants are not alone in driving the trading of commodity derivatives, but equally involved are non-financial firms of international traders. Also, policymakers with the blessings of the World Bank shifted focus from the stabilization of prices via international commodity agreements, centralized marketing boards and cooperative schemes, to private market-based price risk management strategies, and in particular derivatives trading. These larger market players went beyond hedging objectives to include seeking profits from speculative trading.[90] Speculation in commodity derivatives unfortunately contributed to commodity price volatility in practice.

Here, speculators have been heard to have said that they could extract significant speculative profits only where there were significant price volatilities. Oil prices, for example, surged by over 60% in the first half of 2008 to a high of USD 147 per barrel, despite decline in demand and increase in idle production capacity. This suggests that the price of oil is influenced by fictitious barrels in financial markets.[91] This further implied that changing valuations in derivatives markets that do not align with the underlying supply and demand conditions of particular commodities could translate into swings in physical market prices.

Price volatility aside, financialization of commodities contributed to inequality between different market participants. Some speculators would profit a lot from this, but many more others would lose out. Among the main losers could be the conventional users of commodities derivatives, as it has become more costly and unpredictable for hedgers to use futures markets for hedging.[92] Commodity trading now appears no longer serving the use, for which it was designed for, in the first place. Regulatory intervention might now be justified to ensure that these financial instruments cater for traditional hedgers with interests in the physical commodities. Thus far, this has been resisted by strong lobbying from the financial industry. Many small-scale producers and traders in developing economies in practice were excluded from these markets. This is not just a cost participation matter, as participation in derivatives trading requires access to and minimum knowledge of financial markets.

Further, many small firms of traders and producers do not employ futures and options contracts to hedge because of the smaller commodity volumes they handle, relative to the significant lot sizes mandated in international exchanges. These smaller firms, as shown in the case of the coffee markets in Uganda and Tanzania tend to lose, as they have to accept lower prices in exchange for stability, or the risk implied by volatility. Over there, financialization has contributed to increasing inequality in terms

89. *Supra* note [88]. Colbran. 2011.
90. S. Newman. 2009. 'Financialization and changes in social relations along commodity chains: The case of coffee', *Review of Radical Political Economics*, Vol. 41(4): 539-559.
91. M. Labban. 2010. 'Oil in parallax: Scarcity, markets and the financialization of accumulation', *Geoforum*, Vol. 41(4): 541-552.
92. T. Kerckhoffs, R. Van Os & M.V. Stichele. 2010. *Financing food: Financialisation and financial actors in agriculture commodity markets*, Amsterdam: Centre for Research on Multinational Corporations.

of incomes and power within the commodity chain.[93] Big international trading firms with access to large funds and knowledge to participate actively in financial markets profited from price volatility arising from speculation. In contrast, many medium-sized traders became unable to compete financially. They went belly-up or were subject to takeovers.

Controversies over the role of speculative trading have arisen in food crisis in recent years. Prices of internationally traded food items rose sharply by 130% from 2002 to mid-2008. These pose tremendous hardships to people in EMEs where food purchases constituted around 60%-80% of income. Following the food crisis, the number of people considered undernourished and food insecure rose to about 75 million. This induced civil disorders in more than forty different countries around the world, including significant escalation of the costs of food important for the fifty least developed economies.[94] While commodity prices fell significantly in conjunction with the 2008 GFC, from late 2009 onwards, these rose again. It has been argued that the steady injection of speculative money from 2003 to mid-2008 followed by its rapid withdrawal in late 2008 in the commodity derivatives markets were behind the inflation and the sudden bursting of the bubble.[95]

Financialization does not stop in the primary commodity markets, but has also extended to immaterial goods, like greenhouse gas emissions. The practice of emissions trading arose in the US in the 1970s to limit sulphur dioxide contamination via market-based solutions. The financialization of nature is shown clearly in the cap-and-trade notion developed to create a market for pollution permits. In simple terms, a maximum threshold is established for the cap part to form the basis for the generation of a limited number of permits that could then be traded.[96]

The basic underlying premise is to create market incentives for reductions in pollution. Schemes involving carbon offsets allow companies to compensate for their own emissions by reducing them elsewhere, like investing in reforestation or renewable energy projects. Here, more environmentally sustainable companies could gain by selling unused quotas, while those with unsustainable practices would have to pay for additional allowances. Variations of such plays are applied to control air and water quality and similar mechanisms that are supposedly formulated to stop the exhaustion of marine life by creating tradable fishing quotas, or rights. When such initial markets are developed, opportunities for the developments of derivatives like carbon options could enable businesses to hedge against or speculate on the prices of these tradeable permits, quotas or credits.[97]

93. S. Newman. 2009. 'Financialization and changes in social relations along commodity chains: The case of coffee', *Review of Radical Political Economics*, Vol. 41(4): 539-559.
94. *Supra* note [88]. Colbran. 2011.
95. *Supra* note [92]. Kerckhoffs, Van Os & Stichele. 2010.
96. J. Clark & K. Hayes. 2011. 'An emerging geography of intangible assets: Financialization in carbon emissions credit and intellectual property markets', *Georgia Ivan Allen Tech College School of Public Policy Working Paper 66.*
97. L. Kassenaar. 2009. 'Carbon capitalists warming to climate market using derivatives', *Global Research 9/12/09.*

Market-oriented environmentalists support the financialization of nature, as a manner of increasing sustainability, while other financial market participants viewed this as a new profit opportunity. The ethics of pricing and commodifying ecosystem goods and services aside, growing evidence suggests that such market-based financial solutions failed to resolve environmental degradation and might actually accentuate the problem. They might also simultaneously spawn new social inequalities by putting the financial sector in charge of common resources.[98]

Such market-based approaches are argued to be smokescreens giving the appearance of regulations and action, while providing businesses carte blanche to continue using and abusing common resources for profits. Instead of pushing for the expansion, integration, and financialization of water markets and so on, the better option is to implement and enforce regulations that preserve essential resources and promote policies that support water as a human right.[99] There are now growing fears that new forms of volatility and even crises could unfold with the growing expansion of the natural capital derivatives markets, and with existing schemes, such as the EU Emissions Trading Scheme coming under heavy stress.[100]

There were also growing concerns over the impacts of financialization on the wider economy. With financialization of economies, significant levels of profits were now originating from transactions in financial securities and the interest payments they accrue, rather than mainly from the mass production of goods, as in the past.[101] An ILO study covering seventeen economies, for example, suggests that the level of profits represented by the financial sector climbed to over 40% in 2005.[102] These have implications, especially for those economies with good capital and financial markets. When businesses find that they could profit more from trading in financial assets they might focus on this, rather than investing in technologies thereby negatively impacting real investments.[103] This also helps to explain the short-term capitalism problem now troubling the business sector, and in particular, those listed in the capital markets, especially when the board and members of senior management team used this to justify hefty compensation structures.

Households are not free from this orientation either. Many middle-class workers face stagnating real wages and employment instability in many economies. Rather than in the past where productivity drive wages and economic growth, now demand and growth are increasingly propelled by more debts. These are not used only to sustain

98. S. Devlin. 2015. 'Carbon markets have failed', *Resilience 4/9/15*; T. Gilbertson & O. Reyes. 2009. *Carbon trading: How it works and why it fails*. Uppsala: Dag Hammarkskjold Foundation (DHF); Transnational Institute (TNI). 2009. 'Carbon trading', *TNI Menu 11/9/09.*
99. Food & Water Watch. 2012. 'Don't bet on Wall Street: The financialization of nature and the risk of our common resources', *Common Resources Fact Sheet June 2012.*
100. W.F. Spieth. 2015. 'Reform of EU emissions trading system likely to fail', *EU Observer 24/3/15.*
101. D. Basu. 2011. 'Financialization, household credit and economic slowdown in the U.S.', *Research on Money and Finance SOAS London Discussion Paper*; G. Krippner. 2005. 'The financialization of the American economy', *Socio-Economic Review*, Vol. 3(2): 173-208.
102. Freeman. 2010. 'Its financialization', *International Labour Review*, Vol. 149(2): 163-183.
103. O. Orhangazi. 2008. 'Financialization and capital accumulation in the non-financial corporate sector: A theoretical and empirical investigation of the U.S. economy: 1973-2004', *MPRA Paper No. 7724.*

consumption, as many youths have done today, but also to fund financial investments and speculation, such as also found in many money-game schemes that have hurt many innocent investors.

This trend is accelerated by tax provisions in most economies in allowing debt interest as tax-deductible items that enhances earnings per share, and hence share valuations. This, being the case, many financial and non-financial businesses across the world have become increasingly addicted to debts as financial instruments. This is occurring both in the advanced economies of the US, UK, Japan or Ireland, and in various EMEs too. There is hence little evidence of de-leveraging in developed economies subsequent to the 2007 GFC, while debt propagation and addiction in EMEs are becoming serious concerns. The world is awash in debts.[104]

Additionally, MNCs have contributed to widening disparities in income and wealth between the rich and poorer economies as they bring their financialized practices with them to the developing economies.[105] Other than big EMEs, like China and India, which have witnessed significant progress towards convergence with income levels in the developed economies, the difference between average per capita income in other developing economies in Latin America, the Caribbean and the African continent has not altered significantly. This has become a cause of global concern.[106] Of equal concern is the widening income gap between the rich and the poor within economies of both developed and developing economies. This arises mainly because of the increasing concentration of political power among the corporate and financial elites that has been able to influence the policies and laws, by which economies are run worldwide.[107]

Increasingly, and of some concern, is the growing participation of non-financial businesses such as global supermarkets into various finance-related activities. They have ventured into financial rentiers, like speculating in properties and insurance and banking services. This, as seen in the US economy, began sometime in the 1950s, where non-financial businesses turned to financial income streams for greater profits.[108] US non-financial businesses' financial returns, as calculated by interests and dividend income as a percentage of internal funds, escalated from about 20% for most of the 1960s to over 50% from late 1980s on to the early 2000s. The proportion of

104. L.P. McCormick, C. Torres, M. Benhamou & D. Pogkas. 2021. 'The COVID-19 pandemic has added $19.5 trillion to global debt', *Bloomberg 29/1/21*; J. Bilton. 2016. 'Panama Papers: Mossack Fonseca leak reveals elite's tax havens', *BBC 4/3/16*.
105. G. Arrighi, B. Silver & B. Brewer. 2003. 'Industrial convergence, globalization and the persistence of the North-South divide', *Studies in Comparative International Development*, Vol. 38(1): 3-31.
106. UN Department of Economics and Social Affairs. 2015. 'Income convergence or persistent inequalities among countries', *Development Issues No. 5 October 2015*.
107. S. Lynch. 2017. 'Attorney General Loretta E. Lynch delivers remarks at the OECD Anti-Bribery Ministerial Meeting: Paris, 16/3/16', *Justice News US Department of Justice 10/11/16*; R. Reich. 2015. 'The real reason for the growing gap between the rich and poor', *Newsweek 28/9/15*.
108. G. Krippner. 2005. 'The financialization of the American economy', *Socio-Economic Review*, Vol. 3(2): 173-208.

financial assets in relation to real assets expanded, from about 30% in the 1970s to more than 100% in the early 2000s.[109]

This feature and trend appear to be replicated in various ways across other economies.[110] Non-financial businesses over the years have borrowed and lent bypassing banks, when accessing needed resources and invested surplus earnings, at competitive costs, via new sources, like Fintechs.[111] This was also prompted by short-term profitability of finance, relative to real investments that sat nicely with the shareholder primacy form of CG followed in the main capital markets of the world.[112]

The growing significance of the financial sector, together with the growing reliance of non-financial businesses on financial income relative to other productive activities, like manufacturing, suggests the declining role for labour for profits, more so with the accelerating rise of automation and artificial intelligence (AI). In continental Europe, in particular, this was resisted by labour unions and talk of tax on robots. Still, the huge impact of financialization and the corollary persistence of shareholder primacy governance have tilted disproportionate corporate attention on share valuations for existing businesses and for start-ups.

The persistence on the use of securitization to achieve higher profitability means that financialization exerts enormous impact on both business and managerial behaviours towards profit-maximization and average household behaviours in terms of rising financial activities, both quantitatively and qualitatively. In the context of stagnating or falling wages in developed economies, like the US and UK, social pressures for maintaining consumption led to increasing reliance on consumer debts, comprising both hefty housing loans and seemingly convenient credit cards. Household credit consumptions rose to some 160% and 130% respectively in the UK and US, while debt payments relative to household disposable incomes rose from about 8% in 2003 to almost 30% in 2007, but mainly in credit card usage.[113]

Inequality and poverty issues generated by debts and related matters spawned in recent years the need for financial inclusion literacy to help the disadvantaged to channel their small savings into the capital markets. The aim is to foster greater participation, but it has not turned out, as well as intended, with significant challenges persisting. Some estimated 2 billion adults worldwide do not have a basic account, with some 59% of adults globally citing lack of money, accessibility difficulties, and unfriendly documentations, as the primary reasons for financial exclusion.[114] Further,

109. O. Orhangazi. 2008. 'Financialization and capital accumulation in the non-financial corporate sector: A theoretical and empirical investigation of the U.S. economy: 1973-2004', *MPRA Paper No. 7724*.

110. R. Dore. 2008. 'Financialization of the global economy', *Industrial and Corporate Change*, Vol. 17(6): 1097-1112; C. Lapavitsas. 2009. 'Financialised capitalism: Crisis and financial expropriation', *Historical Matrialism*, Vol. 17(2): 114-148.

111. I. Pollari. 2016. 'The rise of fintech: Opportunities and challenges', *Jassa The Finsia, Journal of Applied Finance*, Vol. 3(2016): 15-21.

112. The Aspen Institute of Business and Society (TAIBS). 2010. 'Short-termism and U.S. capital markets: A compelling case for change', *TAIBS August 2010*.

113. E. Curran & D. Roman. 2016. 'Southeast Asia's Debt problems hasn't gone away', *Bloomberg 7/4/16*; J. Montgomerie. 2009. 'The pursuit of (past) happiness? Middle-class indebtedness and American financialization', *New Political Economy*, Vol. 14(1): 1-24.

114. The World Bank. 2017. 'Financial inclusion', *The World Bank 5/4/17*.

more than 200 million formal and informal micro, small and medium enterprises in EMEs lack adequate financing to thrive and grow, with significant many citing lack of collateral and credit histories and business informalities, as the main reasons for not having an account.

Women, the rural poor, other remote hard-to-reach populations, and micro firms were the hardest hit. This issue merits urgent attention and actions as financial inclusion is identified as the enabler for seven of the seventeen UN Sustainable Development Goals (SDGs). For a start, current available tools that measure financial inclusion are either too simple or too academic, and cover mainly transaction accounts. To go beyond transaction accounts, a fresh approach incorporating a user-friendly financial inclusion dashboard that is more sophisticated than common benchmarks, and that measures usage and sustainability, covering credit savings and insurance, are being suggested. Emerging-markets' governments need to take the lead in improving financial inclusion, and financial institutions also need to respond with radical changes in their operating models, while other primary stakeholders have to play their catalytic roles for financial inclusion to succeed.[115]

The disproportionate and excessive impact of financialization on financial institutions, non-financial businesses, and the average households require deep reflections. The positive impacts include the modernization of economies to keep pace with new technology developments, and greater realization of enhanced productivity. Less desirable impacts include the hurting of many households with unsustainable mounting debts, and micro businesses lacking access to much needed funding. Financialization brings with it, both the contradictory problems of financial exclusion for the many, and over inclusion for some. To resist the ill effects of financialization, various novel solutions have emerged. These, among others, include organizing donations to buy distressed personal loans for writing off, moving savings and businesses to smaller institutions with different operating logics, greater use of crowdfunding, lobbying by civil society organizations (CSOs) for new rules to roll back the financialization of agricultural commodity markets, and the strengthening of more financial transaction Tobin taxes to curb excessive speculation.[116]

Also, over the years, financialization and tax havens have witnessed a permanent and simultaneous development.[117] Many governments did not fight against the establishment of tax havens, and instead tried to emulate them by lowering tax rates on profits, developing all types of tax shelters and even suppressed anti-speculative regulations under the pretext of capital mobility. All these, but more, increased the risk for a global catastrophe. Tax havens, for almost five decades now, have assumed the role of exotic outposts for the world of finance. They have been held up as levers with which large multinational banks and the financial elites pressured state authorities. Capitalists became adept at using tax havens to re-route their capital and to continue to

115. K. Kessler, A.S. Ikdal, E. Naidoo, A. Portafaix, J. Hendrickson, A. Boje & D. Rabec. 2017. 'How to create and sustain financial inclusion', *Boston Consulting Group (BCG) 11/4/17*.
116. R. Foroohar. 2016. 'American capitalism's great crisis', *Time 12/5/16*; F. Thomson & S. Dutta. 2016. 'Financialisation: A primer', *Transnational Institute (TNI) 6/1/16*.
117. The Spark. 2013. 'Tax havens: Outpost for the world of finance', *The Spark 26/7/13*.

enjoy making money without any constraints, but not without aggravating the stability of their own systems.

Sure enough, during the GFC, the panic that enveloped global finance came from big bank branches in tax havens. Indeed, Lehman Brothers, Bear Stearns, and Northern Rock were sucked into bankruptcies by their subsidiaries in the Isle of Man, Jersey, the Cayman Islands, or the BVI.[118] The fight against tax havens subsequent to the GFC has been criticized as wishful thinking, because tax havens are at the heart of the financialization of capitalist economies. The financialization of the economy is simply how the system has been operating for more than four decades. It developed because of inadequate profitable productive investments, commencing especially in the 1970s. When seeking for better returns for their money, big corporations and multinationals simply aggravated financial speculation. When they achieved that, many try to conceal the level of their wealth and incomes by routing these to regulatory-light and tax-light OFCs, at times derogatively referred to, as tax havens by policymakers and global regulators. This is the focus of attention of the next chapter.

Meanwhile, the IMF drew the attention of the world on the material impacts of the global financialization process, in particular, the not so small matter of inequality within and between economies and at the micro-level between the financial elites and the disadvantaged. The IMF further drew attention to the issues of financial deepening, financial stability, and financial inclusion.[119] While China and India have been held up, as examples where financial deepening has forged enormous economic gains, research suggests a point, from which it is associated with exacerbated inequality and less-inclusive growth and that is exemplified even in the world largest economy, namely the US. Second, research also suggests that on average a financial crisis such as the 2007 GFC can lead to a permanent output loss of 10%, thereby changing the entire trajectory of a country's future and leaving too many behind permanently; and that inequality tends to increase before a financial crisis, signalling a powerful link between inequality and financial stability.

The link between financial stability and inequality is not confined to the 2007 GFC, as survey insights from seventeen advanced economies between 1870 and 2013 suggest widening income inequality is a strong predictor of financial crises of lasting effects.[120] These rich insights confirmed that while financialization can help spur developments, excessive financial deepening, and financial crises can fuel inequality too, suggesting further the need to find the appropriate balance between too much and too little. Research further suggests a strong association between increasing access to bank accounts and reducing income inequality, that is to say financial inclusion gets more people and businesses to have cheaper and easier access to financial services. For the wider economies, IMF research suggests that there is a 2%-3% point GDP growth

118. *Supra* note [117]. The Spark. 2013.
119. K. Georgieva. 2020. 'The financial sectors in the 2020s: Building a more inclusive system in the next decade', *IMF Managing Director Speech at the Peterson Institute for International Economics Washington, D.C. 17/1/20.*
120. *Supra* note [119]. Georgieva. 2020.

difference over the long-term between financially inclusive countries and their less-inclusive cohorts.

Given these challenges, the IMF has prescribed three policy areas upon which to build a more inclusive system in the next decade that is safer, stable, and smarter.[121] Initiatives towards a safer financial system saw positive steps taken to implement regulatory reform agenda subsequent to the 2008 GFC, demonstrating that in an interconnected global economy, strong financial sector reforms need strong international cooperation. These nevertheless need countries to follow through on the reform agenda and to complement them with new initiatives, as safe developments of financial markets need increasing financial literacy to enable people to fully understand what they are being offered and what it implies for their families or their businesses. With regard to financial stability, building more stable financial systems require the private sector and banking industry to play critical roles. This is where a longer-term business horizon that could crystalize risks and opportunities could help, and where stronger disclosure standards in the business world could help further.

Also, IMF research suggests that lending to small firms increases financial stability and reduces risks compared to lending to large firms, as when risk is spread across many businesses instead of a few conglomerates, a more inclusive and healthier economy emerges. Third, and finally, creating smarter financial systems requires broadening financial access to low-income households and small businesses so as to reduce inequality. A World Bank study showed that lending to smaller firms is directly linked to reductions in income inequality as these firms often hire people needing work the most. This is well exemplified by Kenya's M-Pesa, a peer-to-peer mobile payment service that is now poised to become a pan-African financial platform. This, however, did not just happen overnight, but the outcome of years of work by entrepreneurs, government officials, and importantly, citizens who were searching for new opportunities and is ergo a good model to learn from. Meanwhile, on the other hand, criticisms are levelled at tax havens for not doing its part in curbing the excesses of financialization as highlighted extensively in this chapter, and serve more as reservoirs for surplus capital of questionable origins in many instances. Discussions on this will follow in the next chapter.

121. *Supra* note [119]. Georgieva. 2020.

CHAPTER 3
Tax Havens

§3.01 INTRODUCTION

This chapter draws out the nature and significant of tax havens in global finance and investments. It discusses how and why the OECD put Member States and the world on attention with regard to the harmful effects of lower tax competition. US and EU tax policies in the context of tax havens are discussed in particular as the two jurisdictions combined impact significantly the use and misuse of tax havens across the world. Implications from this provide the background for enhanced discussion on how at the global scale finance interact and intertwined with key activities in tax havens. This is followed by an updated review of how tax havens could be identified using relatively less controversial approaches. This chapter ends with some commentaries on regulatory and enforcement actions against harmful activities going on in tax havens.

§3.02 NATURE AND SIGNIFICANCE OF TAX HAVENS

Various IFCs across the world, whether onshore, midshore, or offshore have been on different occasions referred to as tax havens. These attracted not only the interests of economic entities with focus on cross-border economic activities, but also the attention of national and global regulatory authorities empowered to keep keen eyes on those linked to IFFs. References to tax havens often suggest the notion of jurisdictions where tax obligations of individuals, businesses, and MNCs were minimized and hence beneficial to them, but not necessarily for governments relying on taxes to fund operational and developmental expenditures.

In fact, taxes existed for the purposes of revenue generation to drive human development, for redistribution to reduce poverty and inequality by bridging the gaps between the rich and the poor via its redistributive effect, as price signals to steer economic activities in particular directions, like environmental pollution tax and health protecting tobacco tax, and for inducing civic consciousness about the sourcing and deployment of public funds.[122] Dominant themes in public policies pertain to the aim for neutrality of the tax system of not distorting production or consumption, achievement of the redistribution goals via expenditure not taxation, as governments are assumed to have full range of instruments at their disposals with tax revenues in the order of 15%-20% of GDP.[123]

It appears that poorer economies, like sub-Saharan Africa, are less able to raise revenue in absolute and proportional terms. It would further appear that very similar tax structures and tax rates generate very different revenues in different economies. This has been attributed to different levels of taxpayer compliance and efficiency of tax administration. Governments' discretionary powers to do the right things have been powerfully undermined by international structures relating to flows of finance and goods. Tax leakages arise on account of tax due, but not collected from the shadow economy, tax due from income earned from assets held offshore because of tax havens, tax on income earned by MNCs and then moved without paying appropriately, taxes eroded by tax competition between jurisdictions seeking FDIs, and from underfunded enforcement administration and paltry penalties for non-payments.

Tax Justice Network (TJN) estimated the total annual tax loss due to use of tax havens at about USD 255 billion, of which some USD 50 billion is accounted for by developing economies.[124] Such leakages, in general, exceed aid flows for developing economies. Until such leakages are curbed, tax evasion both onshore and offshore, and those who commit and facilitate would continue to undermine the funding of human development opportunities.

While globalization has opened up vast trade opportunities for many economies, including developing economies, it has the unintended consequence of inducing competition for competition of capital flows for development and related purposes, and this is frequently sought after through the low-hanging fruit provided by tax competition for FDIs. TJN views tax competition as the process by which countries use tax cuts, tax breaks, tax loopholes or tax subsidies to attract investments, hot money, and even from the very affluent communities. These are largely non-cooperative actions to edge out the tax efforts of other competing economies.

§3.03 OECD: HARMFUL EFFECTS OF TAX COMPETITION

The OECD more than a decade ago spotlighted the harmful impacts of tax competition, arguing it has the negative impact of opening up new ways, by which, the affluent

---

122. A. Cobham. 2007. 'The tax consensus has failed: Recommendation to policymakers and donors, researchers and civil society', *The Oxford Council on Good Governance: Economy Recommendation 8*; A. Cobham. 2005. 'Taxation policy and development', *The Oxford Council on Good Governance (OCGG) Project Paper EPP 05-01*; R.S. Avi-Yonah. 2006. 'The three goals of taxation', *Tax Law Revenue*, Vol. 60(1): 1-28.
123. *Supra* note [122]. Cobham. 2007.
124. Tax Justice Network (TJN). 2005. The price of offshore, *Briefing Paper*, London: TJN; Oxfam. 2000. 'Tax havens: Releasing the hidden billions for poverty eradication', *Briefing Paper*, Oxford: Oxfam.

communities and businesses could minimize and avoid taxes, and by which, economies could exploit by designing tax policies targeting principally at diverting financial and other geographical mobile capital.[125] In general, the OECD and others do not intervene, where such policies are undertaken legitimately, and are not over-aggressive tax practices.

Harmful tax consequences, highlighted by the OECD, include the erosion of the tax coffers of non-haven economies, the making-up for these by tax burdens shifting to immobile factors like labour and property leading to inequality issues, the discouraging of tax compliance in general, and restraining the employment of progressive tax rates. It is further claimed that tax competition causes tax rates to be set below their optimal levels.[126] This led to tax harmonization or cooperative tax setting and tax haven eradication suggestions as tax reform initiatives.

The EU, for instance, has a Code of Conduct for business taxation, which though not a legally binding instrument has political force. EU Member States, when adopting this Code of Conduct, undertake to roll back existing tax measures that constitute harmful tax competition, and to refrain from introducing any such measures in the future. Potentially harmful tax measures include having an effective level of taxation that is significantly lower than the general level of taxation in the jurisdiction concerned; tax benefits reserved for non-residents; tax incentives for activities isolated from the domestic economy; granting tax advantages in the absence of any real economic activity; deviations from internationally accepted rules for profit determination of entities in multinational groups; and the general lack of transparency.[127]

The OECD, for its part, following its 1997 Report, created a dedicated forum known as 'Global Forum on Harmful Tax Practices' focusing attention on harmful tax practices in member economies, tax havens, and those involving non-OECD economies. The Global Forum generated various progress reports. In particular, Global Forum together with cooperative tax havens produced a 'Model Tax Agreement on Exchange of Information in Tax Matters', as well as its bigger work on Base Erosion and Profit Shifting (BEPS).[128]

§3.04 EU AND US TAX POLICIES

The EC, in turn, in 2004, adopted a 'Communication on Preventing and Combating Financial and Corporate Malpractice (COM (2004) 611)'. This provided a strategy for coordinated action in financial services, company law, accounting, and tax, and supervision and enforcement areas to lower the risks of financial malpractices. The EC further sought to ensure coherent EU policies pertaining to OFCs, and to encourage these jurisdictions to head towards transparency and effective information exchange.

125. OECD. 1998. *Harmful tax competition: An emerging global issue*, Paris: OECD.
126. N.G. Mankiw, M. Weinzierl & D. Yagan. 2009. 'Optimal taxation in theory and practice', *Journal of Economic Perspectives*, Vol. 23(4): 147-174.
127. European Commission (EC). 1997. 'Harmful tax competition', *EC*.
128. OECD. 2017. 'Background brief: Inclusive framework on BEPS', *OECD January 2017*.

In April 2009, the EC adopted a Communication identifying actions that EU Member States should undertake to promote good governance in the tax area, like more transparency, exchange of information, and fair tax competition. At the global level, the EC calls on Member States to adopt approaches that are more coherent with good governance principles in their bilateral relations with third countries and in international forums. This Communication builds on the existing EU policy on good governance in the tax area[129] and the G20 conclusions reached on 2 April 2009 in London to take actions against uncooperative tax jurisdictions, including tax havens.[130]

More recent developments in the EU include *Directive 2016/1164* on tax avoidance practices that directly impact the internal market and *Directive 2015/2376* on automatic/mandatory exchange of information (AEI) on taxation matters. In respect of tax avoidance, new rules reached at the Economic and Financial Affairs Council on 21 February 2017 set out EU-wide anti-abuse measures against tax avoidance. The rules were designed to help curb tax avoidance, by prohibiting MNCs from escaping corporate taxes via leveraging on the differences between the tax systems of Member States, and those of non-EU economies known as hybrid mismatches. They came into force on 1 January 2020. Member States as of 1 January 2017 were also obliged to AEI, every six months, on all new cross-border tax rulings they issue via a central depository accessible to all EU Member States. This information exchange came into application in 1 September 2017, and also since 1 January 2018, the same information procedures for all cross-border dealings issued since 2012.

It has now been counterclaimed that the assumption that governments would tax optimally in the absence of competition is flawed. Policymakers and governments driven by considerations of re-election prospects tend to overspend and overtax, and tax competition is argued to help keep taxes closer to the optimal level thereby constraining wasteful government excess.[131]

Owing largely to this, international tax competition is very much in play, other than in the case of the US where it lagged far behind, until the significant corporate and related tax reduction to a flat 21% was successfully launched by the Trump administration in 2017.[132] It had been earlier reported that the average tax rate of the US was slightly below the OECD average at 29.2% versus 30.2%.[133] In subsequent years, the OECD average dropped to 20.6%, while that for the US remained relatively unchanged for some years until the tax cut initiated by President Trump in 2017. The OECD 2014 data, for instance, suggests that the combined federal and state statutory corporate tax rate for the US was 39.1%, while the overage of the other thirty-three members of the

129. European Commission (EC). 2009. 'Communication from the Commission to the Council, The European Parliament and the European Economic and Social Committee: Promoting good governance in tax matters', *EC, Brussels 28/4/09 COM (2009) 201 final.*
130. EC. 2009. 'Taxation and good governance: The EC proposed actions to improve transparency, exchange of information and fair tax competition', *EC Press Release 28/4/09.*
131. T. Wiebe. 2011. 'The benefits of tax competition', *Tax Foundation 25/7/11.*
132. M. Hanlon, J.L. Hoopes & J. Slemrod. 2018. 'Tax reforms made me do it', *NBER Working Paper 25283 November 2018.*
133. K.A. Hassett & A. Mathur. 2011. 'Report card on effective corporate tax rates', *American Enterprise Institute 9/2/11.*

OECD was 24.8%, some 14.3% lower than the then US rates.[134] Weighted by country GDP, the average for these thirty-three countries is 28.3%, some 10.8% lower than the US rate, that is until 2017 when the US corporate tax rate became effectively lower.

A different empirical study, on the other hand, suggests that, while the US statutory tax rate was before 2017 higher than much of the rest of the world, the average effective rate was almost similar. The statutory rate differential was relevant for international profit shifting, while effective rates are more relevant for firms' investment levels. The US statutory rate of 39.2% before 2017 compared with 25.5% in other countries suggested a higher 13.7%-point differential, but narrows down to some 9%, when tax rates were weighted to reflect the size of countries' economies.[135] It has been further claimed that because of factors that constrained capital flows, estimates for a rate cut from 35% to 25% suggest a modest positive effect on wages and output, or an eventual one-time increase of less than two-tenths of 1% output. It also seemed unlikely that the rate cut of this magnitude could significantly reduce profit shifting given that these transactions are relatively costless and largely constrained by law, enforcement, and court decisions.[136] Also, output gains and revenue offsets could be reduced, if other economies responded to a US rate cut by reducing their own taxes. The Tax Reform Act of 1986, for instance, triggered rate cuts in other countries.

Still, the US because of this very significant perceived difference in tax liability, coupled with the strategy to enhance their international competitiveness had for long come under real pressure to enact beneficial corporate tax reforms, like the lowering of the corporate tax rate and moving to a territorial system of taxing foreign earnings, as proposed by the Trump administration.[137] The sketchy One-Page Whitehouse Handout sought to cut top individual tax rates from 39.6% to 35%, and top tax rate cut for all businesses to 15% below the current top rates. The suggested tax reform was meant to grow the economy and create millions of jobs, simplify the burdensome US tax code, provide tax relief to American families, and lower the business tax rate from one of the highest in the world to one of the lowest.[138]

Eventually, the Trump administration in lowering corporate and individual taxes in 2017 sought to keep in line with global trends, and to motivate US MNCs to reinvest more of their surplus earnings back into the US, and enhance payments to workers.[139] Thus far, there has been no substantial evidence of countries reacting with similar tax cuts, or US MNCs bringing home much of their surplus earnings held abroad in low-tax regimes or in OFCs. Preliminary analysis though suggests that firms with greater expected savings from the 2017 tax statute were those most likely to announce payments to workers and to plan for increased investments.[140]

134. M. Sullivan. 2015. 'The truth about corporate tax rates', *Forbes 25/3/15.*
135. J.G. Gravelle. 2014. 'International corporate tax rate comparisons and policy implications', *Congressional Research Service (CRS) Report 7-5700 R41743,* 6 January 2014.
136. *Supra* note [135]. Gravelle. 2014.
137. J.H. Davis & A. Rappenport. 2017. 'White House proposes slashing tax rates, significantly aiding wealth', *The New York Times 26/4/17.*
138. Whitehouse. 2017. '2017 Tax Reform for Economic Growth and American Jobs', *Whitehouse Handout 27/4/17.*
139. Tax Cuts and Jobs Act 2017.
140. *Supra* note [132]. Hanlon, Hoopes & Slemrod. 2018.

§3.05 GLOBAL FINANCE AND TAX HAVENS

Jurisdictions with competitive tax rates and tax havens with minimal tax are not that easy to discern, even though the OECD, the EU, and others have targeted these for remedial actions. This is attributed to the absence of a universally accepted definition. The avoidance and minimization of tax liability and the offer of confidentiality bordering secrecy are offered by tax havens, but jurisdictions with competitive tax rates might not offer the latter. Tax havens in general offer the use of shell companies without substantial economic activities to assist in the transfer of tax liability from high-tax home economy to the low-tax havens, while simultaneously offering secrecy for the identities of beneficial owners. They tend also to have some respectable skills in the management of funds and financial flows. Tax havens, as such, could be identified as those jurisdictions with little or no tax on all or particular kinds of incomes, coupled with varying levels of commercial or banking secrecies.[141] In practice, the financial community and others include those that promote themselves, as such, by way of practice and reputation in global tax planning.

Offshore finance grew from a peripheral phenomenon to a pivotal position of contemporary capitalism over the last five decades to enable private investors and businesses to steer clear of taxation and regulation of the onshore jurisdictions, wherein they exist and operate. From a narrower perspective, they could be deemed as countries or jurisdictions that provide financial services to non-residents on a scale that is incommensurate with the size and the financing of its domestic economy.[142] They were also not to be viewed as similar to tax havens, although they are existing as an integral part of the latter. OFCs generally refer to commercial and professional communities set up within tax havens. These comprise solicitors, accountants, financial advisors, tax consultants, bankers, and their associated trust companies that offer services to employ the structures that tax havens have to offer. Tax havens from this perspective are confined spatially. In contrast, OFCs are more mobile with the OFC community largely expatriate and following the flow of funds. For instance, subsequent to the 2016 PP leakage, the OFC community in that jurisdiction could likely move to another tax haven to avoid undue media attention.

Tax havens therefore distinguished themselves as jurisdictions that formulate their statutes and regulations for various entities to escape the relatively more demanding regulatory requirements of their home base or jurisdictions, where they undertake the substance of their economic activities. They are as such marked by little or no tax on particular kinds of incomes, as well as commercial or banking secrecy. In general, they do not require nor provide disclosures of beneficial owners of financial activities or financial assets and also allow the use of nominee directors to perform the day-to-day activities. Further, they do not require disclosures of financial accounts, or

141. D.J. Workman. 1982. 'The use of offshore tax havens for the purpose of criminally evading income taxes', *The Journal of Criminal Law and Criminology*, Vol. 73(2): 675-706.
142. A. Zorome. 2007. 'Concept of offshore financial centers: In search of an operational definition', *IMF Working Paper WP/07/87.*

those that do, with minimum non-current financial data. Tax havens also do not share information of their clienteles with other jurisdictions. In short, they offer secrecy.

These aside, tax havens in general host subsidiaries of big businesses without substantial economic activities. They also tend to have high level of financial services relative to their GDPs, and relatively fewer controls over the financial activities of foreign nationals. These unfortunately tend to attract people and entities with nefarious activities. Secrecy in tax havens therefore occurs in terms of bank secrecy, as found in Switzerland, Austria, and Luxembourg; beneficial ownership secrecy, via the use of shell companies, as exemplified by Wyoming, Delaware and Nevada in the US; and in terms of refusal to cooperate in the exchange of tax-related information with other jurisdictions.[143]

There is no consensus on the numbers and types of tax havens. Much depends on what activities are included, and the kind of taxes being considered. Most tax havens, however, come into being primarily because of the tax advantage they offer, often together with secrecy thrown in. The types and numbers vary depending on the approaches/methods used. They could be two,[144] four,[145] six,[146] or seven.[147] Categorization further depends on the criteria used, whether in geographical terms, targeted types, users' types, or activities types. The OECD basically divides tax havens as those with harmful tax practices and uncooperative in exchange of tax information and those excluding these. Its initial position used the criteria of no or only nominal taxation as the necessary condition coupled with self-promotion as a place of escape from taxation. The burden of proof for this was to be assumed by the tax haven.[148]

Under severe criticisms for dictating the appropriate level of tax rates, the OECD changed its criteria to the lack of effective exchange of information and the lack of transparency.[149] The OECD classification is closely followed, because of its stature, and because it simply tells whether a jurisdiction is or is not a tax haven on the basis of transparency features and effective exchange of information. Most jurisdictions just want to know whether they are on the blacklist, as it could have significant political and economic implications. The TJN claimed that its listings were more comprehensive and included several types of tax haven jurisdictions.[150]

TJN suggests that tax havens could be mere incorporation locations, marked by low effective regulations and minimal information disclosure, as in Montserrat and

143. L. Booijink & F. Weyzig. 2007. 'Identifying tax havens and offshore financial centres', *Tax Justice Network (TJN)*.
144. OECD. 1998. *Harmful tax competition: An emerging global issue*, Paris: OECD.
145. R. Margarida & P.R. Mourao. 2013. 'Tax havens or tax hells? A discussion of the historical roots and present consequences of tax havens', *Financial Theory & Practice*, Vol. 37(3): 311-360.
146. M. Orlov. 2004. 'The concept of tax haven: A legal analysis', *International Tax Review*, Vol. 32(2): 95-111; N.W. Tun. 1997. 'Tax havens', *The George Washington University Institute of Brazilian Business and Public Management Issues Paper Fall 1997*; TJN. 2007. 'Identifying
147. L. Ates, A. Cobham, P. Jansky, M. Meinzer, L. Millan-Narotsky & M. Palansky. 2020. 'The corporate tax haven index: A new geography of profit shifting', *IES Working Paper 38/2020*.
148. OECD. 1998. *Harmful tax competition: An emerging global issue*, Paris: OECD.
149. OECD. 2013. 'Automatic exchange of information'.
150. R. Murphy. 2008. 'Tax havens creating turmoil', *Evidence Submitted to the Treasury Committee of the House of Commons by the Tax Justice Network (TJN) June 2008*; L. Booijink & F. Weyzig. 2007. 'Identifying tax havens and offshore financial centres'.

Anguilla. They could be secrecy locations, like Liechtenstein, the Turks and Caicos Islands and Dubai where secrecy is heavily safeguarded; particular geographic market suppliers, like the BVI servicing Chinese demand for offshore entities, Vanuatu serving the Australian market, and Jersey servicing the London market, and Panama the US market. They could be specialist service providers, like Bermuda and Guernsey serving the reinsurance market; the Isle of Man serving the UK's AIM market; and Cayman serving hedge funds. They could be market conduits, like Malta and Cyprus facilitating transactions between developing economies and the EU; or like Mauritius serving as conduits for investments in India; and the Netherlands, Belgium and Luxembourg serving holding companies investing throughout Europe. They could be high-net-worth providers, like London, New York and Switzerland. Or, they could be tax raiders, like Ireland where low-tax liability comes together with a high degree of financial security and limited risk of being spotted derogatively as tax havens.[151] For some tax havens, they could be combining some of these roles; and these days with the increasing popularities of crypto assets, like bitcoin, as destinations of choice for those engaging in such transactions.[152]

In practice, high-net-worth individuals, big businesses, and MNCs are guided by criteria that serve their interests best. International businesses, for instance, look for those jurisdictions that are economically stable, neutral politically, embracing free trade policies, strength in privacy provisions, ease for conducting operational activities, or minimal or no-tax liability obligations.[153] It merits repeating here, that tax havens and OFCs are not the same thing. While they are related, they have entirely different characteristics.

Tax havens deliberately design legal structures that have little or no benefits for those residents within their own domains, but which and are indeed often exploited by non-residents legally and illegally to avoid obligations placed upon them by the laws and regulations imposed on them in the jurisdictions where they live and undertake their primary economic activities. OFCs are the commercial communities hosted by tax havens, which exploit the structures that could be designed using the legislations of the tax havens for benefits of non-residents.

This means that OFCs are made up of solicitors, accountants, bankers and their associated trust companies that sell services to those wishing to exploit the mechanisms created by the tax havens. This further suggests that tax havens are fixed spatially and has loyalty to a place. In contrast, the OFC community is highly mobile, often collaborating in several tax havens simultaneously, and serving a mobile clientele base that can relocate globally with very short notice, and hence without commitment to geographic space, as they try to achieve the ultimate goal of the tax evader, meaning in nowhere for regulatory purposes and indeed beyond the scope of tax or related laws.[154]

151. *Supra* note [150]. Murphy. 2008.
152. V. Chawla. 2021. 'The top 15 crypto-friendly tax havens', *Crypto Briefing 11/2/21*.
153. P. Hype. 2017. 'The different categories of tax havens', *Paul Hype Page*.
154. *Supra* note [150]. Murphy. 2008.

As a consequence of the activities of some OFCs and tax havens, many business transactions could take place without being effectively regulated by the global financial systems. This undermines the tax coffers of many governments, besides posing serious threats to the stability of the financial system. More seriously, such structures permit the capital flight that is fundamentally undermining development efforts in poor economies. Such capital flights inclusive of illicit activities range from USD 600 billion to USD 1 trillion annually.[155] Much of these activities are enabled by the veil of secrecy that tax havens provide. Tax havens sell secrecy as a valued commodity.

OFCs because of these various developments tend to be tax havens, when competing on tax attractiveness; regulatory havens, when competing on varying secrecy strengths offered; and operational efficiency havens, when competing on economic efficiency grounds. Tax havens are therefore of different stripes. Some focus on tax evasion, others on tax avoidance and secrecy, and yet others on reliable and cost-efficient financial administration, or any combinations of these. But tax havens are more commonly marked by laws and other measures that could be applied to evade or avoid the tax laws or regulations of their jurisdictions.[156]

The key idea is to minimize tax. This could be achieved by the use of shell corporations, trusts, or other suitable legal entities, and coordinated routing and managing financial flows. True blue tax havens generally have laws particularly formulated for these purposes, with the further aim of attracting financial and corporate services business that are or could become a major part of the economy. Secrecy is the attractiveness of most tax havens. These include bank secrecy, where information might not be easily extracted from banks even for official purposes; and secrecy of legal entities where information might not be freely or easily available concerning corporations, foundations, trusts, or with regard to the beneficial owners of financial assets housed in these entities. Importantly, tax havens provide particular advantages like a zero or low tax rate for non-residents, or foreign-owned legal entities.

Since the early 1960s, all major tax havens of the world have spawned financial centres known as OFCs. The Bank of International Settlement (BIS) has estimated that, since the early 1980s, approximately half of all international banking assets and liabilities were channelled through OFCs, while a third of multinationals' foreign direct investments (FDIs) flowed through tax havens.[157] These high levels of FDIs channelled through tax havens have been attributed to the absence of reliable data on corporate tax avoidance. Individual tax avoidance and tax evasion are estimated conservatively between USD 800 billion to a trillion annually.[158] The main choice of channel for the routing of laundered money away from developing economies were, and still are, likely to be tax havens.

Tax havens enable highly affluent financial elites and powerful cash rich multinationals to be elsewhere, ideally nowhere, and therefore away from onshore

155. *Supra* note [150]. Murphy. 2008.
156. S. Botis. 2014. 'Features and advantages of using tax havens', *Bulletin of the Transilvania University of Brasov Series V*, Vol. 7(2): 181-188.
157. R. Palan. 2012. 'Tax havens and offshore financial centres', *Academic Foresights*, Vol. 4(2012): 1-15.
158. *Supra* note [157]. Palan. 2012.

regulatory oversight.[159] Private assets of some USD 6 trillion are registered in OFCs, of which some three-quarters are not in official data.[160] It has also been suggested that, as much as USD 21-32 trillion could be located in tax havens.[161]

As alluded to in the previous chapter, OFCs being important components of the shadow banking system played an important function in the 2007 GFC.[162] Various OFCs operated as legal domiciles for the 'manufacturing' of opaque complex structural financial products, including other asset-backed securities that contributed or accentuated the 2007 GFC.[163] The G20 responded by enhancing the regulation of offshore finance. This did not lower assets logged in OFCs, but merely led to a game of musical chairs between tax havens,[164] and hence merely serving as symbolic gestures of the state doing something. In essence, OFCs are not purely geographic or economic plays, but concerns political sovereignty.[165] In reality, various OFCs are dependent territories applying their inner sovereignty to draw in financial services from overseas via taxation-lite and regulation-lite instruments. These suggest that OFCs, together with the affluent financial elites and global businesses that employ them, are benefiting against the interests of onshore economies' majority inhabitants that do not partake in such offshore activities.[166]

OFCs were and still are controversial, economically and politically. This is because increasingly offshore finance, as a phenomenon, has not been perceived to be confined to small exotic islands, but could include those onshore, such as found in the US state of Delaware and parts of continental Europe. The ICIJ report of November 2014 suggested that the Grand Duchy of Luxembourg assisted some 350 global businesses to contain their global tax bills significantly. Such global entities transferred huge funds through this small jurisdiction thereby saving huge sums in taxes elsewhere.[167] More fascinating was the *Double Irish with a Dutch Sandwich' Tax Model* that cuts down taxes for large global businesses by shifting profits from Irish subsidiaries to the Netherlands and back to Ireland and subsequently to other tax havens.[168]

159. R. Palan & A. Nesvetailova. 2014. 'Elsewhere, ideally nowhere: Shadow banking and offshore finance', *CITYPERC Working Paper Series No. 2014-01*.
160. G. Zucman. 2013. 'The missing wealth of nations, are Europe and the U.S. net debtors, or net creditors?', *Quarterly Journal of Economics*, Vol. 128(3): 1321-1364.
161. I. Henry. 2012. 'The price of offshore revisited', *Tax Justice Network* (TJN).
162. T. Rixen. 2013. 'Why reregulation after the crisis is feeble: Shadow banking, offshore financial centres, and jurisdictional competition', *Regulation & Governance*, Vol. 7(2013): 435-459.
163. P. Lysandrou & A. Nesvetailova. 2015. 'The role of shadow banking entities in the financial crisis: A disaggregated review', *Review of International Political Economy*, Vol. 22(2): 257-279.
164. N. Johannesen & G. Zucman. 2014. 'The end of bank secrecy? An evaluation of the G20 tax haven crackdown', *American Economic Journal: Economic Policy*, Vol. 6(1): 65-91.
165. R. Palan, R. Murphy & C. Chavagneux. 2010. *Tax havens: How globalization really works*. Ithaca: Cornell University Press.
166. N. Shaxson. 2011. *Treasure islands: Tax havens and the men who stole the world*. London: The Bodley Head.
167. L. Wayne, K. Carr, M.W. Guevara, M. Cobra & M. Hudson. 2014. 'Leaked documents expose global companies' secret tax deals in Luxembourg', *ICIJ 5/11/14*.
168. C. Duhigg & D. Kocieniewski. 2012. 'How Apple sidesteps billions in taxes', *The New York Times 28/4/12*.

§3.06 IDENTIFYING TAX HAVENS

As alluded to earlier, there is no universal categorization for OFCs or tax havens, other than some good efforts done on this by two notable researchers in this field.[169] One drew his analysis only on data for portfolio investments and excluded FDIs and foreign bank deposits.[170] Tax havens as generally understood operated since the 1950s. Some governments use their sovereign rights to enact rules to assist successful sectors, or to spur new competitive activities within their economies to compete in the global economy. They employ a menu of fiscal subsidies and sweeteners, including tax reductions by informal and opaque mechanisms and dressing down bureaucracies and regulations to attract footloose global capital.

The fiscal parts of these policy measures are known as Preferential Tax Regimes (PTRs) incorporating wide rules and regulations constructed to attract foreign capital. The European Commission (EC) in the late 1990s, while investigating tax abuse among EU Member States, found 206 such regimes excluding PTRs in dependent territories like the Channel Islands and Gibraltar. Such instances suggest that tax havens are economic zones of a general nature and do not necessarily focus on particular industries or developmental goals. This leads to the probability of smaller jurisdiction tax havens with population of under one million rising from 24% to 63%, and even higher when dependent jurisdictions are included.[171] This though might not apply to onshore tax havens found in parts of the US and continental Europe. Indeed, these days of highly mobile financial environment, together with widespread use of PTRs, could enable any jurisdiction to serve as a potential haven from taxation of other economies. By this token, the US[172] and the UK[173] are considered by many to be tax havens.

On other hand, it has been argued that the US and the UK would unlikely use a tax haven strategy as part of their developmental strategies.[174] Under this intentionality test, both of them could be excluded. As such, tax havens are assigned to those jurisdictions that deliberately formulate legislations to ease transactions undertaken by non-residents in their domains. Such 'international' transactions are subject to minimal regulations with the havens providing legally protected secrecy to ensure that these are not linked to those undertaking them. These then become 'offshore' transactions that occur in legal frameworks that separate the real location of the economic transactions from the perceived locations of occurrence.[175] This perspective is, however, not supported by various CSOs.

---

169. *Supra* note [165]. Palan, Murphy & Chavagneux. 2010; A. Zorome. 2007. 'Concept of offshore financial centers: In search of an operational definition', *IMF Working Paper WP/07/87.*
170. *Supra* note [169]. Zorome. 2007.
171. D.A. Dharmapala & J.R. Hines. 2006. 'Which countries become tax havens?', *NBER Working Paper No. W12802.*
172. V.P. Belotsky. 1987. 'The prevention of tax havens via income tax treaties', *California Western International Law Journal,* Vol. 17(1987): 43-62.
173. C.R. Irish. 1982. 'Tax havens', *Vanderbilt Journal of Transnational Law,* Vol. 15(1982): 449-510.
174. R. Palan. 2009. 'History of tax havens', *History and Policy Papers 1/10/09.*
175. *Supra* note [174]. Palan. 2009.

A brief historical examination of tax havens suggests that they evolved often for reasons that have little to do with their ultimate modern applications. New Jersey and Delaware in the US used the tax haven strategy in the late nineteenth century, but are generally not considered by the US as tax havens for reasons mentioned earlier. They are instead credited as the pioneers of the easy incorporation model that is now replicated and used in all modern tax havens. This model enables business to legally trade in not more than a day by tapping on the use of available off the shelf companies. Parts of Switzerland and Liechtenstein subsequent to 1920 replicated the US practice. While US states pioneered the idea of liberalizing incorporation laws, the British courts are credited for pioneering 'virtual residencies' by enabling companies to incorporate in Britain without paying tax, and this is said to lay the foundation of tax havens. The 1929 case of *Egyptian Delta Land and Investment Co. Ltd. v. Todd* created a loophole that in essence made Britain a tax haven.[176]

This sets the rule not only in the UK, but also across the then entire British Empire, and subsequently leveraged by Bermuda and the Bahamas, before being perfected by the Cayman Islands and expanded across many British Commonwealth jurisdictions. The third leg in the global tripartite tax haven framework was contributed by the Swiss bank secrecy made possible by the Swiss Banking Law of 1934. This legislation insisted absolute silence pertaining to professional secrets, or in this case absolute silence in respect for any accounts held in Swiss banks. It makes enquiry or research into the trade secrets of banks and other entities a criminal offence. In effect, it virtually guarantees capital entering Switzerland enjoying inviolable legal protection backed by the criminal code and the Swiss state.

Banking secrecy in tax matters still exists as an obligation for all Swiss banks. Swiss banks, including Swiss tax authorities, no longer enjoy the right to refuse to provide property data of the taxpayer referring to bank secrecy. But no information would be provided to anyone in the absence of a special request. The supply of information would be secured in court though on the basis of the citizen's rights under Swiss law. This means that banking secrecy would continue to protect banks' clients from illegitimate requests for information by third parties, other than when dealing with cases of criminal activity and inheritance.[177]

Tax havens then evolved into their heydays in 1960s-1990s, because of the emergence of the Euromarkets, rather than because of rising taxation[178] The Bank of England (BOE) ruled in 1957 that transactions undertaken by UK banks undertaken on behalf of lenders and borrowers not domiciled in the UK were not to be officially deemed as having occurred in the UK for regulatory purposes, even though the transactions had taken place in the UK. The Euromarkets, though an inter-bank or wholesale financial market, is not regulated by the BOE. This arose from an implicit understanding between the BOE and the commercial banks. Such transactions therefore became effectively unregulated, even though having occurred in London, as no

176. S. Picciotto. 1992. *International business taxation*, London: Weidenfeld & Nicolson.
177. B. Nuredini & V.P. Dodevska, 2019. 'Protection of privacy and banking secrecy in Swiss banking', *UBT International Conference Paper October 2019.*
178. *Supra* note [174]. Palan. 2009.

other authority regulates the market. The emergence of the Euromarkets gradually became the main force behind an integrated offshore economy in London that came to include former members of the British Empire.

Three big US banks in the 1960s join the British banks, as the latter grew their Euromarkets activities in the Isle of Man, Guernsey, and Jersey. This expanded version of the tax haven model from the 1960s onwards sprouted in the Cayman Islands, as well as various British Commonwealth Member States around the world. Hence, early success of the European and Caribbean tax havens stimulated emergence of others in Norfolk Island, Vanuatu, Nauru, the Cook Islands, Tonga, Samoa, and the Marshall Islands. Nevertheless, as they copied and replicated each other's legislations and procedures they were also 'racing to the bottom' in terms of providing taxation-lite and rules-lite inducements that ended up with most getting the thinnest of margins.

These competitive offerings included zero or near zero taxation for exempt businesses and non-residential businesses, Swiss model of bank secrecy laws, offshore insurance laws, flags of convenience for shipping fleets, aircraft leasing such as found in the Panama, and of late, advantageous laws targeted at facilitating e-commerce and online gaming or gambling, and Irish-style Financial Services with advantageous tax regimes.[179]

The 1970s saw Bahrain and Dubai followed, while the 1980s and the 1990s witnessed emergence of tax havens in the Indian Ocean, Africa, and the post-Soviet Republics. By then, there were some 60-100 tax havens in the world, depending on the working definition for these.[180] The BIS conceded that around 50% of international lending could have been channelled through these havens, including some one-third of FDIs as well. This makes tax havens important conduits for tax avoidance worldwide, and also accounting for the largest drain on developing economies.[181] It also paved the way for various international regulatory responses, especially since the late 1990s. These are exemplified by the OECD 'Harmful Tax Competition' campaigns; by the EU; by the US; and by the G20. These would be discussed further in Chapter 6.

In the meantime, broadly three groupings of tax havens served all the major financial and commercial centres.[182] The biggest, by far, is the British Empire-based tax havens radiating from London. They are fed by the Euromarkets and comprised the Crown Dependencies, Overseas Territories, Pacific atolls, Hong Kong, and so on. The second group, the European havens, specialized as regional headquarters, financial affiliates, and private banking. The third is a disparate group of emulators like Dubai, Uruguay, Panama, or the emerging tax havens from the transition economies and the African continent.

This way of grouping tax havens could help to illustrate problems and opportunities relating to the coordination of international efforts to curb them. The OECD is seen to be ill equipped to dress down tax havens, because many of its members, like the

179. *Supra* note [174]. Palan. 2009.
180. *Supra* note [174]. Palan. 2009.
181. P. Reuter. 2012. *Draining development: Controlling flows of illicit funds from developing countries*, Washington DC: The World Bank.
182. *Supra* note [165]. Palan, Murphy & Chavagneux. 2010.

UK, Switzerland, Iceland and the Benelux countries are themselves perceived by others to be tax havens. The US and Western Europe considerably weakened by the 2007-2008 GFC have left spaces for creditor countries, like the more aggressive Gulf states, Hong Kong, and others to grow as tax havens. Still, with public coffers of most countries in the world, including those mentioned here dwindling, the pressures to recover funds from tax havens persist.

Initially, the UK, despite its rhetoric, is lukewarm in practice towards the taming of tax havens. It, however, started to show growing signs of change since David Cameron assume leadership of both the UK and the rotating G20 leadership. This was no easy matter for the British leader, as the more important tax havens are principally UK dependencies. The EU is seen to be clamping down on the Belgian coordination centres and similar kinds of other special provisions of this sort. Also, all Member States in the EU through the *EU Business Directive* are now required to treat residents and non-residents the same manner for tax purposes, unlike in tax havens where non-residents are taxed relatively less than residents and domestic businesses.

The Gulf States on the other hand seemed to be more preoccupied with Islamic banking, particularly after being insulated from the GFC by the resiliency of faith-based financial products, and less adventurous banking and finance, and hence less ultra-risky. Generally, much of the world was impacted by weak public finances and troubled by the revelations of huge illicit flows of funds globally. Such developments appear to be moving against tax havens.

Designing the fiscal policy to deal with the problems posed by tax havens helps considerably, but more could be achieved by addressing the difficulties posed by opacity or secrecy in tax havens. This is one huge area that draws money launders, potential tax avoiders, and tax evaders to tax havens. This is because in most tax havens, identities of the beneficial owners of the financial assets stored in tax havens are not released, or available. It, incidentally, is also one area where the UK under Cameron's leadership is showing the lead. The reinvigorated efforts of the OECD together with tougher stand from the US and the EU could pave the way for a more concrete global effort to deal with what is essentially a global tax problem.

The 1998 OECD report on harmful tax practices defined a tax haven as a jurisdiction that has no, or only nominal taxes, and offers or is perceived to offer itself as a place to be used by non-residents to escape tax in their country of residence.[183] Second, the laws and administrative practices of the jurisdiction prevents the effective exchange of relevant information with other jurisdictions, or taxpayers benefiting from the low-tax regime. Third, the jurisdiction is also marked by a lack of transparency and the absence of a requirement that the activity be substantial as this could suggest that it is seeking to attract investment or transactions that are purely tax driven.

The fourth criterion of 'no substantial activities' strongly objected by the US was removed in 2001.[184] The OECD also produced a list of forty-seven harmful regimes in

183. OECD. 1998. *Harmful tax competition: An emerging global issue*. Paris: OECD.
184. OECD. 2001. *The OECD's project on harmful tax practices: The 2001 progress report*. Paris: OECD.

twenty OECD countries.[185] The follow-up 2006 report eventually concluded that all were not harmful, other than Luxembourg.[186] The Primarolo Report, commissioned by EU, contained detailed evaluation of tax measures identified as harmful in thirteen Member States. This list coincided with the OECD list.[187]

The OECD identified forty-one tax havens comprising both OECD and non-OECD jurisdictions, of which six made commitments to cooperate. The OECD listing involved making judgments about reputation. This resulted in the inclusion of many small jurisdictions, but excluded Luxembourg, Switzerland, London, and Ireland, and some non-OECD jurisdictions. Disagreements over OECD's initial efforts spawned the OECD Global Forum on Taxation that worked to establish global standards of fiscal transparency for a more level playing field.[188] (By 2007, OECD reported that thirty-three jurisdictions made commitments to improving transparency and setting up effective exchange of information, while five remained uncooperative.).

The Global Forum (GF) on Transparency and Exchange of Information for Tax Purposes was created in the early 2000s. The GF was launched in the context of the OECD's work to address the risks from tax compliance from non-cooperative jurisdictions. The GF comprising OECD countries and jurisdictions that agreed to cooperate was restructured in September 2009 in response to the G20's call for the strengthening of global taxation standards. It now has 139 members on equal status. This is generally perceived as the leading premier international body for ensuring the implementation of tax transparency standards.

The GF reported that as of 23 February 2017, of the one hundred members that have made commitments to the new OECD standard, fifty-three committed to do so by 2017, while forty-seven by 2018 (GF, 2017). The Financial Stability Forum (FSF), the predecessor of the FSB, used similar criteria as the OECD to ferret out tax havens. It also developed a Compendium of Standards relating to regulation of financial markets and institutions.

The FSB was established as the successor to the FSF in April 2009. It promotes international financial stability and has representation from all G20 major economies, FSB members, and the EC.[189] The IMF and the World Bank (WB) monitoring system for compliance by Member States set up in 1999 was extended in 2000 to cover jurisdictions recognized as OFCs.[190] The IMF-WB initiative used the FSF's list of OFCs, but added Dominica, Grenada, Montserrat, and Palau. The IMF in 2007 adopted Zorome's approach that employs the ratio of net exports of financial services to GDP.[191] The 104 jurisdictions identified here, excluded the IMF-WB OFC list that included generally

185. OECD-CFA. 2000. *Towards global tax cooperation*. Paris: OECD.
186. OECD-CTPA. 2006. *The OECD's project on harmful tax practices: 2006 update on progress in member countries*. Paris: OECD.
187. Primarolo Report. 1999. 'Report of the Code of Conduct Group (Business Taxation) to ECOFIN Council 29/11/99'.
188. J. Sharman. 2006. *Havens in a storm: The struggle for global tax regulation*. Ithaca: Cornell University Press.
189. FSB. 2017. 'About the FSB'.
190. IMF. 2000. 'Offshore financial centres: IMF background paper', *IMF 23/6/00*.
191. A. Zorome. 2007. 'Concept of offshore financial centers: In search of an operational definition', *IMF Working Paper WP/07/87*.

recognized tax havens like Andorra, the BVI, Liberia, Liechtenstein, Maldives, the Marshall Islands, Monaco, Montserrat, and the US Virgin Islands.

Zorome's approach has the drawback that particular financial centres within larger economies or countries with harmful PTRs could be omitted. There is also controversy over the use of the number of deviations from the mean to provide the cut-off. For instance, the UK could be excluded when a higher threshold of two standard deviations were applied.[192] Regardless of the approach employed, it appears that by focusing on financial services, the IMF-WB approach could miss out unintentionally important jurisdictions that are significant facilitators of money laundering, tax evasion, or tax avoidance, that operate in unsuspecting situations, as providers of corporate and trust formation and management, instead of financial services. Hence, Zorome's approach mainly captured offshore management of personal wealth, but missed out offshore management of corporate services that are integral parts of the OFC and tax haven criteria.

The TJN generated a lengthy list as it tried to be more comprehensive than the IMF-WB approach. It included OECD countries that offer tax haven facilities or offshore financial services even if these were not significant components of the economy. It therefore included all jurisdictions in the OECD tax haven list. These were generally referred to as true blue tax havens or standard offshore island states that facilitated tax avoidance through low tax rates and secrecy.[193]

The TJN also included OECD member economies with harmful PTRs as tax havens, arguing that nations with wider economic bases have greater responsibility to erase any provisions in their laws which facilitated tax avoidance of the laws of others, and that small jurisdictions should not be the main targets, as was the case previously. The unrelated case of allegations of COVID-19 vaccine hoarding by advanced nations once again suggest the inequitable treatment of small jurisdictions compared to big advanced economies.[194] The TJN also went further by undertaking a reputation test that reviewed tax planning websites and documentation of tax legislations in various jurisdictions.

The above analysis suggests that there does not appear to be a single unambiguous definition for a tax haven, or OFC.[195] The regulatory criteria, like secrecy and low or zero taxes, existed in one form or another. These, together with the different approaches used, resulted in different lists of tax havens or OFCs as the outcomes. In general, both theoretical and practical perspectives used methods differentiating the types of services provided by tax havens, as these were, for instance, relatively more reliable and more informative, than the TJN's general reputation test.

All countries denied existence of tax havens in their domains for obvious reasons. This helped to explain why it had been hard-to-reach consensus on this at the

192. L. Booijink & F. Weyzig. 2007. 'Identifying tax havens and offshore financial centres', *Tax Justice Network (TJN)*.
193. M. Van Dijk, F. Weyzig & R. Murohy. 2006. *The Netherlands-A tax haven?* Amsterdam: Centre for Research on Multinational Organizations (SOMO).
194. S. Meredith. 2020. 'Poor countries set to miss out on COVID vaccines as wealthier nations hoard doses, campaigners warn', *CNBC 9/12/20*.
195. *Supra* note [192], Booijink & Weyzig. 2007.

international level. Even when such jurisdictions were identified as shown in the OECD earlier initiatives, they then promised to make the necessary changes, and were then taken off the black or grey list. This was the main reason why efforts continued to be made to find a more acceptable way to identify and track jurisdictions to ascertain in practice whether they operated as tax havens.

The approach alluded to earlier recognized an OFC as a jurisdiction providing financial services to non-residents at scales that were incommensurate with the size and the financing of their domestic economies.[196] It was seen as relatively simplistic, as it did not ascertain whether they indulged in the lowering of competitive standards to attract foreign capital. Moreover, this approach covered only data for portfolio investments. However, this approach had one great advantage, as it used one single ratio that was convenient for comparison with other jurisdictions.

Building on this said approach, another framework has been proposed that included the other two important components of cross-border global finance, namely FDIs and foreign bank deposits.[197] These three components taken together amounted to USD 96.1 trillion or more than 25 % larger than the global GDP of USD 75.6 trillion.[198]

One model proposed for identifying OFCs (and tax havens) was through the offshore-intensity ratio (OIR).[199] The OIR refers to the aggregated amount of external capital logged in a jurisdiction relative to the size of its domestic economy. This articulated the strength with which a jurisdiction acted as a pull for foreign capital. This approach also complemented the Financial Secrecy Index (FSI), referred to as a qualitative scoring of financial secrecy indicators, weighted by the economic flows of each jurisdiction. The FSI was launched in February 2020 as a politically neutral ranking and mechanism for understanding global financial secrecy, tax havens, or secrecy jurisdiction, and IFFs or capital flights that complemented the Corporate Tax Haven Index ranking most important tax havens for multinationals.[200] Nevertheless, it also suffered from the same weakness found in the earlier models, as it covered only data pertaining to portfolio investments.

The top eighteen jurisdictions in terms of the OIR in 2013 were the Cayman Islands (UK), the BVI (UK), the Marshall Islands (US), Bermuda (UK), Jersey (UK), Luxembourg, Guernsey (UK), Curacao (NL), the Bahamas, Barbados, Cyprus, Mauritius, Isle of Man (UK), Ireland, Hong Kong SAR, the Netherlands, Lichtenstein, and

196. A. Zorome. 2007. 'Concept of offshore financial centers: In search of an operational definition', *IMF Working Paper WP/07/87.*
197. J. Fitchner. 2015. 'The offshore-intensity ratios: Identifying the strongest magnets for foreign capital.' *CIYPERC Working Paper Series 2015/02.*
198. BIS. 2015. 'Locational banking statistics'; BIS. 2015a. 'Consolidated banking statistics'; IMF. 2015. 'Coordinated direct investment survey'; IMF. 2015a. 'Coordinated portfolio investment survey'; IMF. 2015b. *Current challenges in revenue mobilization: Improving tax compliance*, Washington DC: IMF.
199. Fitchner. 2015. 'The offshore-intensity ratios: Identifying the strongest magnets for foreign capital', *CIYPERC Working Paper Series 2015/02.*
200. Financial Secrecy Index (FSI). 2020. 'FSI – 2020 results'. The top three jurisdictions ranked were the Cayman Island, the US, and Switzerland.

Switzerland. However, the distinction between FDI and portfolio investments was argued to be arbitrary.[201]

Further, the novel virtualization of global finance suggests that the US was still by far, the dominant country in cross-border global finance and its centrality is supported by the US-UK axis being the largest financial relation in the world.[202] But, also playing a central role in contemporary cross-border global finance are the large OFCs of the Netherlands, Luxembourg, Ireland, Hong Kong, the Cayman Islands, Bermuda, and the BVI.

§3.07 REGULATING TAX HAVENS

Hence, while mainstream economists argued against a stricter regulation of offshore finance because highly mobile capital could supposedly migrate to other jurisdictions to evade regulatory measures, the findings of this research suggested that a stricter regulation of a few key offshore jurisdictions could generate significant impacts. This was because certain segments of global finance, like FDIs in the Netherlands and Luxembourg, or particular financial actors like hedge funds in the Cayman Islands, or money market funds in Ireland were highly concentrated.

More recently, a global CSO released its report on corporate tax dodging, as a follow-through on its earlier findings, that just eight men owned the equivalent wealth of the bottom 3.6 billion people of the world.[203] It appeared that one of the key drivers fuelling this inequality crisis is tax competition and its consequential race to the bottom in the taxation of big businesses to attract FDIs.

The CSO report suggested that the top fifteen jurisdictions facilitated the more extreme forms of tax dodging. Importantly, the reports examined the harm caused by falling corporate tax rates and tax giveaways in economies across the world. It also ranked the countries by examining their tax rates, whether they offered unfair tax incentives, and whether they cooperated with international efforts to curb tax avoidance, like agreeing to the enhancement of financial transparency. The jurisdictions cited aligned significantly with the earlier findings of, as alluded to earlier.[204] Many other tax havens exist to hide wealth from tax authorities. At least 90% of the world's biggest companies had a presence in at least one tax haven.

Several jurisdictions mentioned in the CSO report have been linked to tax scandals spotlighting some of the world's biggest businesses.[205] With reference to Ireland, for instance, EC in 2016 ruled that the jurisdiction had enabled Apple to pay substantially less tax than other businesses for many years. This was overruled by the General Court that the EC failed to prove that the Irish Government had given the US

201. *Supra* note [197]. Fitchner. 2015.
202. BIS. 2015. 'Cross-border financial leakages: Challenges for monetary policy and financial stability', *BIS Paper No. 82 October 2015*.
203. Oxfam. 2017. 'Just 8 men own same wealth as half the world', *Oxfam 16/1/17*.
204. *Supra* note [197]. Fitchner. 2015.
205. I. Kottasova. 2016. 'These are the world's worst tax havens', *CNN*, 12/12/16.

MNC a tax advantage.[206] Starbucks was similarly ordered by the EU in 2015 to pay back up to EUR 30 million it benefited from the friendly tax deal with the Netherlands, but the General Court later in 2019 overruled this, holding that the EU competition enforcer failed to show that the US MNC benefited unfairly from the Dutch tax deal.[207]

Fiat Chrysler was ordered to pay a similar amount from the same kind of deal with Luxembourg, and this was upheld by the General Court holding that the EC had applied its state aid rules correctly to evaluate if there was an illegal advantage and was not seeking to harmonize tax rules across the bloc.[208] The Bahamas and the BVI were identified among tax haven used by Mossack Fonseca the law firm at the centre of the PP scandals. Indeed, tax dodging by multinationals costs poor economies more than USD 100 billion annually.[209] A global CSO calculated this amount was sufficient to provide education for the 124 million people who are not in school, including the funding of healthcare interventions that could prevent the deaths of at least six million children annually.[210]

The said global CSO report, while drawing good attention to the world's most troublesome tax havens, nevertheless also clarified that tax havens were only part of the problem.[211] This was because countries across the world were bringing down tax rates, as they competed for FDIs. Some twenty-five years earlier, tax rates across G20 economies were 40%, but had since plummeted to less than 30% in 2016.[212] In the developing world in particular, the applications of unproductive and wasteful tax incentives have been rising. Tax incentives, for instance, in Kenya cost USD 1.1 billion annually, almost twice their entire national health budget.[213]

When corporate taxes are trimmed, governments managed their finance by slimming down public spending, or by raising taxes, like the value-added tax (VAT), which impacted disproportionately the poor. For instance, a 0.8% reduction in corporate tax rates across OECD countries between 2007 and 2014 was in part offset by a 1.5% increase in the average standard VAT rates between 2008 and 2015.[214] Esme Berkhout, the tax policy advisor for a global CSO argued that there were no winners in the race to the bottom on corporate tax, with the poor being the hardest hit, and as such governments needed to collaborate to stop this unthoughtful crazy race and ensured that big businesses in particular paid their fair share.[215]

Today, as a global justice organization, the CSO questioned OECD's long and patchy record of not identifying tax havens properly. This has the unintended outcomes of weak islands making the list, while giants in the game like the US and the

---

206. S. Amaro. 2020. 'Apples wins tac battle with EU as a court annuls 2016 order to pay $15 billion in taxes', *CNBC 15/7/20.*
207. F.Y. Chee. 2019. 'Starbucks wins, Fiat loses in EU tax fights', *Reuters 24/9/19.*
208. *Supra* note [207]. Chee. 2019.
209. UNCTAD. 2016. 'UNCTAD world investment report'.
210. Oxfam. 2021. 'Inequality and poverty: The hidden costs of tax dodging'.
211. A. Ratcliff. 2016. 'World's worst corporate tax havens exposed-Oxfam report reveals dangerous to the bottom on corporate tax', *Oxfam 12/12/16.*
212. Said Business School. 2016. 'G20 corporate tax ranking'.
213. TJN. 2016. 'TJN Africa and Action Aid International report: Tax incentives in East Africa'.
214. OECD. 2015. 'OECD revenue statistics'.
215. *Supra* note [211]. Ratcliff. 2016.

UK and traditional jurisdictions like Switzerland and Luxembourg were arbitrarily excluded. It viewed the EU as being likely to follow the OECD's lead on the criteria.[216] The OECD's G20-mandated BEPS project initiated in 2012 sought to deal with corporate lax losses.[217]

The IMF, for instance, estimated tax losses in non-OECD countries arising from the activities of multinationals at between USD 100 and USD 300 billion annually especially with important losses for developing economies.[218] The IMF together with the World Bank, the OECD, and the UN launched the Platform for Collaboration on Tax. The new joint Platform injected an explicit developing country's perspective for this project. It further sought to take the baton for the momentum from the July 2015 Addis Ababa UN Financing for Development (FFD) Conference, by locating domestic resources like tax revenues, as the fulcrum for fulfilling the Sustainable Development Goal (SDG) financing gap of USD 2.3 trillion.

The World Bank in 2011 issued a policy on the employment of OFCs with the principal objective that they will not be used for tax evasions. The initiative suffered from the absence of a specific list of high-risk jurisdictions or practices. Rather, it relied on a weak process of peer reviews and evaluations by the OECD.[219] The BVI, for instance, enjoyed a large compliant status, even though it accommodated over half of the offshore companies referred to in the PP revelations.[220] A global CSO using the wider FSI alluded to earlier suggested that some 25% of International Finance Corporation (IFC), the World Bank's private sector arm's investment projects in the Sub-Saharan region, contracted with businesses incorporated in tax havens like Mauritius, the Netherlands, and Jersey.[221]

Investment analysts MSCI estimated that 22% of companies analysed were taxed substantially below the weighted average concluding that these companies posed a significant risk to investors arising from both reputational and tax litigation risks.[222] Case examples included one of the largest gold mine in Latin America over alleged small tax payments, because of inexplicable distortion between costs and prices as well as BEPS questions over a Northern European jurisdiction's forestry multinational.[223]

The IMF-WB axis is now being urged to revisit its OFC policy and set up a wider tax policy for its lending operations that would allow them to be firm on high-risk jurisdictions, especially those housing OFCs. This would simultaneously enable it to promote good corporate tax planning behaviours. As its current focus on illicit financing touched only on the criminal and corrupt aspects of the problems, commercial transactions facilitating these, like tax avoidance and trade mispricing, should also

---

216. TJN. 2016. 'Will the OECD tax haven blacklist be another whitewash', *TJN 20/7/16*.
217. OECD. 2013. 'Action plan on Base Erosion and Profit Sharing', *OECD 19/7/13*.
218. M. Kohonen. 2016. 'World Bank and IMF: Where do they stand on progressive and responsible taxation?', *Bretton Woods Project Paper 5 August 2016*.
219. *Supra* note [218]. Kohonen. 2016.
220. Transparency International. 2016. 'British Virgin Islands: Have they cleaned up since the Panama Papers', *Transparency International 14/10/16*.
221. Oxfam. 2016. 'The IFC and tax havens: The need to support more responsible corporate tax behaviour', *Oxfam 11/4/16*.
222. *Supra* note [218]. Kohonen. 2016.
223. *Supra* note [218]. Kohonen. 2016.

be examined. It is these and other related issues that ushered in the Platform for Collaboration on Tax. This should be employed not only to promote OECD economies' agenda as frequently occurring during the OECD-led BEPS process but also to accommodate the urgent concerns of developing economies.[224]

Despite the persist existence of tax havens and their corresponding activities, a global CSO noted some signs of actions at regional and international levels, but argued that further positive actions could be taken, especially in the launching of a new generation of comprehensive international tax reforms. Further analysis of this would be covered in Chapter 6.

The different methodologies used in identification of tax havens and the apparent use of tweaking suggested clash of agenda at the global level. This was not something new, as research a decade ago suggested that the international political economy was largely a matter of the strong regulating as they would and the weak suffering as pressured. Indeed, 'The interplay of rhetoric and reputation may just as readily entrench inequalities as undermine them.'[225]

Some OFCs and tax havens facilitated significant illicit capital flows from poor economies to an estimated USD 1 trillion. The fast-rising figure annually is almost ten times the total amount of foreign aids these economies were getting from international sources.[226] The African continent alone lost some USD 850 billion between 1970 and 2008, money badly needed for various economic development purposes.[227] It is mainly for this reason, that countering measures were put into actions. The more widely used was the 'naming and shaming mechanism'.[228] This was a soft law mechanism formulated to enforce the norms of international law against a non-compliant state to get it to comply with its obligations under international law.

In 2002, for instance, Seychelles launched the Economic Development Act to attract foreign investments, but with total disregard on whether the source was from money laundering or tax evasion.[229] This legislation granted immunity to anyone, including those undertaking nefarious activities, as long as their investments came to USD 10 million or more. The financial assets were also protected from compulsory acquisitions or sequestrations, other than when it involved acts of violence and drug trafficking committed in the Seychelles. The Financial Action Task Force (FATF) and the international banking community condemned this. The FATF invoked its powers to get Seychelles blacklisted. This and subsequent other pressures compelled Seychelles to retract the legislation.

224. *Supra* note [218]. Kohonen. 2016.
225. J. Sharman. 2016. *Havens in a storm: The struggle for global tax regulation*. Ithaca: Cornell University Press, pp. 161.
226. C.L. Biron. 2013. 'Developing countries lose US$1tn a year from illicit financial flows: Watchdog cites poor governance and lax regulation for huge outflows, which have increased by almost 10% each year', *The Guardian 13/12/13*.
227. T. Anderson. 2017. 'How Trump's new tax reforms proposal may impact every income bracket', *CNBC 27 April 2017*.
228. N. Mugarura. 2017. 'Tax havens, offshore financial centres and the current sanctions regimes', *Journal of Financial Crime*, Vol. 24(2): 200-222.
229. *Supra* note [228]. Mugarura. 2017.

Earlier in 1997, the IMF collaborated with Nordic countries in suspending aid to Kenya for failures to prosecute alleged corruption scandals by senior Kenyan public officials, ministers, and businessmen who manipulated procurement contracts via overpriced or fake contracts. The 'stolen' funds were estimated at a staggering 16% of the country's annual national budget. The OECD launched reforms to enhance individual states' abilities to share and exchange financial information on money deposited in tax havens. Naming and shaming have been applied against blacklisted economies for not implementing desired tax reforms to curtail the flow of illicit funds.

Though the approach has been criticized for lacking credibility in many economies, it still nevertheless impacted public perceptions of blacklisted jurisdictions and motivated many economies to implement desired changes. Some blacklisted jurisdictions, like Guernsey and Zimbabwe, protested being included, as they claimed to have instituted the desired levels of reforms, while Switzerland touted as the worst offenders, they argued, were excluded. These were serious implications, as the IMF, the World Bank, and major international banks usually avoided doing business with blacklisted economies.[230]

The FATF, in June 2000, subsequent to its review process, provided a list of all nineteen non-cooperative jurisdictions. It instigated sanctions mechanisms that were reinforced by the nine UN Security Council Regulations adopted in 2001. Earlier, in 1996, the FATF formalized a policy of imposing sanctions on members who fail to adopt measures to translate its forty Recommendations into practice. These comprised a series of graduated steps formulated to pressure member economies into enacting required reforms to achieve compliance. These graduated from highly publicized visits, getting financial institutions to scrutinize transactions, and ultimately to suspension of FATF membership. The most severe sanctions were thus far imposed on Turkey and Austria.[231] Both these economies eventually chose to comply. Other than this, the FATF extended the work of the Basel Committee, by stressing the importance of requiring Member States to implement its standards.

The EU operated specific sanctions involving the implementation of the UN Resolutions, like economic sanctions and the use of force of the UN Charter. EU's autonomous sanctions regimes, included arms embargo, trade sanctions, and flight bans. The association between the EU Directives and the FATF Recommendations was evident. When the FATF adopted new Recommendations, the EU responded by adopting measures to transpose those obligations within EU Member States. To ensure that the EU was equipped with measures to deal with OFCs, the EC Anti-money Laundering (AML) Directive was not only confined to candidate economies, or offshore jurisdictions, but also continuously sought to incorporate agreements to bind Member States.[232]

Thus, international laws incorporated a wide scope of legal regimes, principles, codes of conduct and transactional rules of state practice, that were recognized in

230. *Supra* note [228]. Mugarura. 2017.
231. *Supra* note [228]. Mugarura. 2017.
232. *Supra* note [228]. Mugarura. 2017.

formal or informal multilateral agreements.[233] The use of such soft law instruments in multilateral agreements generally underscored the willingness of the state to employ them, but they lacked opinions and jurisdiction to render them legally binding as rules of customary international law.[234] While soft law instruments were legally non-binding, they nevertheless created guidelines for dealing with particular business exigencies by contributing to the development of international rules, standards, and legal principles that could over time graduate into hard laws.[235]

The adoption of soft law norms was powered by the quests for a common framework applicable across different economies. Though in theory non-compliance did not equate with the breach of international law, it could be badly construed thereby generating tensions between those not complying, and those which did. The IMF and the World Bank did not in general work with those that did not comply. Soft law norms as such were introduced to fill gaps that might not have been envisaged when treaties of international laws were adopted.[236]

Soft laws helped to create pressures for even advanced economies to act. For instance, Switzerland shifted its attitude towards bank secrecy laws and indicated willingness to stop operating as a safe haven for unlawful wealth from corrupt political leaders from around the world. It reached consensus with the OECD in exchanging data with sixty other economies.[237] This would effectively end its banking secrecy. This was of huge implications, as Switzerland is the world's largest offshore wealth centre, with an estimated USD 2 trillion in assets, compared to its USD 632.2 billion in GDP.[238]

Previously, the lack of transparency of Switzerland's banks undermined global AML laws, because it is the seat of the BIS. The BIS champions the adoption of the Basel Committee regulatory and supervisory standards. By signing the Convention, Switzerland confirmed its commitment to the fight against tax fraud.[239] UBS, Switzerland's biggest bank's acknowledgement of helping some 52,000 American evading taxes have led US authorities to investigate a dozen other Swiss banks.

At this juncture, the twin issues of bank secrecy and private wish for confidentiality merit reflection, as they revolved around the important matter of fundamental human rights. The challenge concerned whether these exchanges of information were confined only to legitimate purposes, and not abused by some jurisdictions. Then, there were further concerns over the new corporate offence of failure to prevent tax evasion, enacted on 27 April 2017, as part of UK's Criminal Finances Act 2017. Under this legislation, corporations could be held accountable in situations where those associated with them have engaged in the criminal facilitation of tax evasions.

---

233. K. Alexander, R. Dhumale & J. Eatwell. 2006. *Global governance of financial systems: The international regulation of systematic risk,* Oxford: Oxford University Press.
234. P. Alliott. 1999. 'The concept of international law', *European Journal of International Law*, Vol. 10(1999): 31-30.
235. *Supra* note [233]. Alexander, Dhumale & Eatwell. 2006.
236. *Supra* note [233]. Alexander, Dhumale & Eatwell. 2006.
237. J. Manning. 2013. 'Switzerland signs deal to end banking secrecy', *The International Banker 20/10/13.*
238. *Supra* note [228]. Mugarura. 2017.
239. *Supra* note [228]. Mugarura. 2017.

The rules essentially covered two offences: criminal tax evasion and the criminal facilitation of such evasion. Businesses that did not have reasonable procedures in place to prevent such facilitation run the risk of committing this offence. The legislation appeared to cover not only corporates incorporated or formed in the UK, but also those with business presence in the UK. It also included businesses wherever located, if a step in the facilitation offence took place in the UK, implying a wider extraterritorial effect than UK's Bribery Act 2010.

The deleterious impacts of OFCs and tax havens need careful analysis of relevant financial data flows available. This includes the Net Resource Transfers (NRT) or the net recorded flows into and out of a country less outflows of illicit capital.[240] It is interesting to note that, since the early 1980s, NRTs in most developing economies were primarily large and negative, suggesting sustained and significant outflows from the developing world. It has been estimated that illicit outflows accounted for about 82% of all NRTs from developing economies.[241] Illicit flows, financial secrecy, and tax evasion via offshores tax havens since the 1930s have delayed or diverted equitable economic participation by all.

Various OFCs have contributed to the facilitation of criminal, corrupt, and commercially tax evading financial flows, with haemorrhaging impacts on the world's poor or under-classed. Benefits from the relatively smaller levels of legitimate transactions undertaken did not diminish the far more damaging roles of intermediating illicit flows that were the primary drivers of NRTs from developing economies. Research suggests that residents of developing economies held some USD 4.4 trillion in assets in tax havens in 2011, or even higher.[242] It has been further argued that there was unlikely greater driver of inequality in developing economies than the toxic cocktail of offshore tax havens and IFFs. These enabling mechanisms and facilitating entities benefit the affluent, but harm the middle class and the poor. These IFFs would be addressed in the next chapter.

240. Global Financial Integrity (GFI). 2015. 'Financial flows and tax havens: Combining to limit the lives of billions of people', *GFI December 2015*.
241. *Supra* note [240]. GFI. 2015.
242. *Supra* note [240]. GFI. 2015.

CHAPTER 4

Global Financial Flows and Illicit Financial Flows

§4.01 INTRODUCTION

Many tax havens have been criticized or even censured by global financial watchdogs for enabling the concealment of surplus capital of dubious origins by various entities and individuals. This chapter examines the likely or suspected sources of those likely ill-gotten gains, why they occur, and why OFCs or tax havens are their preferred destinations. The usefulness of having more insights on this phenomenon is also discussed. Given the alleged scale and magnitude of IFFs, attention is directed to the need and ways of curbing or controlling their flows across the global financial system. Attention is also given to the extensive use of transfer price manipulations (TPMs) by multinationals and others engaged in cross-border transactions, as well as on matters going on in the illegal markets.

§4.02 USEFULNESS FOR FOCUSING POLICY ATTENTION ON IFFS

IFFs, in general, are referred to as illegal movements of money or capital from one jurisdiction to another. Global Financial Integrity (GFI) identified these movements as illicit flows, when funds were of illegal origins, transferred, and/or utilized.[243] These could include, for instance, a drug cartel using trade-based money-laundering mechanisms to mix legal money from trade sales with those illegal from drug sales; importers applying trade mis-invoicing to evade custom duties, VAT, or income taxes; corrupt public officials employing anonymous shell companies to route illegal money to bank accounts in another jurisdiction; human traffickers carting cash across borders and

243. Global Financial Integrity (GFI). 2017. 'Illicit financial flows'.

depositing this in foreign bank accounts; and terrorists wiring money from one jurisdiction to another operative in another jurisdiction.

A 2013 GFI estimate suggests USD 7.8 trillion being drained from developing and EMEs in IFFs and is growing at an alarming rate of 6.5% annually.[244] This was almost two times, as fast as global GDP. The estimate was considered highly conservative, as it excluded movements of bulk cash, mispricing of services, and many kinds of money laundering. The problem was huge. For instance, the USD 1.1 trillion that was drained from developing countries in 2013 exceeded the aggregate total of FDIs and net official development assistance (ODA) which these countries received in that year.

Aside from the damaging economic impact on the overall capital flows, IFFs inflict terrible subversive consequences on governments, victims of crime, and society. They facilitated transnational organized crimes, foster corruptions, undermine governance, and weaken tax revenues. Commonly, these outflows eventually ended up in well-protected jurisdictions, like in the US, the UK, and in widely perceived tax havens, like Switzerland, the BVI, and so on. GFI further estimated that, some 45% of IFFs ended up in OFCs, and the balance 55% in developed economies.

GFI maintained that this happened, not by chance, but was the outcome of jurisdictions and their institutions actively facilitating and extracting huge profits from leakages of enormous amounts from developing economies. Stemming from this, GFI took the position, that developed economies had a responsibility, together with developing countries to curb IFFs. These, among others, could involve formulating and implementing policies and measures that could detect and deter cross-border tax evasion; elimination of anonymous shell companies; enhancing further current AML laws and practices; curbing trade mis-invoicing; and enhancing transparency of big businesses and in particular multinationals.[245]

Research on IFFs generated four principal observations. These were as follows:[246]

(1) IFFs from developing countries were substantial, even if the correct data was one-tenth of GFI's estimate of USD 1 trillion annually, or USD 100 billion,[247] as this was relatively significant to either the ODA of USD 70 billion, or total FDIs in developing economies of about USD 250 billion in 2004.[248] Curbing this large outflow would mean an enormous benefit for developing economies. However, this on its own would not imply a good target for policy. IFFs were outcomes of more fundamental problems of grave concerns. To development agencies, like the World Bank, bribery and corruption to government officials was a troubling issue, since the mid-1990s. This was also seen as a

244. J. Spanjers & D. Kar. 2015. 'Illicit financial flows from developing countries: 2004-2013', *GFI 8/12/15.*

245. *Supra* note [243]. GFI. 2017.

246. P. Reuter. 2012. *Draining development: Controlling flows of illicit funds from developing countries,* Washington DC: The World Bank.

247. D. Kar, D. Cartwright-Smith & A. Hollingshead. 2008. *Illicit financial flows from developing countries 2002-2006,* Washington DC: GFI.

248. D. Kar & J. Spanjers. 2015. Illicit financial flows from developing countries: 2004-2013. *GFI December 2015.*

major failure of developing economies to effectively collect taxes, but instead to conveniently rely on ODA.[249] The complementary strategy was therefore to resolve the fundamental underlying problems of corruption, tax evasion, and so on.

(2) Giving attention to causes, rather than symptoms, was useful in many remedial policy measures. To be even more comprehensively effective, this needed to be complemented, by treating the symptoms as well. For instance, IFFs exacerbated the underling harms from tax evasions, corruptions, and criminal markets, if left unattended.[250] Trapping funds in the source countries cuts down the attractiveness of briberies, corruptions, and tax evasions. Attention on the consequences could also then reduce the underlying activities. This could be achieved by lowering the incentives to plunder from state coffers, and by making money less secure domestically, than abroad. Conversely, there were potential negative impacts of preventing international transfers, as when compelled to keeping the illegal money domestically. Beneficial owners could be incentivized to pay more bribes regularly to protect their assets, compared to one-time payment when moving funds abroad illegally.

(3) Some still took the position that IFFs could be the erroneous focus for policy initiatives,[251] as the IFFs were the consequences of the more fundamental failures of governance that generated grand corruption and a reduced willingness to pay taxes. This had very much to do with feasibility, as it is only possible to reduce outflows from developing economies, by improving governance, which incidentally generated other benefits, as well. Such efforts even, if not at the desired pace, had seen some successes, especially with the contributions from well-established entities, like the FATF, or via forums, like the G8 and G20. Still, the fundamental problems were mainly domestic.

(4) There were so much global developmental agencies, like the IMF or the World Bank, could do to resolve corruptions, tax evasions, or criminal markets. The failure of international coalitions to support the Government of Afghanistan represented an extreme narrative of the limits of intervention on such matters, especially when some 150,000 troops made little impact with respect to heroin production and widespread corruption in that economy.[252] Still, a focus on IFFs would enable developed economies to assume more direct

249. D. Brautigam, O-H, Fjeldstad & M. Moore (eds.). 2008. *Taxation and state-building in developing countries: Capacity and consent*, Cambridge: Cambridge University Press.

250. M. Moore. 2012. 'The practical political economy of illicit flows', in P. Reuter (ed.), *Draining development? Controlling flows of illicit funds from developing economies*, Washington DC: The World Bank.

251. S. Blakenburg & M. Khan. 2012. 'Governance and illicit flows', in P. Reuter (ed.), *Draining development?*, Washington DC: The World Bank; M. Everest-Phillips. 2012. 'The political economy of controlling tax evasion and illicit flows', in P. Reuter (ed.), *Draining development?*, Washington DC: The World Bank.

252. J.P. Caulkins, M.A.R. Kleiman & J.D. Kulick. 2010. *Drug production and trafficking, countering policies, and security and governance in Afghanistan*, New York: New York University Center on International Cooperation.

participations. In this connection, as mentioned earlier, these IFFs did not just disappear, but significantly flowed into legitimate and frequently highly respected financial institutions in the developed world. Hence, governments of affluent economies could via legislations pressure these institutions not to encourage the intakes of these IFFs.

§4.03 CONTROLLING THE FLOWS

TJN, GFI, and others sought to curb IFFs, while yet others sought to reduce the extent of transfer mispricing practices.[253] Tightening the regulation of tax havens and other mechanisms broadly target all methods behind IFFs.[254] AML efforts, on the other hand, helped to build on existing initiatives. Practical realities diverged from rhetoric, when political and economic governance are weak in various developing economies.[255] Past cases showed that the courts and police in Switzerland and the UK have helped to return stolen assets to Nigeria,[256] but in contrast, the systems in other African economies, like Kenya, have failed in dealing with their corruptive practices.[257] Consequent upon the remedy actions in Nigeria, there were sharp reversals in flows of illicitly generated funds.

Arguments are now raised that AML systems could be made more effective globally, so that those who transmit illegally secured funds are at greater risk of losing the assets, or of being prosecuted. In countries without a tradition of independent and vigorous prosecution, there were concerns about the difficulties of creating effective systems. This was compounded in the case of IFF, due to the plethora of channels by which money could be laundered. FTF guidelines showed that AML controls initially targeted only banks, but soon expanded to financial institutions in general, and in most businesses. In the UK, for instance, all businesses must report cash purchases of more than USD 10,000. Incidentally, no country had been able to comply with the 2004 FATF 40 + 9 regulations. Even if a country was in compliance, there were informal channels in certain Asian countries, for example, that could be available to money launderers.

This helped to explain why there were suggestions that perhaps the controlling of IFFs could achieve more. Country-by-country (CbC) reporting, transparency rules for traditional secrecy jurisdictions, and better monitoring of politically exposed persons (PEPs) were all major problems that could help with the job. In this respect, better

253. R. Murphy. 2012. 'Accounting for the missing millions', in P. Reuter (ed.), *Draining development*, Washington DC: The World Bank; R. Murphy. 2009. *Country by country reporting: Holding multinational corporations to account wherever they are*, Washington DC: Task Force on Financial Integrity and Economic Development.
254. TJN. 2007. *Closing the floodgates: Collecting tax to pay for development*, London: TJN.
255. M. Levy. 2012. 'How well do anti-money laundering controls work in developing countries', in P. Reuter (ed.), *Draining development*, Washington DC: The World Bank.
256. J. Maton & T. Daniel. 2012. 'The kleptocrat's portfolio decisions', in P. Reuter (ed.), *Draining development*, Washington DC: The World Bank.
257. M. Wrong. 2009. *It's our turn to eat: The story of a Kenyan whistle-blower*, New York: HarperCollins.

outcomes could be expected, given that major businesses, both financial and non-financial, for their own interests, are incentivized to work with rules, both soft and hard, in the international financial system.

This was reflected in some respects with the trade isolation of certain economies. However, these were well-defined targets, whereas IFFs, by definition, were not so narrowly targeted, and hence the effectiveness of such reforms remained to be seen. The significant exposures of developing economies to secrecy jurisdictions, or tax havens, in terms of the share of capital flights passing through financial institutions domiciled in these locations were viewed as threats to the effectiveness of financial regulations and macroeconomic policies globally.[258] The OECD, the EU, and the US have taken initiatives to make them more transparent, though with varying outcomes.

The high level of rhetoric from world leaders on this matter had limited impacts on the fundamentals mentioned earlier.[259] The barrier to change for tax havens was synonymous to the standard ones for global economic policy reforms. This referred to protectionisms by various countries. This was accentuated by policy actions of the Trump administration in 2016,[260] as well as by other administrations across the world, all being pursued to protect national economic welfare and other domestic agenda.[261]

Even with the strengthening of firewalls across many advanced economies, this might not be adequate to deal effectively with a phenomenon that thrived on weak governance. For the longer perspective, tackling IFFs from developing countries need to focus on improving governance at the source through the developments of sound business environments, as well as providing more opportunities for citizens, like in giving them incentives to partake in legal economic activities, paying their taxes and dues and reinvesting their profits domestically. In this regard, governments in developed economies have been urged to link their aids to support emerging and developing economies willing or committing to address these various challenges alluded to earlier.[262]

§4.04 TRANSFER PRICE MANIPULATION

TPM is both the means, by which illicit funds are generated, and a method for transferring illegal funds generated by other economic activities.[263] There were some

258. A. Cobham. 2012. 'Tax havens and illicit flows', in P. Reuter (ed.), *Draining development*, Washington DC: The World Bank.
259. European Network on Debt and Development (Eurodad). 2016. *Survival of the richest: Europe's role in supporting an unjust global tax system in 2016*, Brussels: Eurodad; K. Hansen. 2014. *Illicit financial flows from developing countries: Measuring OECD responses*, Paris: OECD.
260. M. Noland. 2018. 'US trade policy in the Trump administration: US trade policy', *Asian Economic Policy Review*, Vol. 13(2); 262-278.
261. M.E. Ferracane & H. Lee-Makiyama. 2017. 'China's technology protectionisms and its non-negotiable rationales', *European Centre for International Policy Economy (ECIPE) Paper June 2017*.
262. *Supra* note [259]. Hansen. 2014.
263. L. Eden. 2012. 'Transfer price manipulation', in P. Reuter (ed.), *Draining development*, Washington DC: The World Bank; C. Fuest & N. Riedel. 2012. 'Tax evasion and tax avoidance: The role of international profit shifting', in P. Reuter (ed.), *Draining development*, Washington

general indications that TPM was reasonably monitored and controlled among and between developed economies. This implied that developing countries might want to take this path by seeking assistance form the OECD and so on, as TPM required technical skills both to understand and to tackle. TPM occurred because multinationals have superior skills and resources relative to the systems found in developing economies and because of underlying corrupt systems. As TPM usually involved two or more economies and likely with an advanced economy as one, assistance and cooperation from affluent economies could help a lot.

§4.05 ILLEGAL MARKETS

The case of illegal markets was best illustrated through the problems posed by illegal drugs.[264] Producers and transit economies were mostly from developing economies, with rich economies accounting for most of the consumption expenditures. Funds generally flowed from consumers in rich economies to traffickers in the poor economies. This did not necessarily imply that all earners were from developing economies, as usual exposures of prominent personalities would suggest, because comparable rich US and European traffickers could have been better at concealing their identities. Of greater concerns were the fiscal problems faced by economies, like Colombia arising from this trade. The problems posed were significant, but detecting the magnitude and setting up effective remedial measures were formidable, and required international cooperation between countries from around the world. This was especially so, when illegal markets crossed borders and involved wide range of activities from drugs to human trafficking,[265] counterfeiting, prostitution, or the use and exploitation of modern slavery.[266]

The above four were not the only issues that policymakers had to contend with, when dealing with IFFs. There were unintended outcomes over the alarm bells generated by the crude estimates provided by global justice CSOs, like the GFI, to show the magnitude and scale of the problem.[267] While generally effective in drawing attention of policymakers, especially from developing economies, these also attracted the attention of affluent economies, that were providing assistance in the form of ODA, as they reflected over the alternative of curbing IFFs that could be likely both constrictive and less expensive. This prompted more reliable measures of IFFs so as not to cause problems associated with either overestimation or underestimation of the scale of the problem.

DC: The World Bank; C.A. Leite. 2012. 'The role of transfer pricing in illicit financial flows', in P. Reuter (ed.), *Draining development,* Washington DC: The World Bank; R. Murphy. 2012. 'Accounting for the missing millions', in P. Reuter (ed.), *Draining development,* Washington DC: The World Bank.

264. F.E. Thoumi & M. Anzola. 2012. 'Illicit capital flows and money laundering in Colombia', in P. Reuter (ed.), *Draining development,* Washington DC: The World Bank.
265. P. Kopp. 2012. 'Human trafficking and international financial flows', in P. Reuter (ed.), *Draining development,* Washington DC: The World Bank.
266. Home Office. 2020. *2020 UK Annual Report on Modern Slavery,* London: Home Office.
267. P. Reuter (ed.). 2012. *Draining development: Controlling flows of illicit funds from developing countries,* Washington DC: The World Bank.

To begin with, the term itself could be defined differently in different contexts. One definition offered included income and wealth transferred from both legal and illegal sources.[268] Another definition offered by Blakenburg & Khan in the context of capital flight was said to be legalistic with focus on formal laws and did not distinguish between illicit and illegal.[269] The illicit term covered the notion of morality.

No good efforts have yet been made to ascertain the impact of the distinction between the two terms. While the legal perspective was favoured, it was taken at the expense of conceptual clarity. This generated controversy when identifying and tracking economies with huge IFFs, such as China and the next seven in the hierarchy, which happened to be oil exporting countries. Nevertheless, these concerns did not necessarily invalidate current efforts for identifying and tracking of the IFF phenomenon, but certainly raised questions over what the numbers really implied.

There were, for instance, particular problems posed by economies relying on remittances from workers abroad, such as found in many Asian economies. Whether undetected or un-regularized, these could count as illicit flows, even though the real benefits went to very poor people. In short, the focus on aggregate data obscured the dynamics of the phenomenon. 'IFFs have complex origins and varied consequences and present difficult policy options.'[270]

Fast forward from 2009 to 2015, the GFI and experts at the Centre for Applied Research at the Norwegian School of Economics, Jawaharlal Nehru University, *Instituto de Estudos Socioeconomicos,* and the Nigerian Institute of Social and Economic Research collaborated their research initiatives in IFFs. Their combined findings suggest that tax havens have been key facilitators of movements of licit and illicit capital out of and into developing economies.[271] This report further suggested the following:[272]

(1) Since the 1980s, developing countries lost USD 16.3 billion through broad leakages in the balance of payments, trade mis-invoicing, and recorded financial transfers. Such resources had immense social costs that were being borne by people in developing economies. Developing economies, as such, have effectively functioned as net creditors to the rest of the world with tax havens playing important role in the flight of unrecorded capital. By example, in 2011 tax haven holdings of total developing country wealth were estimated

268. D. Kar & D. Cartwright-Smith. 2008. 'Illicit financial flows from developing countries', *Global Financial Integrity (GFI) 14/12/2008.*

269. S. Blakenburg & M. Khan. 2012. 'Governance and illicit flows', in P. Reuter (ed.), *Draining development?,* Washington DC: The World Bank.

270. P. Reuter. 2012. 'Policy and research implications of illicit flows', in P. Reuter (ed.), *Draining development,* Washington DC: The World Bank, pp. 96.

271. GFI. 2015. 'Financial flows and tax havens: Combining to limit the lives of billions of people', *Centre for Applied Research Norwegian School of Economics/GFI/ Jawaharlal Nehru University/Instituto de Estudos Socioeconomicos/Nigerian Institute of Social and Economic Research December 2015.*

272. C. Clough. 2016. 'New report on unrecorded capital flight finds developing countries are net creditors to the rest of the world', *GFI 5/12/16.*

at USD 4.4 trillion. This aggravated inequality and undermined good governance and economic growth.

(2) NRTs for all developing economies have been significantly large and negative, since the early 1980s, suggesting sustained and significant outflows from the developing world. NRTs were defined as net recorded outflows of illicit and unrecorded capital. In contrast to previous studies that limited their analysis to financial flows, this study included in its measure of NRTs; non-financial transactions, like debt forgiveness and write-offs; unrequited transfers, like remittances; and unrecorded capital outflows. As financial institutions did not differentiate between recorded or licit, and unrecorded or illicit capital, this study followed likewise.

(3) Special attention was given to China's capital flows in the examination of NRTs for all developing economies. This impacted the magnitude of cumulative net transfers, but not the overall conclusions. Keeping out China from the developing world's NRTs brought down the magnitude of cumulative NRTs from the remaining developing countries to around USD 11.7 trillion. The hefty reduction was attributed to China's large current account surpluses, associated capital and reserve asset outflows, and large unrecorded outflows. It appeared that while China has had significant recorded and unrecorded financial flows, the data showed that NRTs were concerns for all developing countries.

(4) As of 2011, USD 2.6 trillion of developing countries' private wealth was held in tax havens, and more than 50% of the USD 4.4 trillion of total developing country assets was also in these same jurisdictions. Sub-Saharan Africa's assets held in tax havens grew at over 20% annually from 2005 to 2011. This was faster than that of any other region, developed or developing. GFI President Raymond Baker argued that overall, there was perhaps no greater driver of inequality within developing countries, than the combination of IFFs and offshore tax havens.

(5) This report argued further that much improved statistical compilation and reporting were necessary to achieve a more adequate picture of global financial flows. It recommended this task to be undertaken collaboratively by the World Bank, the IMF, the OECD, the BIS, and the UN. In the meantime, there was need for enhanced transparency in domestics and global financial systems, especially pertaining to tax haven jurisdictions. The GFI called upon governments to create public registries of beneficial ownership to prevent corporations and individuals from keeping secret accounts to transfer and utilize funds, illicit or otherwise. Financial institutions and state agencies should from this perspective be alerted to transactions without verified beneficial ownership information and look into applying additional scrutiny in these cases.

The above alluded to report highlighted that some USD 16.3 trillion have been drained from developing economies, with a large chunk of this accounted for by illegal capital flight, that was facilitated by tax havens, with sixty operating across the world, and with a significant majority of these controlled by a few advanced economies. The European tax havens comprised Luxembourg and Belgium, the US has Delaware and Manhattan, while by far the biggest network of tax havens radiated from the City of London. The latter controls secrecy jurisdictions throughout the British Crown Dependencies and Overseas Territories. In short, economies that said a lot about their foreign aid contributions appeared to be the ones also facilitating financial thefts from developing countries.[273]

It is further clarified that when the reverse financial flows are taken into consideration, this would additionally suggest that aid does little but mask the maldistribution of resources around the world. In this sense, poor economies do not need charity but justice rather. This could be quickly achieved by writing off excess debts of poor countries to free up financial resources used in debt servicing to spend on economic development. Secrecy jurisdictions could also be put into oblivion. Heavy financial and criminal sanctions could also be imposed on financial institutions and professionals that facilitate illicit outflows. The solutions looked clear and not too difficult to do, especially in the context of global cooperation for economic and social justice so often said by global development agencies and others. These, on the other hand, risk running counter to the entrenched interests of powerful multinationals, highly affluent financial elites, and even some economies bent on keeping their national agendas protected.

§4.06 GLOBAL TRADE, OFFSHORE WEALTH AND PROFIT SHIFTING

Already, some doubts have been raised over the quality of the data gathered and analysed in the report. These cited the thoughtful opinions of other experts, as well as a study by the UN University of World Institute for Development Economics Research that compared different methods of measuring illicit capital flight. These researches concluded that the methods were imperfect and ran the risk of misinterpreting ordinary investments.[274] The complexity was demonstrated by a hypothetical example where cocoa was being exported from the Ivory Coast bought by a Dutch trading company. This would be reported as an export to the Netherlands, despite in practice it could be warehoused at the docks in Amsterdam, before being purchased by a chocolate manufacturer in Cologne. This was where it would be reported as an import from the Ivory Coast to Germany. Researchers examining the trade data might interpret this as an illicit flow of finance out of the Ivory Coast to Germany and simultaneously an illicit flow of finance into the Ivory Coast from the Netherlands.

Indeed, the absence of universal agreement on the definition of IFFs, what to be included within their scope, or how the components could be measured, and the

273. J. Hickel. 2017. 'Aid in reverse: How poor countries develop rich countries: New research shows that developing countries send trillions of dollars to the west than the other way round', *The Guardian 14/1/17*.

274. M. Forstater. 2017. 'It's not aid in reverse, illicit financial flows are more complicated than that: It's meaningless to bundle up countries like China and Saudi Arabia with poorer economies such as Bangladesh and Ethiopia', *The Guardian 18/1/17*.

absence of consistent statistics on IFFs contributed to uncertainty as to how large these flows have been, how and where they originate as well as their impacts on developments, while hampering policy actions to tackle these flows. To this end, United Nations Conference of Trade and Development (UNCTAD) and the United Nations Office on Drugs and Crime (UNODC), the two custodians of indicator showing total value of inward and outward IFFs have started methodological work and broad consultations to develop statistical definitions and methods to measure IFFs.[275]

Finally, from current insights and analysis of trade-based estimates of IFF, three main conclusions could be drawn.[276] First, international trade grew to be an active channel for IFFs, and research leading to trade estimates had been useful. Insights from numerous case studies and review of a number of aggregate studies demonstrated clearly the application of trade mispricing for transferring funds illicitly across borders. Second, there were improvements in the methodology applied by GFI and other researchers in their mission to provide more reliable trade data-based estimates of IFFs. However, there appeared to be a trade-off for the trade estimates; either they were available for many economies, but not credible, or they were of relatively high quality, but available only for a few countries. Third, options could be explored for improving the current methods, either at the country level, as exemplified by recent GFI changes, or by extending the existing transaction-level methods to more countries.

Pertaining to offshore wealth, five main findings were identified. First, their estimates were and should be an integral part of the aim for estimating the scale of IFFs. Wealth is stored in tax havens as a direct outcome of some of the IFFs migrating from onshore to offshore. The PP and PRP, the *LuxLeaks*, and other offshore leaks drew good attention to the importance of financial secrecy and offshore wealth. Second, offshore wealth is explicitly important, and the scale appeared to be substantial, with recent estimates putting the scale of offshore wealth at some 10% of global GDP, with some economies more vulnerable.[277] Third, undeclared offshore wealth could be reduced making this policy pertinent as a basis for the sustainable development goal (SDG) target indicator. Offshore wealth estimates varied widely across economies and tax havens. There appeared to be a lot of heterogeneity among economies having wealth in tax heavens, while the role of Switzerland appeared to be receding due to changes in international regulations governing offshore wealth, like the exchange of information to which Switzerland finally agreed.

Fourth, the SDG target was formulated in terms of IFFs, whereas official wealth was usually estimated as a stock. This posed a technical challenge when harmonizing the expectations of the target and the actual estimates. A potential solution would

275. UNCTAD. 2020. 'Recent conceptual and methodological developments on measuring illicit financial flows for policy action'.
276. A. Cobham & P. Jansky. 2020. *Estimating illicit financial flows: A critical guide to the data, methodologies, and findings*, Oxford: Oxford University Press.
277. A. Alstadsaeter, N. Johannesen & G. Zucman. 2018. 'Who owns the wealth in tax havens? Macro evidence and implications for global inequality', *Journal of Public Economies*, Vol. 162(2018): 89-100.

involve estimating the income streams that might accrue on offshore assets.[278] Fifth, the offshore wealth estimates pertaining to the indicator of the SDG target were of very high quality.[279]

With respect of international corporate tax avoidance, there were six main observations.[280] Foremost, profit shifting by MNCs to tax havens and associated international tax avoidance fell under IFFs. These could be treated as illicit rather than illegal flows and ergo the inclusion of profit shifting would be apt, as the practice of profit shifting would be considered illicit, while the matter of legality would be left mostly to others. The main concern could focus on the harm done, especially so when many developing and EMEs were found to be more intensively and expansively impacted by profit shifting. Also, as articulated in the G20/OECD BEPS project, the international policy consensus has been for MNCs' profit misalignment to be curbed.

Second, profit shifting has been a real and substantive phenomenon with large tracts of supporting evidence demonstrating MNCs shifting profits illicitly from where economic activities occurred to tax havens. It appeared that the current international tax systems provided the avenues for lowering their tax obligations via intra-company transfer prices and deceptive management of the location of intangible assets or corporate debt structures distortions. That many MNCs indulged in the shifting of incomes to tax havens have grown from speculative commentaries to well-founded research insights.[281] Though research insights had been less conclusive with respects of scale and revenue implications, the quality and coverage of estimates had improved significantly over time, no doubt in part due to the efforts of the BEPS and other related initiatives.

Third, research insights had suggested that the scale of shifted profits and revenue losses had been widely distributed across countries, with the highest values in affluent economies, but relatively heavier losses in proportion to GDP and particularly to tax revenues. A small number of economies in contrast were consistently the recipients of outsized profit volumes relating to economic activities somewhere else. Various research had estimated that some seventy-three economies alone lost more than USD 125 billion in annual tax revenues across the world each year,[282] with some estimating[283] that profit shifting on macroeconomic aggregates, like the GDP, were statistically material.

278. N. Johannesen & J. Pirttila. 2016. 'Capital flight and development', *UNU-WIDER Working Paper Series*, Vol. 2016(9): 1-18.
279. *Supra* note [277]. Alstadsaeter, Johannesen & Zucman. 2018.
280. *Supra* note [276]. Cobham & Jansky. 2020.
281. K.A. Clausing. 2016. 'The effect of profit shifting on the corporate tax base in the United States and beyond', *National Tax Journal*, Vol. 69(4): 905-934; H. Huizinga & L. Laeven. 2008. 'International profit shifting within multinationals: A multi-country perspective', *Journal of Public Economics*, 92(5): 1164-1182.
282. P. Jansky & M. Palansky. 2019. 'Estimating the scale of profit shifting and tax revenues losses related to foreign direct investment', *International Tax and Public Finance*, Vol. 26(2019): 1048-1103.
283. T. Torslov, L. Wier & G. Zucman. 2018. 'The missing profits of nations', *National Bureau of Economic Research (NBER) Working Paper 24071*; F. Guvenen, R. Mataloni Jr., D.G. Rassier & K.J. Ruhl. 2019. 'Offshore profit shifting and domestic productivity measurement', *NBER Working Paper 23324*.

Fourth, profit shifting could be curbed. While the academia and policy experts had been paying some attention to this phenomenon, no clear and specific recommendations have been made thus far. Historical analysis had demonstrated that profit shifting had been of less significance in the 1980s, thereby suggesting that the global economy could function well in its absence;[284] but for various reasons, not least the maximum profit-seeking motivations of global corporations for competitive power had scaled its magnitude and importance.

Fifth, when deliberating on a feasible indicator for the SDG, main research thus far applied straightforward methodologies to publicly available, official, government-sponsored, and official statistics of foreign affiliates of MNCs. Despite mixed outcomes, they shared many similarities thereby making them desirable for an indicator of the SDG target; and ergo no doubt useful when designing a new indicator that could overcome remaining limitations these estimates might have.[285] Sixth, this augured well that feasible or workable SDG indicators could be within reach.

Finally, for close to two decades, important progress had been made towards a global agenda for enhanced transparency, propelled in part by the TJN's tax transparency guide drawing attention to automatic multilateral exchange of information; beneficial ownership data in public registers for corporations, trusts and foundations; and CbC reporting by MNCs in the public domain. One proposed policy target for SDGs for complementing the scale-based target could be appealing in that it identified explicitly the accountabilities of jurisdictions that resisted transparency thereby raising IFF risk levels for others; but suffered from the drawbacks that the approach neither generated scale measures as SDG 16.4 required nor provided an immediate premise for policy decisions in locations suffering from IFFs.

The risk-based approaches as offered by the Bilateral Secrecy Index and the vulnerability measures pioneered in the High Level Panel on IFFs from Africa could empower policymakers to carry out more effective responses to the particular IFF risks encountered, while simultaneously enabling progress to be shown, as well as for greater attention be beamed on economies of risks to others. Hence, the evaluations of policy and risk-based measures would suggest that SDG indicators could best support accountability where they were fully separated to the jurisdiction levels and enable progress monitoring by those aggravating IFF from elsewhere, and those suffering from IFFs. The two proposed indicators[286] could include those relating to the profit shifting of MNCs, while the second could capture a core outcome of other illicit flows, as exemplified by the generation of undeclared assets of some USD 21-32 trillion squirreled offshore under conditions of low or zero tax and substantial secrecy.[287]

284. A. Cobham & P. Jansky. 2019. 'Measuring misalignment: The location of US multinationals' economic activity versus the location of their profits', *Development Policy Review*, Vol. 37(1): 91-110; T. Torslov, L. Wier & G. Zucman. 2018. 'The missing profits of nations', *NBER Working Paper 24071*.

285. *Supra* note [284]. Cobham & Jansky. 2019. *Supra* note [283]. Torslov, Wier & Zucman. 2018.

286. *Supra* note [276]. Cobham & Jansky. 2020.

287. N. Shaxson. 2014. 'The price of offshore revisited'.

The above illustrations and analysis showed that IFFs were more complicated, than ordinarily thought, with *kleptocrats*[288] tending to use varied methods to conceal their ill-gotten wealth. However, their preferred option appeared to be simply transferring money to anonymous shell companies. Taking this into account, wealthy economies should enforce anti-bribery rules and prevent the use of anonymous companies as getaway vehicles, such as being increasingly done in the UK, while aid should be transparent and focused on outcomes. Additionally, global developmental agencies and governments from advanced economies should support institutional reforms in developing economies that sought to mobilize domestic resources, like the enhancing of tax collection, improvements in public procurements procedures, improvements in natural resource governance, as well as enabling public examinations of revenues and budgets. The solutions appeared obvious and considerably simple in rhetorical terms, but difficult to implement in practice, because of vested political and economic interests.

Still, CSOs, national governments, and global development agencies by collaborating together could gradually make the difference. Tax and secrecy havens could in this way be pressured to change their modus operandi, or faced global isolation. So far, there had been isolated small outpourings of not so good things done in some tax havens.

Serious analysts have begun to propose indicators for the UN SDGs 16.4 that could provide the single best strategy for global progress against the damaging harm from IFFs undermining both the resources available for developing economies to support development, and the capacity of these and other economies to apply inclusive, politically representative initiatives. The US and the EU on the other hand had increasingly sought in UN negotiations to exclude MNCs from the scope of any measures relating to IFFs; but this to some extent had been counterbalanced by OECD initiatives to reform international tax rules that sought to address in particular the distribution of taxing rights between economies.[289]

Appreciating that progress on indicators for SDG 16.4 could be uncertain, two other policy instruments had been proposed.[290] One pertained to a convention on tax and transparency that could include commitments around the tax rules for MNCs, but would at a minimum formulate international standards for the full inclusion of economies at all income levels in the application and benefits of the bolts and nuts of transparency.

The other pertained to the idea for a UN centre for monitoring tax rights that could be empowered to curate and published data with global scope on the cross-border patterns of profit misalignments and financial asset ownerships; and with responsibility for annual reports revealing the degree within which each jurisdiction was able to exert taxing rights over profits linked to economic activities therein, as well

288. N. Sibley & B. Judah. 2021. *Countering global kleptocracy: A new US strategy for fighting authoritarian corruption*, Washington DC: Hudson Institute; T. Sutton & S. Clark. 2020. 'The treasury department should lead the fight against corruption and kleptocracy', *Center for American Progress* 10/10/20.
289. *Supra* note [276]. Cobham & Jansky. 2020.
290. A. Cobham. 2019. *The uncounted*, Cambridge: Polity Press.

as over the offshore financial assets of their tax residents. Finally, evaluation of methodologies for estimating IFFs would be ongoing; simultaneously international progress would be ongoing against financial secrecy. Both in tandem could open up new avenues and possibilities for quality data providing better guidance to policymakers in search for effective solutions to the persistent headaches posed by IFFs and tax havens.

The PP meanwhile, as released in April 2016 for the first time provided strong evidences of who actually used tax havens and the extent of their employment for wealth concealment in a big way. These included big corporations and highly affluent political and financial elites from across the world. The PP was quickly followed by the equally attention-grabbing PPR. Both of these would be discussed in Chapter 5.

CHAPTER 5
Panama and Paradise Papers

§5.01 INTRODUCTION

This chapter begins with discussions on some of the more stunning revelations from the PP. Analysis of the implications of these revelations included those impacting various senior political leaders, senior officials of international sports associations, and other financial elites. While acknowledging the good contributions from leaks of such magnitude and scope towards the containment of IFFs, some reflective thoughts and analysis drawn from research suggest the usefulness of having a better understanding of the nature and origins of such leak-driven insights for the law-making process to avoid the design of socially costly laws. These are discussed in some details in this chapter to avoid excessive exuberance over the stunning revelations, and not giving enough thought on the best way forward when framing global policy responses. Key insights from the equally stunning revelations of the PPRs are also discussed together with some analysis for national and international policy responses.

§5.02 KEY REVELATIONS FROM THE PP

News organizations around the world in April 2016 published investigations drawn from a massive cache of leaked documents suggesting corruption and questionable business transactions of world leaders, politicians, sports mega-stars, and other financial elites. The source of this was the encrypted internal documents from Mossack Fonseca. This being a Panama-based company that sold offshore shell companies across the world. The leak amounted to around 11.5 million documents or 2.6 terabytes worth of data on 214,000 shell companies, extending from the 1970s to 2016.[291] To put

291. M. Koren. 2016. 'What are the Panama Papers?: A year-long investigation has revealed millions of classified documents that point to corruption among world leaders, politicians, and others', *The Atlantic* 3/4/16.

this in perspective, 1 terabyte of data could be stored in around 1,400 CD-ROMs or 220 DVDs. An anonymous source had in 2015 offered the document to well-known German newspaper Suddeutsche Zeitung (SZ), without financial compensation, but simply for the expressed purpose of revealing the purported crimes in public. SZ shared the records with the ICIJ based in London.

These documents known as the PP contained mostly emails, PDF files, and photo files belonging to Mossack Fonseca. This Panamanian law firm was well known as one of the biggest providers of offshore financial services. The firm's website claimed it offered comprehensive legal and trust services. The website went on to add that it provided research, advice, and legal services in Belize and other known tax havens in other jurisdictions. This was not the first leak of its kind, nor the last on the activities going on in tax havens.

Nevertheless, it was, by far, the biggest-ever leak of classified information eclipsing in size the WikiLeaks dump of American diplomatic cables in 2010 and Edward Snowden's expose in 2013. Previous leaks included the UBS and LGT leaks, the Swiss leaks, the Julius Baer leak, the British Havens Leak, the *LuxLeaks,* and subsequent leaks from the Bahamas.[292] The PP leaked data offered rare insights into a world that only existed in the shadow. It gave evidence of how the global financial service industry comprising banks, legal firms, and asset management businesses secretly managed the wealth of the world's highly affluent community.

The modus operandi usually involved the use of anonymous shell companies that were not illegal, but were very easy to set up one in most jurisdictions of the world, including tax havens.[293] There was even, one example, of a journalist using her cat as an anonymous owner in a US state known for its corporate-friendly privacy laws. Shell companies enabled their owners to hold assets that were subjected to minimal government oversights. Though not all, but some are employed to dodge taxes, particularly in tax havens. The latter as alluded to earlier referred to jurisdictions offering foreign businesses little or no-tax liability and other dubious economic services.

It needs to be emphasized that owning an offshore company or creating an offshore trust is not illegal or illicit. It is perfectly legal in almost all jurisdictions, including the US, UK, and elsewhere. It is illegal, however, when using such offshore trusts to conceal assets from known creditors, or for evading taxation.[294] Failures to disclose offshore assets and report offshore income are nefarious activities. The US Internal Revenue Service (IRS) in this connection annually released a list of common tax schemes in its 'name and shame tactic' known as the *Dirty Dozen,* and this clearly identified the hiding of money or income offshore as one of these. There are significant reporting requirements for offshore assets, Foreign Bank Account Report (FBAR) and Financial Accounts filings. Taxpayers without proper reports and disclosures of such accounts are said to be breaking the law and could potentially face civil and criminal

292. S-Y Oei & D. Ring. 2017. 'Leak-driven law', *Tulane Public Law Research Paper No. 17(1)*: 1-69.
293. *Supra* note [291]. Koren. 2016.
294. K.P. Erb. 2016. 'What are the Panama Papers?', *Forbes 4/4/16*.

penalties and fines. The IRS though provided those failing to report in the previous years with the Offshore Voluntary Disclosure Program (OVDP) option.

Those qualifying on this scheme are allowed to catch up on filing and payment requirements and avoid having to pay hefty fines and criminal prosecutions. Also named in the tax schemes shaming lists were abusive tax shelters that might not have to be multimillion-dollar tax schemes, as they could merely involve simple trust arrangements, offshore tax schemes, and the employment of multiple pass-through companies, like limited liability companies and limited liability partnerships. This implied that it might not pay to legally avoid taxation, by creating multiple layers of companies, or trusts, or by manipulating the ownership of assets, as sometimes advised by professional consultants.[295]

Hence, when advisors like lawyer, accountants, and financial advisors worked to set up offshore accounts, they were supposed to carry out serious due diligence to ensure that money was not being transferred for illegal purposes, like tax evasion, money laundering, or to avoid existing creditors, like ex-spouses or victorious plaintiffs.[296] Offshore accounts with legitimate concerns about asset protection or estate planning were therefore not unusual. Moving funds out of a jurisdiction like the US did not extinguish the compliance obligations for the beneficial owners who might still live in or are US citizens. Where the US is concerned, taxpayers must still report the existence of the accounts on tax returns, as well as income generated from the accounts. Failures to do so could render both the beneficial owners of the accounts and the financial advisors who facilitated the opening of such accounts with big accountability problems.

In the initial months of the PP revelations, the Panamanian law firm regretted any misuse of its services and announced steps to prevent this, including defending its world-class services in global financial markets. In fact, three years earlier, when ICIJ published a series of report on tax havens based on leaks of confidential documents, the firm assured its clientele that their secrets locked in offshore companies were safe as its data centre was state of the art, and its encryption algorithm world-class. Still, the firm's founders were in February 2017 subsequently arrested on money-laundering charges.[297]

Preliminary research outcomes from collaborative efforts of ICIJ and SZ were reported by the media across the world.[298] Interestingly, such big data analysis using graph database technology were the confines of big financially strong tech corporations, like Facebook or Google, but for this occasion, support was being provided by Neo Technology, a start-up from Silicon Valley. Neo's technology was employed to sift

295. K.P. Erb. 2016. 'IRS issues "dirty dozen" list of tax schemes & tax scams for 2016', *Forbes 17/2/16*.
296. *Supra* note [295]. Erb. 2016.
297. W. Fitzgibbon, E. Diaz-Struck & M. Hudson. 2017. 'Founders of Panama Papers law firm arrested on money laundering charges', *ICIJ 11/2/17*.
298. *Supra* note [291]. Koren. 2016.

through more than 11 million records revealed in the PP leak, and to locate evidence of corrupt offshore tax activities.[299]

The ICIJ revealed that the documents named at least thirty-three individuals and companies blacklisted by the US. These included those that had business dealings with Mexican drug lords, terrorist organizations, and countries with which the US imposed sanctions, such as Iran and North Korea. The leaks revealed confidential financial information about twelve current or former heads of states.[300] There were also revelations about how Russian leaders and their associates secretly moved about USD 2 billion through offshore accounts,[301] while others reported how a president of a national soccer team and Federation Internationale de Football Association (FIFA) ethics experts managed companies through which FIFA members could receive bribes.[302] In other words, offshore companies identified in the PP were reported to be linked to several individuals closely involved in the massive FIFA corruption charges.

The files were also said to contain twenty-one billionaires featured in Forbes Magazine list of the 500 richest people on the planet.[303] These reports, including others published across the world barely touched the surface of the leaked materials. More are expected over the coming months and years. There were a lot more beyond Mossack that could be leaked, as the firm had only 5%-10% of the global market for shell companies. Some professional wealth advisors have thus been telling their clientele to assume anything they transacted offshore could become public and to prepare to answer this when required.[304]

§5.03 IMPLICATIONS OF PP LEAKS

The PP revelations stunned the world. However, its preliminary impacts have been mixed. The Prime Minister of Iceland stepped down on account of the revelations, but most of the individuals and institutions identified have naturally denied any wrongful involvements, with some linking it to various conspiracies. The various repercussions flowing from the PP revelations are discussed in this chapter, but they have immediate impact on the reputation of tax havens with the public mood hardening against offshore shenanigans. They have been earlier lambasted for their enabling role in various illicit activities connected with 2002 Enron debacle, the 2007-2009 GFC, and now the PP.

299. M. Kendall. 2017. 'They are no Palantir: Smaller startups with new ideas take on big data', *Mercury News 27/3/17*
300. R. Bilton. 2016. 'Panama Papers: Mossack Fonseca leak reveals elite's tax havens', *BBC 4/3/16.*
301. L. Harding. 2016. 'Revealed: The $2bn offshore trail that leads to Vladimir Putin', *The Guardian 3/4/16.*
302. T. Kistner, F. Obermaier, B. Obermaier & M. Much. 2016. 'Playing both sides', *Suddeutsche 3/4/16.*
303. *Supra* note [295]. Erb. 2016.
304. The Economist. 2016. 'Panama Papers: A torrential leak: A huge trove of documents has revealed the secrets of offshore business, presaging tougher times for tax havens', *The Economist 9/4/16.*

As the tide surged, more whistle-blowing of this nature was expected, particularly these days with enhance protections for whistle-blowers following proper procedures. This might appear to have also curbed interests in the use of shell companies. The Panamanian law firm was reported to be closing down more than it opened in recent years. The PP revelations showed how much more collaborative journalism could achieve by working together. In fact, the ICIJ had enlisted some 400 journalists to analyse the leaked data to ensure that important items were not missed out.

Even though the analysis to date has been preliminary, it mattered.[305] Legal and financial services providers, such as Mossack, specialized in helping foreigners to conceal wealth. These individuals and corporations might respectively want to steer money from soon-to-be ex-wives or launder money to evade taxes. The main mechanisms for achieving this were through anonymous shell companies that existed only on paper and offshore accounts in tax havens that came with perks, like banking secrecy and low to no taxes. Such structures obscured the identity of the beneficial owners of financial assets hidden in or routed through secrecy jurisdictions, like the Panama.

The PP were said to contain information about 214,500 companies in twenty-one offshore jurisdictions and names of over 14,000 middlemen, like banks and law firms, with whom Mossack has allegedly worked with. It was probable that those using these structures for illicit purposes, like human trafficking, drug cartels, and terrorism could be called upon to answer in civil or criminal suits. The not so obvious miscreants include service providers in the global financial industry that flogged financial secrecy to those able to afford them. It has been estimated earlier that some 8% of the world's wealth were squirreled away in offshore accounts.[306]

These could be done legally for some or illegally for others. Those making money from facilitating tax evasions might want to take note of UK's Criminal Finances Act 2017 that now makes such activities a criminal offence and which has wider than extraterritorial reach than its Bribery Act 2010. Legal or illegal, the PP revelations aligned with contemporary sentiments on the fundamental disconnect between the global political and financial elites and the rest for whom taxes were as certain as death.[307]

The attention of policymakers, regulators, and CSOs would likely extend beyond Mossack or Panama. Giants of corporate services like *TMF* and *Intertrust* based in the Netherlands could fall under increase public attention.[308] While the business for forming companies was not huge for them, with estimated annual revenues around USD 6 billion, the pre-tax margins at 30%-40% were high and growing by some 7% annually, but importantly the average life span of eight to ten years provided a

305. The Economist. 2016. 'The Economist explains: What are the Panama papers and why do they matter?', *The Economist 5/4/16.*
306. G. Zucman. 2013. 'The missing wealth of nations, are Europe and the U.S. net debtors or net creditors?', *Quarterly Journal of Economics*, Vol. 128(3): 1321-1364.
307. *Supra* note [304]. The Economist. 2016.
308. The Economist. 2016. 'After the Panama Papers: Who next?: Mossack Fonseca and its homeland are not alone in facing closer scrutiny', *The Economist 14/4/16.*

comfortable annuity-like earnings stream.[309] This perhaps explained why savvy institutional investors, like *Blackrock* had a stake in *Intertrust*, while Doughty Hanson owned TMF. Panama's resistance against the international move for greater tax transparency would likely melt with the occurrence of this April 2016 incident. Panama aside, the most heat could likely be on the UK and offshore territories, like the BVI that host close to half of the 214,000 companies alluded to in the PP.

Close to a dozen of the world's fifty-sixty active OFCs were current or former British colonies.[310] These though have been spruced up significantly in terms of transparency, since the 1990s, when they were mentioned as being linked to nefarious financial activities. They are now operating as well as other bigger places in reviews by the OECD and the FATF. These two bodies set tax transparency and AML standards. David Cameron, the previous Prime Minister of the UK has since 2013 when assuming leadership of the rotating G20 urged these British protectorates to provide central registers of company ownership available to the taxman and law enforcers, like what Bermuda and Jersey had earlier done. This could put them ahead of FATF standards that as yet to require such centralized data collection. While seemingly likely to follow suit, they were lukewarm to the idea of making their registers public.

The BVI, the home to 450,000 companies, endeavoured to deflect criticisms with its new requirements on corporate agents. One of these would force these corporate servicing agents to collect and verify beneficial ownership information on clients.[311] This had been largely left to 'introducers' in the client's home country that often failed to do so. There were concerns in the UK that when British outposts are squeezed excessively business could flow to jurisdictions with shell-company-friendly laws, like the Seychelles and Samoa. Other jurisdictions, like Hong Kong, are already home to many offshore firms.

Other jurisdictions with competing features included US states with lax regulation of registration agents and ironclad corporate anonymity jurisdictions, like Delaware and Nevada. Then, there are also other parts of the UK itself, as well as, other parts of the US. There have been reported links between British shell companies and criminals, like the USD 1 billion swindle in Moldova, involving Scottish limited partnerships. Various criminals engaged in illegal business transactions operated through the UK and the US, because they have attractive status as being cost-effective, anonymous, and having good names. These made them subject to less due diligence, as they are generally not perceived to be of high-risk.

The economic repercussions and implications from the revelations of the PP were enormous. The loopholes provided by tax havens, such as Panama, were typically accessible to the rich and famous, including powerful businesses. They used this access to game the system. Others, of lower economic rankings, and in particular from the middle class downwards were financially less capable of doing so. Those gaming the system, included people engaging in harmful economic activities, like drug peddling, human trafficking, money laundering, and terrorism. This implied that the rich and

309. *Supra* note [308]. The Economist. 2016.
310. *Supra* note [308]. The Economist. 2016.
311. *Supra* note [308]. The Economist. 2016.

powerful and those undertaking criminal activities were benefiting in different ways, at the expense of the wider poorer population.

This narrative was illustrated by offshore holdings of twelve current and former world leaders and details on the hidden financial dealings of 128 political and public officials around the globe. This also alternatively implied that economies drained by this financial leakage became less able to invest in health, education, badly needed infrastructure, or to create more economic opportunities for the young. This was the immediate reaction of the then US President in relation to the PP.

The then UK Prime Minister was stung by clarion calls for a government inquiry and allegations of bad hypocrisy, even though he had since 2013 to the early part of 2016 championed for greater global financial transparency. This was because the PP disclosures implied that his family and other distinguished UK families held undisclosed wealth in offshore tax havens. Simultaneously, there were also calls for the UK to impose direct rule on its overseas territories and dependencies to get them to comply with UK tax laws. These calls included those from Transparency International UK not to allow corrupt individuals to continue acquiring assets and enjoy life in the UK. Many leading politicians in Asia, Africa, Eastern Europe, and in Central and South America were also implicated by the PP.

Global reactions in general to the PP have been relatively swift.[312] There were, for instance, graphic descriptions of French prosecutors searching the offices of Societe Generale, Peruvian authorities seizing documents from the Lima office of Mossack, El Salvador's top prosecutor overseeing a raid on Mossack's office in that jurisdiction, New York's Attorney opening criminal investigations arising from the PP, and with US senators seeking assurances from the US Treasury that it too was looking at potential involvements of US and US-linked banks, financial service institutions, and other businesses, or individuals with the Panamanian law firm. The US Inland Revenue Service (IRS) was reported to have participated in a special meeting of the Joint International Tax Shelter Information and Collaboration (JITSIC) network on the day the PP were released.

The OECD declared that the JITSIC meeting brought together senior tax officials of more than forty jurisdictions to deliberate on opportunities for obtaining data, cooperation, and information sharing in view of the PP revelations. The World Bank President announced that financial transparency would henceforth be moving forward, while a lot of leaders from across the world were additionally telling the World Bank that they would work with the global financial development agency to identify and track down IFFs to ensure that fair shares of taxes were being borne.

Initially, there were serious concerns over the PP public disclosures, especially with regard to national security implications flowing from abrupt regime changes, and the higher risk of political instability. Somehow, firm and vehement denials by many named and the limited outpourings of public outrage over the implied injustice revealed by the disclosures were generally contained, apart from some isolated cases of resignations of political leaders implicated. To be fair, not all those named are

312. L.J. Trautman. 2017. 'Following the money: Lessons from the Panama Papers Part 1: Tip of the iceberg', *Penn State Law Review*, Vol. 121(3): 807-873.

necessarily engaged with illegal activities, as the anonymous shell companies used to conceal their identities are perfectly legal instruments commonly used onshore, or offshore in tax and secrecy havens. Some of them could have legitimate reasons to protect their identity.

The nine most popular tax havens publicly disclosed by the PP in order of significance were the BVI, Panama, the Bahamas, Seychelles, Niue, Samoa, Nevada, Hong Kong, and the UK. This showed that tax havens could come from onshore and offshore jurisdictions, as well as, from developing to advanced economies. This together with other data from the PP suggested that a considerable part of IFFs moved around and between tax havens. Such data also suggested that a wider view was necessary for bribery and corruption oversight. For example, the World Bank alerted the world to the existence of bureaucratic or administrative corruptions. This referred to the intentional imposition of distortions in the prescribed implementation of existing laws, rules, and regulations to provide benefits to individuals internal or external to the state, via illicit opaque mechanisms. This could be exemplified by payments to tax officials for reduction of tax liabilities.

There were also problems relating to patronage and nepotisms, exemplified by the granting of personal favours, sole-source contracts, or the making of unmerited appointments to public office; state capture or intentional actions of individuals or groups in public and private sectors to influence laws and policies in particular direction; and extortions by public officials in terms of collection of unlawful fees. The incidence of such illegal sources of funds as unmasked by the Panamanian law firm was not all there is, as research alluded to earlier suggested about 8% of the world's financial wealth or around USD 7.6 trillion being held in tax havens.[313]

The PP leak reminded but more importantly accelerated the calls for global tax reforms and related measures to curb and to retrieve financial assets leaked from the many coffers of governments of all stripes. These drained funds rightfully belonging to the people around the world of some USD 100-USD 240 billion annually by OECD estimates. This is likely to have fuelled voter anger, as many governments of the world need the leaked funding source for development purpose. Very importantly, tax evasions could destroy trust in public institutions and the rule of law, while shrinking fiscal flexibility for investing in the delivery of public services.[314] Corruptions stretched from global multinationals to manufacturers, agricultural producers, and service providers, including those profiting from harming the environment, engaging in all kinds of labour abuses, delivering shoddy infrastructures, and dispensing unsafe medication around the world.[315]

The ill-gotten gains from these practices, including others, were laundered across the world to hide their origins. The US through the US Foreign Corrupt Practices Act

313. *Supra* note [306]. Zucman. 2013.
314. H. Watt. 2016. 'Panama Papers: Global tax officials to launch unprecedented inquiry', *The Guardian 12/4/16.*
315. L.J. Trautman & K. Altenbaumer-Price. 2013. 'Lawyers, guns and money: The bribery problems and the U.K. bribery Act', *The International Lawyer*, Vol. 47(3): 481-517; F.X. Donnelly & S. Kellog. 2011. 'Understanding corruption', *GW Business: The George Washington University*, (Fall 2011), p. 9.

(FCPA) appeared to have pioneered the criminalization of money laundering. Its initiative paved the way for OECD's Anti-Bribery Convention, the UK's 2010 Bribery Act, as well as other legislations elsewhere. Subsequent to the FCPA, the US in 2010 launched the Kleptocracy Asset Recovery Initiative (KARI), that had thus far recovered some USD 63 million in bribery proceeds, forfeitures of some USD 480 million embezzled by a Nigerian dictator, and including collaborative actions with other jurisdictions.[316]

Tax evasions, the other major kind of financial leakage, were clearly illegal as it implied wilful intention not to pay obligated tax liabilities. But, tax avoidance by legal instruments was a very controversial matter. While legal, it had moral implications, together with the larger issues of unfairness and inequality, as it was usually undertaken by the wealthy with the support of enabling service providers. Nevertheless, technology had begun to whittle away secrecy shields employed by both criminals, and the wealthy, as clearly seen in recent Internet-based leakages, including that from the PP. Such leakages, including others found in the social media were going to help in making financial transactions more transparent. Transparency was argued to be the best disinfectant, or remedy for social and industrial diseases. This contention was raised more than seven decades ago by a prominent judge.[317]

Tax authorities were spurred by enhanced disclosures and leaked data of those contributed by the PP and the like to examine the potentials for prosecutions of offshore tax cheats to recoup lost revenues, enact new laws, and promote international agreements that enhanced 'sunshine' or greater transparency, and AEI between jurisdictions. The benefits were clearly seen in the 2008 leaked information about improprieties at Switzerland's UBS bank that alerted the US to the extensive use by US taxpayers of secret offshore bank accounts to conceal assets and evade taxes.

This led the US to prosecute tax cheats and develop voluntary disclosure initiatives to recoup revenue.[318] From this viewpoint, such leaks were socially and economically beneficial. Such tax leaks were not one-off events, but rather recurrent. There were no indications of these abating. They were being perceived as playing undeniable roles in the development of international tax law and policy.[319] However, questions were raised over the implicit assumption that these kinds of leaks would turn out to be beneficial, socially and economically.

---

316. L.E. Lynch. 2016. 'Attorney General Loretta E. Lynch delivers remarks at the OECD Anti-Bribery Ministerial Meeting: Paris, 16/3/16', *Justice News US Department of Justice 10/11/16.*
317. L.D. Brandeis. 1914. *Other people's money and how the bankers use it*, New York: Frederick Stokes Company.
318. L. Browning. 2008. 'Ex-UBS bankers pleads guilty in tax evasion', *The New York Times 20/6/2008*; R. Jackson. 2008. 'Former UBS banker indicted in tax evasion cases', *Tax Notes International*, Vol. 50(2008): 472.
319. A. Rettman. 2013. 'EU Commissioner: Offshore leaks transformed tax politics', *EU Observer 5/6/14.*

§5.04 BENEFITS AND RISKS OF TAX LEAKS

The last ten years well-publicized data leaks such as those from the PPs revealing secret offshore reservoirs of MNC taxpayers and high-profile high net worth of senior politicians and celebrities have spiked cross-border tax enforcements. Drawing on these leaked data, tax regulators began prosecuting tax havens' tax cheats, took initiatives to recoup tax revenues, promulgated new laws, apart from signing international agreements promoting the exchange of information between countries and between financial institutions. The popular idea claims that data leaks enable governments and regulators to identify and discipline offshore tax evasion more forcefully, and in that sense are economically and socially beneficial. That has been argued to be too simplistic, as while leak-driven law-making could deliver positive outcomes, tax leaks could generate unintended negative outcomes like hijacking of purpose by agenda setting third parties with particular interests, as well as the revelations' capacity to stimulate non-rational responses. While on balance, leak-driven law-making are likely to generate overall benefit, it would be helpful for policymakers and regulators to be also mindful of their pitfalls when ascertaining the appropriate response.[320] Research has demonstrated that under particular circumstances, this kind of leak-driven law-making could generate negative social welfare outcomes. In other words, they could induce the opposite effect, depending on how enforcement resources were allocated, and how taxpayers, governments, havens, and others reacted. The outcomes would depend on which of these behaviours and alternative choices would dominate. It has been further suggested that systematic and recurrent features of leaks and their aftermaths could lead to social costly outcomes when not properly managed.[321]

Foremost, it would be helpful to recognize the value and limitations of different species of information leaked. In general, they provide information about particular taxpayers; observations of the practices and cultures of facilitators; and reflections on policies, practices and priorities of governments. The LuxLeaks spotlighted Luxembourg's ruling practices in facilitating MNCs' tax strategies; the Bahamas and Panama revelations suggest these as preferred destinations for those seeking offshore secrecy; and in the HSBC leak the whistleblower encountered extradition and criminal charges in Switzerland, despite being celebrated elsewhere, thereby highlighting differences between Switzerland and other jurisdictions when it comes to bank secrecy and tax compliance. Additionally, it pays for policymakers, regulators and others to appreciate that leaked data have various imperfections; ranging from incompleteness, different degree of preciseness, and false positives. Such differences could generate powerful public sentiments to drive kneejerk reforms that failed to differentiate between tax avoidance and tax evasion behaviours.[322] Data leakages do not originate merely from the PPs even though they are more stunning in scope and scale. More often, as demonstrated in earlier corporate scandals they could originate from internal and

320. S.Y. Oei & D. Ring. 2018. 'Leak-driven law', *University of California Los Angeles Review*, Vol. 65 (2028): 532-618.
321. *Supra* note [320]. Oei & Ring. 2018.
322. *Supra* note [320]. Oei & Ring. 2018.

external whistleblowers, and ergo not from hackings. These different sources of transmissions caused delays in enforcement actions and on the comprehensiveness of policy and regulatory responses.

In general, and undoubtedly, leaked information would provide authorities with data not hitherto available, dissuade offshore tax evasion, and prompt policymakers and regulators to probe the nature and forms of tax impropriety so as design more effective response. Tax leaks from whatever source could generate benefits in terms of enhanced access to vital information to enable more effective enforcement, the lowering of enforcement costs, and dissuasion of noncompliance, besides stimulating the pace for needed tax reforms.[323] However, when dealing with the cross-order tax enforcement and evasion space, jurisdictions seeking to tax including tax havens deliberate on decisions about how to enforce, while taxpayers deliberate on decisions as to whether to comply or evade given the background of imperfect information, limited resources and their corresponding objectives. Specifically for enforcement-minded agencies, leaked information provides, in general, costless data sources, high relevancy for policymaking, and counterweight to policymaking lobbyists. The potential distinctive risks of tax leaks include the risk of regulatory capture, and the triggering of disproportionate and ill-conceived knee-jerk public and policymaking responses. This is because intermediaries and information gatherers might select, withhold, falsify, or curate data in manners that make their release timing and content suspect.[324]

This strongly suggest the benefit of appreciating the potential distinctive risks alluded to earlier to ensure that regulatory agencies to respond with better designed policies and enforcement actions. The distinctive risks of relying on tax leaks could arise from the ways in which agenda setters have decided how the public and the authorities receive, access, and respond to leaked data, the hesitations and procrastinations arising from data transmission within and among economies, and knee-jerk laws enacted in responses to highly -charged emotional information. This form of leak-driven law-making is argued to be impacted by the roles of various agenda setters; the messiness of leaked data transmission, and leak-driven laws occurring elsewhere. These are accordingly discussed in further details discussed below.[325]

[A] Agenda Setters

The following are the three better known agenda setters:

(i) Agenda-setting behaviours by leakers and media organizations that might be seeking to direct public reactions and policy outcomes according to their agenda or missions. Take the case of the role of ICIJ in the PP case. Here, it has been observed, first, that the ICIJ chose to present the leaked material in a searchable Internet database. This required it to format and combine

323. *Supra* note [320], Oei & Ring. 2018.
324. *Supra* note [320]. Oei & Ring. 2018.
325. *Supra* note [320]. Oei & Ring. 2018.

the Panama data with data from the BVI leaks and those from the Bahamas data. This approach carried the implication, that all of this leaked information fell under a broad set of offshore secrets, or offshore misconducts. Second, it only released a fraction of the leaked information suggesting that the ICIJ could have had an underlying metric for deciding what to release, and might have been done in conjunction with the anonymous leaker. Third, it did not release the underlying original documents. Though, justifiable by journalistic standards, it also implied that the ICIJ's framing and characterization of data largely controls the narratives received by the public. Where the priorities of the media organizations shifted or were captured by particular interests' groups, the welfare impacts of their actions could also alter. For instance, media framing and publication choices could distort policy responses by causing governments to over- or under-react to leaks.

(ii) Leakers are said to enjoy discretionary powers over information sources, the time of collection, the kinds of information to gather, and what data ranges to retrieve. Unlike media entities and journalists, identities of leakers could be anonymous or secret, making it difficult to know the leakers' motivations. In the case of the PP, it was widely held to be the result of a hacker who could be driven by different agendas. In this case, a leak to the ICIJ was likely to trigger a wider set of responses, than leaks to particular agencies. It has been seen in some instances, how the ICIJ's intervention in publicizing leaked data contributed to a surge of interest and activities by countries that have not previously acted.

(iii) These would include CSOs, non-profits, social enterprises, international entities, secondary media outlets, and the general public. Such participants processed, interpreted and commented on the leaked data and government responses to leaks. Some agenda setters, for example, could be keener on transparency, poverty reduction, or fairness, and prioritized these over the more comprehensive social welfare maximization objective of tax policy. In the case of others, they could be driven by a wider mission to expose systemic flaws to drive fundamental legal changes. The above disparate agendas could create agency costs for a jurisdiction, or tax authority, that sought to optimize enforcement of existing laws, but had to rely on the contributions of the media and leakers to access information. Since the underlying agendas of external agents would drive leaks, and leaks would drive legal and regulatory responses, welfare-maximizing tax policymakers might need to appreciate how these agendas could inadvertently shape, or manipulate wider government priorities.

[B] Messy Transmission of Data

The narrative over how a global UK-based bank data worked its way from its original data holder to multiple tax authorities and governments across the world and to the public suggested, generally, that the transmission of leaked data was neither seamless nor costless.[326] There were issues arising from time lags, intra-jurisdictional sharing, varying responses by different countries, and the agenda-driven roles of media organizations in data transmission. Hence, the uneven transmission of information across jurisdictions eventually suggested that welfare impacts of leaked data could also be messy and varying for different countries. It further implied that, because one jurisdiction could access leaked data in relatively costless manner, this did not mean that other jurisdictions could achieve the same. Others might have to incur larger costs to access, verify, and effectively apply the data. Therefore, even after agenda setters decided when and what to leak and how to frame the leak, the unsmooth transmission causeway suggested that additional costs and distortions might be incurred in the arduous and lengthy process of turning leaks into regulatory responses.

[C] Leak-Driven Socially Costly Laws

The triggering of knee-jerk responses by governments and agencies is argued to be exemplified by the US' enactment of the 2010 Foreign Account Tax Compliance Act (FATCA) in response to the UBS and LGT leaks.[327] While these leaks may have exposed the tax evasion strategies used by high-net-worth taxpayers and holding them accountable through the groundbreaking FATCA legislation, the high salience of the leaks and the egregious behaviours exposed could have inadvertently diverted attention away from the potential costs and pitfalls of FATCA, not least the risks of ensnaring less wilful populations, imposition of high costs on others, including the imposing of disproportionate burdens on those immigrants and expatriates with less ability to complain, comply or substitute out of the law's grasp.[328]

There no simple solutions for governments and tax authorities to guard against the downside risks of leak-driven law-making as alluded to above. Three suggestions though have been made for managing the pitfalls alluded to above so as to be able to achieve better policy decisions:[329]

- Government and tax agencies at the most basic should become more sophisticated consumers of leaked data. They should be cognizant of the hidden risks inherent in such data, and as such should verify the data's authenticity, understand how the data has been curated and stored, including understanding the motivations underlying the leak, besides also analysing the opportunity costs of responding to the issues highlighted by the leak.
- It is conceivable that, in practice, publicly posted leaked data could generate significant outrage and pressures for authorities to execute particular enforcement actions that could lead to populist or reactionary policies. As the conduct that is revealed by a leak might be more salient to tax agencies than the costs,

326. D. Gauthier-Villars & D. Ball. 2010. 'Mass leak of client data rattles Swiss banking', *Wall Street Journal 8 July 2010.*
327. SY. Oei. 2018. 'The Offshore tax enforcement dragnet', *Emory Law Journal*, Vol. 67 (4): 655-735.
328. *Supra* note [327]. Oei. 2018.
329. *Supra* note [320]. Oei & Ring. 2018.

impacts or collateral outcomes of a post-leak policy change; more comprehensive clarification of objectives and evaluation of impacts before enacting laws might help to restrain knee-jerk leak-drive law-making.

- Tax agencies should avoid allowing leaked data to overwhelm wider enforcement agendas or principles. As such, they should regularly review whether their overall enforcement agenda remains on track, despite the impacts of high-salience leaks.

§5.05 LEAKED-DATA MANAGEMENT: EXISTING AND FUTURE DIRECTIONS

Leaked-data law-making though should not overwhelm the pre-existing priorities and areas of focus that have been carefully developed. This implies avoiding sunshine in one place, while casting shadows in others. The future developments of leak-data driven legislation could continue to cause upheavals, or merely entrenching existing positions. The extent, to which, later-occurring leaks continue to induce dramatic legal changes remains to be seen. The impacts could unlikely be nothing, but if these exerted less systematic impacts moving forward, it could likely impact the decision of leakers, media platforms, and other participants.

The current push at transparency has not stopped at disclosures to governments, but there could be risks attached to this, including apprehensions about privacy, cybersecurity, data and identity thefts, frauds, and hackings. For instance, multinationals raised confidentiality concerns in response to CbC reporting in the OECD BEPS project. Where the trend focused on transparency, then leaks could become less relevant, as much of the information were already known; but there could be continuing roles for leaks, both as an enforcement tool for government, and as a behavioural control for taxpayers, where the pendulum could swing towards privacy. There could also be the further dilemma of monopolies versus competitive markets for leaked data. Either trend could have accompanying welfare impacts.

For now, the competition would appear to be between government authorities and the ICIJ, as media repository and disseminator. Leaks to the government could yield financial compensations, as in most whistle-blowing laws, asylums for the leakers, or a more concrete pathway towards enforcement actions by the government. By contrast, a leak to the ICIJ, or the equivalent, could enjoy a wider global impact, leading to swifter actions, as seen in the PP case, together with enhanced pressures on multiple governments to act. Still, these remained uncertain, as the differentiation would lead to systematic differences in the selection, transmission, reception, and therefore the eventual welfare impacts of the leak.

Moving forward, thoughts must be given to how market factors would affect the provision, transmission, and use of leaked data. Markets could generate competing alternatives to the existing dominant pathways alluded to earlier. This was exemplified by the European Parliament's (EP's) competing 'EU Leaks' website allowing whistleblowers an alternative platform for submitting leaked information securely. On the other hand, existing pathways could create incentives to attract leakers to select them over others. Arising from such possible future developments, these could create incentives for governments and media organizations to act swiftly and reduce time lags to provide more comprehensive data to the public. In this sense, policymakers might find it beneficial to consider how to optimize the design of existing markets for leaked data, so as to improve the probability that a leak could eventually generate a positive welfare outcome. Overall, the issue might not be about how governments could apply leaked information to discipline bad behaviours, make decisions, and design laws, but rather, how the actions and responses of leakers, private citizens, governments, and the media collaborated to generate and promote particular policy outcomes, and how these should be evaluated, supported, or resisted.[330]

Also, the immediate impact might not just be about the scale and magnitude of the leak. There could be at least three major implications.[331] First, many politicians and businesses in Asia, Africa, South America, and Europe were impacted with varying consequences. The leak proved to be most bothersome in Europe, coming at a time, when economic barometers were tough, and where its populations were most demanding of accountability. For starters, Iceland's Prime Minister resigned because of conflicts of interest between his offshore dealings and banking negotiations, while UK's Prime Minister came under severe criticisms over shares owned by his family before assuming office, as this clashed embarrassingly with his administration's transparency advocacy to the G20 and the world. The impacts in authoritarian regimes, like Russia and China, were relatively less damaging dismissing these as Western conspiracies, or via censorship campaigns curbing public online discussions of the leak.

Second, the leak implied that corruption was much more widespread than perceived, and not confined to poor economies. The leak while confirming bad corruptive practices in the usual suspect economies, like Africa and South America, grew to be an international problem. It also implied that the leak was not confined to governments, but private individuals and corporations undertaking morally dubious transactions. For the larger part though, the US did not appear to come into play, as Panama was not a tax haven of serious choice for US people, but as mentioned earlier, there could be probable instances of people using secrecy-friendly jurisdictions in the country.

Third, people across the world, especially, the middles class got upset. Public figures swore to do the necessary. Investigations were immediately launched. Policymakers and regulators sought to pass laws to curb such corruptive practices. Pressures for tax reforms in particular escalated especially at the international front. Tax investigators from around twenty-eight countries met in Paris to launch an international inquiry and promised to collaborate towards a global strategy to crack down on tax evaders. They argued further that a global mindset would be needed for tackling essentially a global problem, and that they would aggressively go after those who had

330. *Supra* note [320]. Oei & Ring. 2018.
331. B. Golodryga. 2016. '3 major implications of the Panama Papers leak', *The Huffington Post 21/4/16.*

structured aggressively.[332] In short, there were massive calls to individuals, businesses, and governments to clean up their acts.

The social and economic implications were unlikely to be the only considerations of the PP leakages. There could also be legal implications. Claims pertaining to the leak could potentially be significant involving criminal, regulatory, and civil suits. For starters, banks and financial institutions and services providers implicated in the leak could likely be exposed to investigations. The US DOJ, instead of looking at legal tax avoidance, such as said to have been perpetuated by Mossack, could be examining this and others for possible involvements in the employment of offshore companies to go round international trade sanctioned economies, and other kinds of illicit activities, like money laundering and bribery.

UK's Financial Conduct Authority (FCA) has begun requesting financial services entities to provide information on accounts linked to the Panamanian law firms to ascertain the degree of exposures. In the process, the FCA could be evaluating the quality and effectiveness of AML controls in these institutions. The source leak, namely Mossack, besides being already charged by the Panamanian authority might possibly have to face claims from its clientele for breach of confidence, loss of privacy, and reputational damage, particularly if it could be established that the firm was not using state of the art technology, as claimed by it, but systems with known weaknesses.

Tax authorities could also be working on the clamping down of tax avoidance schemes. In turn, impacted clientele of Mossack could also be filing claims for negligent tax advice against it, as well as, other service providers working together with it. In the UK and other Commonwealth jurisdictions, which have replicated UK corporate laws might be looking at the possibility of filing claims against board members who used these perceived unethical structures that might not be in the best interest of their companies.

There could also be the possibilities, that under current conditions, businesses, financial institutions, service providers, and senior personnel helming them could be subject to legal suits for not managing pertinent potential risk threats, when relying on operating systems without careful deliberations and maintenance procedures. In other words, whether the regulatory compliance systems they have in place were adequate to protect their interests and welfare of their entities, and whether they had undertaken adequate due diligence, when entering into these major transactions. They might need to be forewarned that, in recent years, violations of the 1970 Bank Secrecy Act (BSA), otherwise known as the Currency and Foreign Transactions Reporting Act,[333] have culminated in several high-profile prosecutions, and millions in penalties against banks.

Many business entities might also not be fully aware of the extent of their direct and indirect exposures to Mossack and could find themselves in legal spotlights, because of the employment of tax havens by agents, contractual counterparties,

332. H. Watt. 2016. 'Panama Papers: Global tax officials to launch unprecedented inquiry', *The Guardian 12/4/16*.
333. M. Treanor. 2021. 'Alleged BSA violations do not support civil negligence/fraud claims-again', *National Law Review*, Vol. XI(58), *27/2/21*.

venture partners, and others with whom they have transacted businesses with. Unknowingly, investigations by competent authorities could extend beyond tax evasion or tax avoidance to breaches of export controls, corruptions, and existing international sanctions against particular economies.

Regulators and prosecutors around the world, because of the leak, have in fact began analysing whether and how Mossack, the Panamanian law firm, concealed the true beneficial owners of the various enormous financial assets, and in the process helped them to avoid paying rightful taxes. They would probably also be examining how banks, other regulated entities, as well as shadow banking institutions might have assisted Mossack in accomplishing these aims. It was entirely possible that these institutions might not have undertaken, or conveniently forgot to do sufficient due diligence on their clientele or those of their business associates, when designing shell companies intentionally.

With reasonable work, querying, and help from the courts, people who owned the financial assets in shell companies could be detected other than just learning these from those managing them. It was also by no coincidence that these anonymous shell companies were likely to be situated in secret and tax-friendly IFCs offshore or onshore. Some of these could be located in very affluent countries like parts of the US, UK, and continental Europe, where they were favoured because of their fine reputations and political stabilities, but yet, could still fall short of global transparency rules pertaining in particular to taxes and corporate ownership details.

In general, banks, other financial institutions, and professionals engaged in financial services were likely to be already familiar with the practice of beneficial ownership due diligence to ward off criminals, terrorists, and others with ill-gotten gains. In practice, occasionally business pressures and other motivations could weigh against carrying out the required due diligence. The PP revelations suggested in reality there were still weaknesses to overcome, where these were concerned. Financial institutions and connected professional service providers might need to be reminded that the absence of sufficient, reliable, and timely ownership data could have helped to enable money laundering and sanctions evasions. These could be achieved, by concealing the identities of criminals and others with bad intentions, obscuring the real purposes of the financial assets held by corporate vehicles, and the sources or applications of funds linked to corporate vehicles.

Recognizing these problems, the international FATF, which most jurisdictions followed to avoid being called out, had already designed transparency standards to deter and prevent the abusive use of corporate structures. The FATF required jurisdictions from across the world to ensure that adequate, reliable, and timely information on beneficial owners of corporate structure be made more accessible.[334] Regardless of the levels of national commitments to the FATF agenda, those tasked to carry out the job would need to be more vigilant than ever, given the fiascos unleashed by the PP. This implied that they needed to be both prudent and risk-sensitive. In this connection, the

334. Financial Action Task Force (FATF). 2019. 'Best practices on beneficial ownership for legal persons', *FATF October 2019*; FATF. 2020. 'Recommendation 25: Transparency and beneficial ownership of legal arrangements', *FATF October 2020*.

US has recently enacted the Corporate Transparency Act (CTA) in 2020 within the larger National Defense Authorization Act that henceforth would require the US Treasury Department to gather the names of beneficial owners at the time of entity formation.

The Financial Crimes Enforcement Network (FinCEN) will be required, a year after the CTA comes into force, to set up a registry to gather the names, addresses, and birth dates of beneficial owners. The CTA defined a beneficial owner as a person who exercises substantial control over a corporation or limited liability company; owns 25% or more of the equity interests of a corporation or limited liability company, or receives substantial economic benefits from the assets of a corporation, or limited liability company.[335] This information though would only be available to law enforcement and financial institutions in the private sector upon request and with customer consent. Further, investment funds, banks, credit unions, charities, and any entity with more than twenty employees, USD 5 million in annual sales, and a physical presence in the US would be exempted from these requirements.[336]

This legislation, when viewed in the global level context, suggested that the secrecy of US laws surrounding forming corporations and other legal entities have been deployed to facilitate extensive corruptions, as exemplified in a reported case alleging laundering of millions of dollars of public money via shell companies including those in the US,[337] and domestically, the using of anonymous shell companies to defraud relief funds for the ongoing COVID-19 pandemic,[338] including the US PPP loan initiative.[339] The CTA might not though end criminals' ability to apply the US financial system to facilitate their crimes and conceal their ill-gotten gains, as a registry might not be fool-proof, as observed in the UK, which already has this in place. Criminals could file false information to registries, and verifications could be challenging, even with criminal penalties in place against those providing false information. There could be other legal loopholes needing attention, such as the Geographic Targeting Order (GTO) Programme[340] requiring title insurance entities to provide the Treasury Department with the beneficial owners of all residential real estate cash transactions beyond USD 300,000.

From another perspective, though somewhat provocative, was the notion that shell companies and other offshore vehicles could be created within minutes with just an Internet connection and a few thousand US dollars. Apparently, it would require heavy liftings to dodge taxes, debts, child support, and so on, by injecting financial

335. L.-A. Basha & D. Ransom. 2021. 'Congress passes the Corporate Transparency Act with veto-proof majority', *National Law Review*, Vol. XI(58), *27/2/21*.
336. *Supra* note [335]. Basha & Ransom. 2021.
337. S.P. Freedberg, S. Alecci & W. Fitzgibbon. 2020. 'How Africa's richest woman exploited family ties, shell companies and inside deals to build an empire', *ICIJ 19/1/20*.
338. Department of Justice (DOJ). 2020. 'Three men who allegedly used existing shell companies and prior fraud experience to exploit COVID-19 Relief Programs charged in South Florida Federal Court', *DOJ Press Release 7/8/20*.
339. S. Shah & A. Amico. 2020. 'Washington targets beneficial owners with the Corporate Transparency Act', *FCPA Blog 21/12/20*.
340. Financial Crimes Enforcement Network (FinCEN). 2020. 'Geographic Targeting Order', *FinCEN 4/11/20*.

assets in one of these structures. This, however, underestimated the risks of getting caught, audited, and maybe even prosecuted.[341] The highly affluent financial and political elites could on the other hand game the system by stacking the odds in their favours, as they could afford the relatively expensive services of financial institutions and financial services firms to enjoy the privilege of defeating the spirit of the laws, without violating them formally.

The Panamanian law firm and its counterparts from across the world serviced this need of the rich, by providing the knowledge and skills that enabled these privileged people to keep well within the right side of the law, or with sufficient legal distance into legal grey zones, such as associated with widely known tax havens where they could have higher chances to prevail, should they end up in court. This was probably why, despite the leak, thus far, there have been no corresponding levels of prosecutions, given the scale of the allegations, but then again, such matters could be slow to resolve. Incidentally, many of the bad financial practices alleged to be linked to the 2007-2008 GFC were only seeing resolutions, some ten years later. Putting into context, the PP case was only about one year old, when much was being undertaken.

Mossack was speedily charged for facilitating money-laundering and related activities. This was to be expected, given the high profile attached to the PP. The local jurisdiction needed to show to the world, that it was serious about maintaining and rebuilding its reputation as a responsible member of the global financial and business community. Still, Mossack initially tried to maintain its innocence to give credence to its business model of keeping their clientele out of legal trouble. If anything, it could be arguing that it was not legally wrong to sell a product, known as secrecy. No doubt, in time, some of the activities disclosed in the PP could eventually turn out to be illegal. However, going by past events associated with financial crises, it was entirely possible that the bulk of the leak could merely embarrass those exposed, and suggesting them to be opportunistic and perhaps unethical, but not criminal. There were some good examples of these. The higher echelons of many financial institutions said to be linked to the financial scandals in the 2007 GFC in contrast were relatively left largely financially undamaged, besides being generally free from prosecutions or civil suits, despite having recklessly led the institutions under their care into massive financial problems.

However, many named in the PP documents, including sitting political leaders, sport superstars, and big screen stars were unlikely to be hauled up in courts, despite the rather shady services provided to them by Mossack. This was not because of the power to squash prosecutions, other than perhaps an isolated few, but because back then they had the wisdom and resources to employ expert advisors with the skills, knowledge, and global connections to design their tax avoidance strategies.[342] The PP case showed how various household name global multinationals together could be

341. B. Harrington. 2016. 'Panama Papers: The real scandal is what's legal. Mossack Fonseca kept its client largely on the right side of the law. Indeed, that's entirely the point', *The Atlantic* 6/4/16.
342. *Supra* note [341]. Harrington. 2016.

saving as much as USD 260 billion annually by setting up businesses in low-tax regimes that were perfectly legal.[343]

Buying secrecy could be an expensive affair accessible only to the wealthy, depending on which laws to avoid, but those who needed this could get it, when they pay. This was why some 140 politicians and public officials from more than fifty jurisdictions were involved. Still, in some cases the price for this went beyond money. The then Prime Minister of Iceland resigned merely because he was once part-time owner of an offshore entity set up with assistance from Mossack, but had since 2009 been wholly owned by his wife. This was because this company could profit millions from the deal he negotiated for claimants on Iceland's bankrupt financial institutions. It was to be all the more painful for him, as reports showed no evidence to suggest tax avoidance, evasion, or any dishonest financial gains on his part. In other word, his mere association with Mossack and an offshore firm were adequate to cost him his reputation and career.[344]

Stopping offshore financial activities is an uphill battle owing to entrenched conflicts of interest. As shown in the PP, there were cases of those, who publicly criticized the use of such financial strategies, were themselves beneficiaries. This was because such activities were commonly formally legal and extremely lucrative, especially in jurisdictions that relied a lot on these to spur economic growths. The gains to be had were not necessarily realized from far-strung offshore islands as popularly propagated, but could be from expensive real estates in New York and London.

The UK economy had been argued to be closely tied to the offshore world, via its property markets. The wealthy from former Soviet states and from Asia in particular snapped these up to avoid taxes and launder the proceeds of corruption.[345] They achieved this normally through offshore corporations and trusts. The 'Global Laundromat' revelations[346] provided more evidence of how weaknesses in the country's AML system have been exploited in the property market. Here, fictitious companies were registered in London to perpetuate the scam. The London housing stock at the time the PP unfolded has been claimed to exceed the entire GDP of Brazil.[347] This meant the UK economy could be hit hard, if things were made difficult for such transactions to continue. This was said to be even of larger importance to the City of London that contributed some USD 64 billion to UK's GDP. Noteworthy was that London, besides being UK's capital, also operated as the centre of the most significant part of the global offshore system. While the general rhetoric has been UK's global call for disengagements with over-aggressive tax havens and that under the separation trade agreement with the EU, the country would work cooperatively with the EU regarding such and

343. A. Ali. 2016. 'Panama Papers: Why some of this is perfectly legal. What is the difference between tax avoidance and tax evasion?', *Aljazeera 4/4/16.*
344. *Supra* note [341]. Harrington. 2016.
345. D. Kavakeb. 2017. 'Russian laundromat revelations underline UK role in facilitating global corruption', *Transparency International 21/3/17.*
346. L. Harding. 2017. 'What is the Laundromat?', *The Guardian 20/3/17.*
347. J. Kelly. 2015. 'London-centric: London is a city of immense prosperity and power. But has it succeeded at the expense of the rest of the UK', *BBC 30/9/15.*

related matters,[348] it is relatively unclear as to the pace of disengagements given some insights from the PP and subsequent PRP.

On balance, the UK did not appear to be the only advanced economy to have this dilemma connected with the world of offshore or inshore IFCs. New York in the US has been argued to have traces of this kind of real estate issues, while Delaware and Nevada have tax and secrecy-friendly regimes. Continental Europe through Switzerland had enjoyed this kind of business much longer than any in the world, but 'new Switzerland' was now being used in various other European jurisdictions. The OECD has taken note of this development and warned against the race to the bottom by all forms of tax and secrecy havens. Still, Mossack together with other equivalent service providers grew to be a web of 'legal corruption' that touched the four corners of the world. So far, the world of tax havens has not been brought down, despite the PP leak. Despite rhetoric and measures against them, most are still functioning, albeit many with declared intentions to follow the rule of law in general, and ironically servicing those needing secrecy or wholesome confidentiality, a much sought-after service.[349]

Indeed, as mentioned several times earlier, the PP leak was not the first leak of its kind, as there had been in recent years, leaks coming from Luxembourg and Switzerland, and elsewhere. On this occasion though, a much longer list of names was provided as fodder for prosecutions, but if not held out as embarrassments for individuals, corporations, and some governments. The more crucial issue pertained to the underlying point of anonymous whistle-blowing, and why this became helpful for prosecutors and regulators in having better insights on the opaque activities occurring in OFCs, and in particular tax and secrecy havens. Research inputs provided these insights, as nations even when working together did not muster enough power and resources to effectively regulate the Teflon-like world of anonymous offshore finance. This has been attributed to the following three reasons:[350]

(1) Foremost, the service providers who facilitated the setting up of these anonymous shell companies were not at all incentivized to provide the zealously guarded information. The modus operandi here rested on secrecy. The financial institutions, the service providers from lawyers to accountants, and the local jurisdictions exploited the use of the international legal system and the protections afforded to sovereign states to obscure/conceal information from authorities and thereby providing advantages to their clientele for hefty financial compensations. Research by activists and others suggested that these occurred in major tax haven across the world, and not just confined to far-flung islands, as generally perceived, with some ironically, rich OECD Member States.

348. EC. 2020. 'The EU-UK Trade and Cooperation Agreement'.
349. P. Yeoh. 2018. 'Secrecy in Teflon international financial centres', *International Journal of Law and Management*, Vol. 60(56): 777-797.
350. D. Wigan & L. Seabrooke. 2016. 'The question behind the Panama leak: Why aren't international rules stopping offshore tax evasion?', *The Washington Post 5/4/16.*

(2) Second, existing institutions for information exchange were generally bureaucratic, inadequately resourced, and not sufficiently efficient. Research disclosed that even exchange of bank account information between OECD Member States for investigating possible tax evasions could take around half a year under a best-case scenario between friendly countries backed by well-developed bureaucracies. The lengthy process was therefore likely to be way longer, when information flow was transacted between unfriendly jurisdictions, with small organizational resources. This contrasted sharply with perpetrators who could mobilize financial assets at will and at phenomenal speed. Given this, local law enforcers hunting key performance indicators (KPIs) were likely to focus on purely domestic cases that were relatively easier, than dealing with complex and thorny international investigations, even though, the latter might lead to where the big financial assets were hidden.

(3) Third, the big more powerful states from large emerging and advanced economies might not be in sync to push for tougher rules. These jurisdictions were generally known to be benefiting immensely from the 'hot' money flowing various other jurisdictions. Think London, New York, Belgium, and Switzerland. Indeed, as mentioned several occasions already, the UK effectively commanded control over 50% of the jurisdictions that provided secrecy for mobile elite wealth. Recent research showed that it could relatively easier to set up anonymous shell companies in Delaware and Nevada, than even Panama.

It has been further contended that the first and second problems could only be resolved when the third has been taken care of.[351] There was good momentum, right after the 2007 GFC. European states and the US were, for instance, searching for funds to beef up their financial coffers to take care of their financial gaps, especially at a time when austerity was being preached. The US unilaterally and boldly initiated FATCA in 2010 requiring foreign financial institutions to report to the IRS on US held-accounts.

The G20 mandated the OECD in 2013 to set up a standard for AEI between participating tax authorities. The progress was nevertheless patchy. The OECD did in 2015 release a new standard for information sharing among various tax authorities, but Panama for example backtracked on the new OECD standard. It was only in February 2016 that Member States were informed of this. Significantly, the US, while insisting on information from the rest of the world and in particular the European states, was on the other hand proving to be less reluctant to share what its regulators knew about foreign accounts in its jurisdiction. Questions were also raised on whether developing economies said to be suffering the most from IFFs and tax abuse could really benefit from the process. It was still unclear, whether advanced economies would chip in financially, or provide technical assistance to developing economies that would enable them to participate effectively in the new AEI.

351. *Supra* note [350]. Wigan & Seabrooke. 2016.

Still, it was entirely possible that the PP case could help to drive and reinforce a policy trajectory towards enhanced regulations and information, like what happened subsequent to the *LuxLeaks* that led to political actions in the EU and the OECD. The data provided was relatively less important for the information it provided, than the high profile it raised on the matter of tax evasions. This could incentivize more economies to work together to resolve the problem.

A more concrete plan could lead to greater transparency. The UK in recent years have shown greater enthusiasms for transparency of information to enable the quicker revelation of beneficial owners to reduce the opportunities for criminals and people with bad moral intentions to exploit the use of shell companies. The UK has already taken preliminary steps for disclosure of beneficial owners in the property sector, even though with access only to competent authorities and appeared also to have taken further initiatives to 'persuade' its Crown dependencies, like the Channel Island and the Isle of Man that thrived on tax avoidance to do the right thing. Indeed, in this connection, the US could also restrain secrecy- and tax-friendly jurisdictions like Delaware and Nevada. Earlier moves have, as seen in the PP data, lessened the number of shell companies in formation. Such moves and more could accelerate a more significant decline in their existence.

In the likely ensuing battle between the financial elites who might have engaged lobbyists and global tax experts to protect their interest against the socio-economic agenda of policymakers, it could be helpful for policymakers to ally with CSOs and regulators to turn the tide in their favour for the good of their respective economies and for the poorer strata of society. In the meantime, it needed to be said again, that the PP, though the largest information leak of its kind was unlikely to be the last, given current trends in whistleblowing. As further revelations continued to unfold from the PP, the PPR and others, the calls for greater global transparency could only get louder.[352] Four years down the road, corporate secrecy globally persisted, despite these and other initiatives.[353]

§5.06 THE PARADISE PAPERS

The PPR, like its PP predecessor, but on a relatively smaller scale, were leaked again to the *Suddeutsche Zeitung*, the German newspaper shortly after the PP. The PPRs comprising 14.3 million documents led to investigations by 381 journalists in 67 countries covering the period 1950-2016, culminating in a global coverage rolled out by 95 ICIJ media outlet partners.[354] Most of these 6.8-meters-high documents pertained to Appleby, a law firm and corporate services provider operating across 10 jurisdictions. The fiduciary arm of its business was the subject of a management buyout in 2016, and it is now known as Estera. There were also details from 19 corporate registries

352. Stratfor. 2016. 'Those who are (and are Not) sheltered from Panama Papers', *Stratfor 8/4/16.*
353. T. Van der Merwe. 2020. 'Beneficial ownership registers: Progress to date', *Transparency International 8/4/20.*
354. N. Hopkins & H. Bengtsson. 2017. 'What are the Paradise Papers and what do they tell us?', *The Guardian 5/11/17.*

maintained by governments in the secrecy jurisdictions of Antigua and Barbuda, Aruba, the Bahamas, Barbados, Bermuda, the Cayman Islands, the Cook Islands, Dominica, Grenada, Labuan, Lebanon, Malta, the Marshall Island, St. Kitts and Nevis, St Lucia, St Vincent, Samoa, Trinidad and Tobago, and Vanuatu.[355]

The leak contained the names of more than 120,000 people and companies of the said law firm from 1993 to 2014, but not all are necessarily linked to companies registered offshore, with the data from the firm indicating the involvements of some 25,000 offshore companies. This still offered a good demonstration that many of the firm's clientele came from the UK, China, and Hong Kong, with the largest of more than 30,000 from the US.[356] It would appear that the most popular jurisdictions for incorporations were the UK-ruled tax havens of the Cayman Islands and Bermuda, as well as the British Virgin Island, a UK overseas territory, and the British crown dependency of the Isle of Man.[357]

The PPRs concentrated on celebrities in the silver screen and royalties, apart from mega global corporations, like Apple, Nike, and Facebook. The leaked documents showed the varied and extensive ways corporations and individuals designing and relying on artificial structures to minimize or even avoiding taxes altogether. These could be legal when managed properly, but some did not appear to do so. These disclosures raised questions as to whether tax avoidance in its various forms have gone too far.[358] Indeed, the revelations showed that the law firm in question had been red-flagged by some regulators in various areas, including those to do with flawed compliance procedures in twelve confidential audits over a decade in the BVI, Bermuda, the Cayman Islands, and the Isle of Man.[359] The firm in question rejected these allegations and insisted its adherence to lawful procedures, despite being challenged on insights from several business cases.[360]

Noteworthy revelations included the following:[361]

- Extensive offshore transactions by various Cabinet members of the previous US administration.
- Profitable transactions of senior royalty members in various offshore investments.
- Million-dollar investments by Russian financial institutions in some US global MNCs.
- Use of a tax-avoiding Cayman Island trust by senior politicians from Canada.
- Participation of a Formula One driver in an Isle of Man tax avoiding structure.
- Use of an offshore trust for wealth sheltering by a well-known UK politician.
- Managers profiting in the managing of Angola's sovereign wealth funds.

355. *Supra* note [354]. Hopkins & Bengtsson. 2017.
356. *Supra* note [354]. Hopkins & Bengtsson. 2017.
357. *Supra* note [354]. Hopkins & Bengtsson. 2017.
358. N. Hopkins. 2017. 'Why we are shining a light on the world of tax havens again? After explosive leaks from an offshore firm last year, others in the sector insisted it was a bad apple. Now that claim can be tested', *The Guardian 5/11/17*.
359. *Supra* note [358]. Hopkins. 2017.
360. *Supra* note [358]. Hopkins. 2017.
361. *Supra* note [354]. Hopkins and Bengtsson. 2017.

- Secret Glencore dealings.
- Complex Russian offshore financial schemes used in the acquisitions of UK football clubs.
- Schemes deployed to avoid tax on UK property transactions, and so on.

These revelations and more suggested the rise of a global fourth estate marked by a global outlook on social reality that is embedded in a networked rationale. This could pave the way for the media's role as a global fourth estate, responding to the budding demand for a new kind of reporting influencing political decisions and articulating society's development towards an internalized sense of globalization, illustrating in the process how this form of networked collaboration operates in real time generating simultaneous coverage in many jurisdictions.[362]

Thus, other things apart, the beneficial ownership transparency agenda gained significant progress over the past decade. This began in a big way when in 2014 the G20 leaders adopted the High-Level Principles on Beneficial Ownership building upon the 2012 FATF recommendations for the global standard for AML, together with the 2013 G8 action plan principles to prevent the misuse of companies and legal arrangements.[363] The fallout prompted by the Panama and Paradise global controversies highlighting the need for beneficial ownership transparency provided the opportunity to drive for further reforms at the Anti-Corruption Summit in 2016. Such developments at the global level, together with various national-level policy pressures induced many economies to commit to implementing beneficial ownership registers.[364]

Since 2016, centralized registers of beneficial ownership have achieved important milestones, with the Fifth EU Directive on AML and Counter-Terrorist Financing, as its foremost example. Nevertheless, progress on the ground has been uneven, with uptakes generally lagging behind national and international policy commitments.[365] Fully public registers remain few in numbers, with the majority concentrated in the EU. Still, emerging evidence suggests registers have important roles to play in helping in the detection and prosecution of money laundering cases by enforcement agencies, the world over. This could likely serve as a powerful deterrent on the supply side of financial crime. Additional to ensuring implementation, further progress would be needed in embedding verification elements into the design of registers to help avoid regulatory arbitrage.[366] For sure, effectiveness for this transparency measure, as well as other policy responses, to address the problems of tax evasion and the roles played by tax havens would require similar global responses. These and more would be discussed in Chapter 6.

---

362. P. Berglez & A. Gearing. 2012. 'The Panama and Paradise Papers: The rise of a global fourth estate', *International Journal of Communication*, Vol. 12(2018): 4573-4592.
363. M. Martini. 2015. 'Technical guide: Implementing the G20 beneficial ownership principles', *Transparency International* 2015.
364. Open Government Partnership. 2019. 'Beneficial ownership'.
365. T. Van der Merwe. 2020. 'Beneficial ownership registers: Progress to date'. *U4 8 April 2020.*
366. *Supra* note [365]. Van der Merwe. 2020.

§5.07 ROBUSTNESS OF PANAMA AND PARADISE PAPERS

Drawing on network modelling and analysis techniques, it was possible to map out the connectivity structure for the top twenty-two economies in the ICIJ database, and to identify the central actors and their influence in the offshoring network.[367] The network was developed from the different relations taking place between emitting and receiving entities in the ICIJ database and aggregated for their corresponding economies. These networks of entities have been represented intermediately at the level of countries and geographical regions, and their intra- and inter-relationships accordingly mapped.

The findings yielded of important conclusions:[368]

- The main offshoring regions/countries were identified, including how they are related to the rest of the worldwide actors. The most significant regions identified as the offshoring receptors are the Oceania, Eastern Asia, South East Asia, and the American Antilles. The most prevalent offshore receiving jurisdictions were identified as the Samoa, the Cook Islands, Indonesia, Hong Kong and the BVI. The last-named jurisdictions are the most significant actors, serving as a hub in the offshoring network linking countries from different regions.
- The internal relationships space is important, as it could provide a measurement of the internal network deployed by the jurisdictions to frustrate the tracking of money in tax havens. The main general conclusion is that the offshoring size of regions and the number of offshoring countries has advanced and diversified. Second, these regions and countries have a different role and important. Hence, the conventional tax havens in the Antilles and Central America continue to ply a relevant role; but Switzerland (perhaps because of various recent high-profile banking scandals and the impact of tax information exchange agreements) appears to have lost relevance, while Asia has strongly emerged as a tax haven, and accordingly justified close monitoring.
- Drawing on insights of existing linkages, national and international regulatory agencies could act in these networks with the objective of increasing their control and eliminating fraudulent behaviour. While the historical origin of tax havens was premised on the search for capital investments, this initial origin has tended to deviate from its purpose to hide transfer and concealment of illicit capital.

Another empirical study drawing on network science and existing relational version of the PPs selectively constructed various networks for examining the properties of the underlying system. These methodologies taken together yielded results showing that the PPs constituted a distinct class of networks differing significantly

367. D. Dominguez, O. Pantoja, P. Pico, M. Matcoes, M. del Mar Alonso-Almeida & M. Gonzales. 2020. 'Panama Papers' offshoring Network behavior', *Heliyon*, Vol. 6 (2020): 1-10.
368. *Supra* note [367]. Dominguez et al. 2020.

from ordinary social and information networks.[369] Hence, this study supports the claim that the PPs are fundamentally different in structure than other networks of organization, intermediaries and officers, or some combination thereof.[370]

The leaked data from the PPs was used in another empirical study to examine whether and how business enterprises used secret offshore vehicles. Drawing on insights from the leaked data, 338 listed firms were identified as users of secret offshore vehicles (SOVs).[371] Such vehicles were found to be deployed to finance corruption, avoid taxes, and expropriate shareholders. Subsequent to the enhanced transparency brought about by the leak, implicated corporations experience lower sales from perceptively corrupt countries and avoid les tax. The study further estimated that one in seven corporations have offshore secrets.

Hence, some of the benefits of using offshore vehicles may be offset by diversion of firm resources by insiders, who appear to exploit the opaque structures that offshore vehicles provide. This study further gives support for the anecdotal evidence about the deployments of SOVs for at least partially illegal activities. Offshore service providers appear to play important roles in facilitating such activities. While the study spotlights on the benefits and costs of SOVs to shareholders, the deployments of SOVs might also yield important welfare implications, their roles in enabling hidden bribe payments, for instance, may contribute to the substantial social costs of corruption, estimated at USD 2.6 trillion, or 5% of global GDP annually according to World Bank Institute's 2001-2002 survey data.[372] An equivalent argument is applicable for SOVs as a mechanism to avoid, or evade taxes. Simultaneously, prior research has demonstrated that tax haven activities may also promote regional growth[373], and create employment in the corporations' home economies.[374]

Tapping on published macroeconomics data, an empirical study estimated that the equivalent of 10% of world GDP is held in tax havens globally, this average though conceals a lot of heterogeneity, ranging from a few percent of GDP in Scandinavia, to some 15% in continental Europe, and some 60% in Gulf economies, and some Latin American countries.[375] The research conceded that while their country-by country estimates of offshore wealth involve a margin of error, they are globally reliable because the country figures sum up to the world's offshore wealth, that by itself is by design fully consistent with the international investment positions of countries, central bank data, and official stats published by tax havens. To further asses their reliability,

369. M. Kejriwal & A. Dang. 2020. 'Structural studies of the global networks exposed in the Panama papers', *Applied Network Science*, Vol. 5 (2020): 63-86.
370. *Supra* note [369]. Kejriwal & Dang. 2020.
371. J. O'Donovan, H. F. Wagner & S. Zeume. 2019. 'The value of offshore secrets: Evidence from the Panama Papers', *The Review of Financial Studies*, Vol. 32 (11): 4117-4155.
372. *Supra* note [371]. O'Donovan et al. 2019.
373. M.A. Desai, C.F. Foley & J.R. Hines. 2004. 'Economic effects of regional tax havens', *National Bureau of Economic Research (NBER) Working Paper 10806 October 2004.*
374. J.C. Suarez Serrato. 2018. 'Unintended consequences of eliminating tax havens', *NBER Working Paper 24850 December 2019.*
375. A. Alstadsaeter, N. Johannesen & G. Zucman. 2018. 'Who owns the wealth in tax havens? Macro evidence and implications for global inequality', *Journal of Public Economics*, Vol. 162 (2018): 89-100.

a robustness check was undertaken where estimates of offshore wealth to data that have become available in 2016 in the context of the PPs.

Panamanian law firm Mossack-Fonseca at the time of the leak was one of the world's give largest purveyors of shell companies, and enhanced information on the owners of these shell entities created by this firm would be insightful. There are strong similarities between the amount of the study's offshore wealth estimates and the use of tax havens as disclosed by the PP. Economies having a lot of shell companies relative to the size of their economy include Kenya, Zimbabwe, Venezuela, UAE, Taiwan, Russia, and Jordan. These all have high offshore wealth to GDP ratios.

China appears to be the main exception that is overrepresented in the Mossack-Fonseca data. One understanding is that Chinese residents do not use shell companies to hide wealth in foreign banks, but to circumvent regulations restricting cross-border investments in and out of China, while another interpretation is that the study undertaken under-estimate the amount of Chinese offshore wealth, maybe precisely because an abnormally high fraction of it is held through shell companies. Examining the subset of high-tax OECD economies, data analysis demonstrates a strong correlation between how much each economy owns in wealth offshore, and the number of owners of Mossack-Fonseca shell entities. For instance, Greece is estimated to owing the equivalent of 40% of its GDP in offshore wealth, and this is featured incidentally in the PP. Scandinavian economies at the other end of the spectrum have low stocks of offshore wealth and few owners of Mossack-Fonseca shell entities. These findings overall corroborate the view that the country-by-country estimates of offshore wealth as undertaken by this study are likely to be reliable. The estimates though could be further improved upon when new leaks or improvements in financial transparency become available.

Top wealth shares have been estimated in prior studies using tax data over the last few years, and these contributed to insights on wealth distribution estimates that are reasonably comparable for ten countries (namely, the US, UK, Sweden, Spain, Russia, Norway, the Netherlands, France, Finland and Denmark) that in combination accounted for up to half of world GDP. Taking offshore wealth into account modifies inequality in these respective economies.[376] This is because a great deal of evidence showing that the vast majority of offshore wealth was not typically reported on tax returns. For example, two US Senate reports revealed that 90% of the wealth held by US citizens at UBS and Credit Suisse was undeclared in 2008,[377] while other studies suggest that 90% of the wealth held by Europeans in Switzerland was undeclared,[378] and 90%-95% of the wealth owned by Danish and Norwegian households at HSBC

376. A. Alstadsaeter, N. Johannesen & G. Zucman. 2018. 'Who owns the wealth in tax havens? Macro evidence and implications for global inequality', *Journal of Public Economics*, Vol. 162 (2018): 89-100.
377. US Senate. 2014. *Offshore tax evasion: The effort to collect unpaid taxes on billions in hidden offshore accounts*. Staff Report of the Permanent Subcommittee on Investigations. Washington, DC: US Senate.
378. N. Roussille. 2020. 'Tax evasion and the "Swiss Cheese" regulation'.

Switzerland was undeclared either.[379] Thus, even when no illegal tax evasion is involved, offshore wealth is usually structured in manners that these do not generate taxable income nor reportable assets. This is achieved by combining trusts, foundations, and holding entities so as not to link assets with their beneficial owners.[380] Such arrangements could be legal or illegal, but typically would imply that tax authorities would not observe much offshore wealth or investigate income earned offshore, other than in exceptional circumstances, like a taxable and properly declared intergenerational transfer of assets.

Accounting for offshore wealth increases the top 0.01% wealth share substantially, even in Scandinavian economies that do not use tax havens extensively; but the magnitude of the impact varies a lot across economies.[381] Offshore wealth has a larger impact on inequality in France, Spain, and the UK, where it has been estimated that some 30%-40% of all the wealth of the 0.01% richest households is held overseas. Some 60% of the wealth of the richest in Russia is held outside the country. Offshore wealth in the US also increases inequality, but the impact is toned down in Europe, as the US top wealth shares are already very high even disregarding tax havens. These findings highlight the significance of going beyond tax data when examining wealth accumulation among the very affluent in the globalized world.[382] More broadly, offshore wealth is likely to have major implications for the concentration of wealth in many developing and emerging economies. Estimates such as undertaken could be friend when new data emerges on the level and distribution of offshore assets. Not much though has been achieved in terms of statistical transparency, despite some progress in curbing bank secrecy. No major financial centre publishes comprehensive stats on the level of foreign wealth managed by its banks, with the exception of Switzerland.[383] Opacity like this makes it difficult to measure the evolution of global wealth and its distribution, suggesting that the improving of statistics on offshore wealth ought to be a priority for policymakers in the immediate coming years.

379. A. Alstadsaeter, N. Johannesen & N. Zucman. 2017. 'Tax evasion and inequality', *NBER Working Paper No. 23772 September 2017.*
380. B. Harrington. 2016. *Capital without borders,* Cambridge: Harvard University Press.
381. *Supra* note [376]. Alstadsaeter et al. 2018.
382. *Supra* note [376]. Alstadsaeter et al. 2018.
383. *Supra* note [376]. Alstadsaeter et al. 2018.

CHAPTER 6
Global Tax Reforms

§6.01 INTRODUCTION

This chapter begins with a brief discussion on global tax reforms initiatives in the modern era as countries sough a fairer and more equitable international tax system. As financialization spurred global finance through the increasing presence of OFCs, the particular roles of tax havens became more and more controversial as it impacted the international tax system considerably. This stimulated initiatives to reform the international tax system. These, together with initiatives launched by the OECD, as well as OECD-linked tax reform initiatives are also addressed in this chapter.

Other matters examined in some details in this chapter include business tax-related matters like beneficial ownership transparency; country-by-country (CbC) reporting; tax havens categorizations; multinationals' BEPS practices; controversial advanced tax agreements (ATAs); special purpose acquisition companies (SPACs), and US influence on the global tax systems. Considerable attention given to discussions on reform initiatives for the international tax system is justified by the need to balance the economic interests of advanced, developing and emerging economies.

§6.02 GLOBAL TAX REFORMS INITIATIVES IN THE MODERN ERA

Public trust was battered on several major occasions by the 2001 Enron saga and the 2007 GFC, and these financial risks came to some degree under threat across the world with the unfolding of the PR and PRP scandals in 2016. Public trust thus fell under threat of being breached when various political and financial elites could conceal their questionable wealth in secrecy and tax havens, both via legal tax avoidance schemes and illegal structures. CSOs and others advocated for a fairer national and global tax systems collaborated with others to take more concrete actions towards the diminished deployments of suspected illegal or illicit corporate structures or vehicles. This turned out to be a serious and highly important agenda, given that some 50% of developing economies raised less than 15% of their GDP in taxes, with many still significantly dependent on natural resources. This compared poorly to the OECD average of around 34%.[384]

Interestingly, the worldwide average statutory corporate income tax (CIT) rate weighed by the GDP was 25.85%, with Europe having the lowest regional average rate of 24.61%, and conversely Africa at 28.16%, OECD countries at 23.51%, and G7 economies at 27.24%.[385] Indeed, worldwide average statutory rate has consistently decreased since 1980s, with the biggest taking place in early 2000s. Equally interesting was the argument that, despite the enactment of the 2017 Tax Cuts and the earlier 2012 Jumpstart Our Business Startups Act (JOBS Act), current rules would still encourage US multinationals to earn and report profit in low-tax foreign economies thereby enabling both US and foreign-based firms to shift profits earned in the US to other countries, and importantly also motivating companies to incorporate in foreign jurisdictions.[386] Tax reforms at the national levels could therefore be crucial for the strengthening of public finances in developing and EMEs.

This was appropriately demonstrated in Indonesia, where those paying taxes climbed from 4.35 million to about 16 million, after some five years of tax reforms implementation, and from thereon growing by about 20% annually. The proceeds together with a stronger economy bolstered the national budget and decreased national debt, besides enhancing the national capacity to provide essential services. This was pivotal to the strengthening of trust the private sector required to invest and create jobs.[387] At the international level, worldwide condemnation of the various implications of the PP discussed earlier could probably lead to louder calls for a stronger and fairer tax platform underpinned by sound tax systems, good institutions, good CG, and integrity.

The US working on its own and on occasions with the IMF, the World Bank, the OECD, the EU, and G20 economies sought international mechanisms to deal with the kind of tax leakages shown by the PP revelations. This chapter would examine in general as to how tax and secrecy havens have helped businesses and individuals to escape legal tax obligations legally and illegally, and how policy measures could be coordinated internationally to curb these financially harmful activities that deprived the public coffers of many economies for development purposes. Global efforts are and would be essentially needed to address tax-escaping activities crossing borders.

In the global financial architecture, British Overseas Territories are of good significance.

Drawing on their inalienable right to self-determination, many developed OFCs to achieve sustainable economic development. It becomes therefore particularly important to consider in their context including those other tax havens, the viability of

384. S.M. Indrawati. 2016. 'Panama Papers underscore need for fair tax systems', *The World Bank 14/4/16.*
385. E. Asen. 2020. 'Corporate tax rates around the world, 2020', *Tax Foundation Fiscal Fact No. 735 December 2020.*
386. Tax Policy Center (TPC). 2020. 'What are the consequences of the new US international tax system'.
387. *Supra* note [384]. Indrawati. 2016.

international standards on suspect wealth emanating from financial crimes like corruption, money laundering, and tax evasion; as well as controversially, tax avoidance, as to how willing or able they are to comply with them, as well as how their financial centres could better prevent receipt of suspect wealth. It has been contended that despite the desirability for universalism in modern approaches, a one-size-fits-all approach is inappropriate for these and other relevant jurisdictions. It is further argued as to whether the extent of criticism levelled that these offshore jurisdictions have encountered is merited in the light of their apparent willingness to engage in the enactment and administration of internationally accepted laws and cooperating with international institutions.[388]

§6.03 TAX HAVENS AND GLOBAL TAX REFORMS INITIATIVES

For starters, a revisit of the listings of tax havens would be necessary. Whatever ideas would work only, if those seriously involved in such activities are recognized. This, of course, would not be something new, as there had been previous good efforts made in this direction. A narrower take of tax havens could help limit these to those jurisdictions that have the combined features of low or no tax, low transparency, bank secrecy standards, lack of information sharing, and no substantial economic activity requirements for an entity to obtain legal status.[389] The OECD used this approach in its initial 2000 tax shelter initiative in 2000.[390]

Developmental economists consider tax havens as those jurisdictions competing with competitive tax breaks to attract foreign capital, or just simply economies with low or no taxes. International tax avoidance features became differentiated on the basis of legality, between individuals and businesses, or whether originating from narrow or broad definitions of tax havens. They could also be differentiated by what policy measures are employed to curtail the financial leakage. Revenue losses from individual taxes would likely be generally linked to evasion in narrowly defined tax havens, whereas business tax avoidance would likely occur in both narrow and widely defined tax havens and could be evasion, or legal avoidance. Evasions had a lot to do with data flow weakness. These implied remedies called for resources for enforcement, together with incentives and sanctions formulated to foster and expand the information-sharing base.

The OECD initial list of tax havens in 2000 was adopted by the US, with exception of the US Virgin Islands. This 2000 OECD list excluded low-tax jurisdictions that included OECD members generally perceived as tax havens, like Switzerland and

388. D. Thomas-James. 2021. *Offshore financial centres and the law: Suspect wealth in British Overseas Territories*, Abingdon: Routledge.
389. O.B. Skeie. 2017. 'International differences in corporate taxation, foreign direct investment and tax revenues', *Economics Departments Working Papers No. 1359 OECD;* J.G. Gravelle. 2014. 'International corporate tax rate comparisons and policy implications', *Congressional Research Service (CRS) Report 7-5700 R41743 6/1/14*.
390. OECD. 2000. 'Towards global tax co-operation: Report to the 2000 ministerial council meeting and recommendations by the committee of fiscal affairs. Progress in identifying and eliminating harmful tax practices'.

Ireland. These two jurisdictions were included on the other hand in another examination of tax havens.[391] These sources aligning, on a broad level, suggested some fifty tax havens, with concentrations in the Caribbean and West Indies, and those within and adjacent to Continental Europe.

This list could also be differentiated from the OECD's black list. The OECD referred to tax havens, as those unwilling to cooperate on information exchange. Initially, there were some thirty-five jurisdictions included, but over time, as more tax havens committed to cooperate, the numbers fell to three, namely Andorra, Liechtenstein, and Monaco. This was not attributed to actual progress towards cooperation, but due mainly to withdrawal of US support in 2001 that led to the OECD concentrating on information on request without requiring reforms, until all participants signed on.[392] Big economies, as such, were unable to contain tax havens, or to reducing their practices.[393]

Interests on international tax information reporting and individual evasion surged when the fiascos surrounding UBS AG (UBS) and the Lichtenstein Global Trust Group (LGT) surfaced that attracted legal actions from the US and other nations. Bailouts of several US and European banks using public funds subsequent to the 2007 GFC kept public interests focused on the theme. This was edged up again at the G20 2 April 2009 Summit. Here, the G20 threatened tax havens that included a fresh list of nations with sanctions to end an era of banking secrecy so as to root out the hundreds of billions of dollars said to be concealed from tax authorities in offshore banks.[394]

The OECD designated countries in four domains, based on the actions they have taken to comply with its internationally agreed tax standard. These comprised those that have substantially implemented the standard, like the UK, US, France, Germany and China; tax havens that have committed to the standard, like Andorra, Monaco, Gibraltar, and Lichtenstein; financial centres that have committed to the standard, like Switzerland, Singapore, Chile, and the three EU Member States of Belgium, Luxembourg, and Austria; and those that have not committed to the standard, like Costa Rica, the Philippines, and Austria.[395]

Apprehensive of the prospects of penalties that could make it harder for their businesses to transact internationally, Austria pledged to comply without delay, and the Philippines and Monaco committed to do the necessary to get themselves off the blacklist. Switzerland and Luxembourg stood their grounds maintaining that they were no-tax havens, but agreed on the matter of more transparency. This and the alleged incomplete and flawed list made global tax advocacy groups unhappy, as they claimed that some alleged tax havens found in twenty major jurisdictions were not included.

391. J.R. Hines & E.M. Rice. 1994. 'Fiscal Paradise: Foreign tax havens and American business', *Quarterly Journal of Economics*, Vol. 109 (February 1994): 149-182.
392. J. Sharman. 2006. *Havens in a storm: The struggle for global tax regulation*, Ithaca: Cornell University Press.
393. D. Spencer & J.C. Sharman. 2008. 'International tax cooperation', *Journal of International Taxation*, February 2008: 39-58.
394. A. Faiola & M. Jordan. 2009. 'Tax-haven blacklist stirs nations: After G-20 issues mandate, many rushed to get off roll', *Washington Post 4/4/09*.
395. N. Watt, L. Elliott, J. Borger & I. Black. 2009. 'G20 declares door shut on tax havens: OECD publishing list of member countries that do not comply with its rules', *The Guardian 2/4/09*.

These notably included the special Chinese administrative zones of Hong Kong and Macau that China claimed are not tax havens, as well as the British banking enclaves of the Isle of Man and Jersey. Serious offenders designated in the 2009 OECD list included Uruguay, the Philippines, Costa Rica, and another thirty-eight, including the Cayman Islands, Panama, the Bahamas, and Lichtenstein. This time, leaders of several major economies and large EMEs agreed to develop a toolbox of countermeasures to pressure these tax havens to comply, that included obstacles for receiving development aid for EMEs.

There were doubts on the effectiveness of these announcements. But it was claimed that this was unlike previous occasions, as this time, the US administration was supporting the initiative. Moreover, the 2007 GFC had made investors more edgy about risk of using tax havens in the context of the fresh initiatives from the OECD. This probably explained why those on the original blacklist protested as they claimed that they had signed agreements to negotiate tax information exchange agreements (TIEAs) or negotiated agreements.

After various adjustments, as of May 2012, Nauru appeared to be the only tax haven listed on OECD's grey list, or those that have committed to the OECD standard, while Guatemala is the only one on the grey list for financial centres. They were differentiated from those on the OECD's black list of jurisdictions that have not committed to the OECD standard, and of which there were four that migrated to the grey list; and those on the white list, or those jurisdictions implementing an agreed-upon OECD standard. Apart from unwanted media publicity, there were legal implications for jurisdictions declared in the blacklist. This was because of laws and sanctions, especially at the global level, being imposed on those blacklisted, apart from the US relying on this identification for its unilateral actions.

§6.04 OECD, GLOBAL FORUM, AND OECD-LINKED GLOBAL TAX REFORMS INITIATIVES

The OECD has advanced further with its BEPS initiative. A constituent of this is the Global Forum on Transparency and Exchange of Information for Tax Purposes (GFTEITP). The GFTEITP comprising OECD countries was set up in 2000, but expanded in 2009 to include jurisdictions that agreed to implement tax connected transparency and information exchange. The fifteen-member Steering Group comprised representations from both advanced and developing economies.[396] The same makeup was found in the twenty-four Peer Review Group. The Global Forum operated under the directions of the OECD and the G20 to deal with tax evasions, tax havens, OFCs, double taxation, money laundering, and tax information exchange agreements (TIEAs).[397]

396. Global Forum (GF). 2014. 'Tax transparency 2014: Report on Progress'.
397. GF. 2017. 'About the Global Forum'.

Since 2009, the GF grew to be the main international body moving the implementation of the international standards on tax transparency.[398] It sought to ensure that high standards of transparency and exchange of information for tax purposes would operate across the world, via its monitoring and peer-review activities. To ensure worldwide participation, the GF provided technical assistance programmes for its members, including developing economies. The international agreed standards comprised the Exchange of Information on Request (EOIR) and the AEI. The GF currently has 161 members participating on equal footing, inclusive of fifteen international organizations as observers.[399] All Global Forum members have committed to implementing the new standard on AEI. Jurisdictions undertaking AEI numbered forty-nine in 2017, fifty-one in 2018, fifty-three in 2019, fifty-seven in 2020, sixty by 2021, sixty-two by 2022, and sixty-seven by 2023; while developing countries not asked to commit and that have not yet set a date for the first year of exchanges numbered forty-five.[400] The US has undertaken AEI pursuant to FATCA from 2015 and entered into intergovernmental agreements (IGAs) with other jurisdictions to do so.[401]

At the 2009 G20 London summit, tax havens were bracketed under four categories. Here, countries were rated, based on various standards, as being compliant, largely compliant, partially compliant, or non-compliant. The US enacted the FATCA in 2012. This compelled foreign financial firms to disclose their American clientele base.

International initiatives were expanded in the same year to cover automated exchange of tax information (AETI) to curb tax evasions, while expanding the coverage to developing economies. By 2014, the Global Forum completed 150 reviews. This included seventy-nine Phase 1 reviews, twenty-six Combined Phase 1 + 2 reviews, and forty-five Phase 2 reviews.[402] Overall, one hundred and five jurisdictions completed Phase 1 reviews, while seventy-one received a rating after finalizing both phases. Compliance with the international standard was generally high for most criteria. In terms of overall rating, a majority of jurisdictions received a largely compliant rating. Availability of ownership information was the only element where less than 50% rated jurisdictions scored a fully compliant rating.

The GF released results of the AEI peer reviews for 100 jurisdictions showed that almost all committed jurisdictions had commenced the AEI, and that the legal frameworks of 88% of the jurisdictions that committed to exchange financial account information by 2017 or 2018 have been determined to be 'in place', or 'in place but needs improvement'.[403] The jurisdictions' performance on the EOIR standard remained strong, with 86% of jurisdictions reviewed in the second round of the EOIR per reviews having received a satisfactory overall rating of compliant or largely compliant. The demand for capacity building support, commitment to the transparency agenda, and engagement with jurisdictions remained strong during the COVID-19 pandemic. The

398. *Supra* note [397]. GF. 2017.
399. OECD. 2021. 'Global Forum (GF) members', *OECD February 2021*.
400. Global Forum (GF). 2021. 'AEOI: Status of commitments', *GF 17/2/21*.
401. *Supra* note [400]. Global Forum (GF). 2021.
402. Global Forum (GF). 2014. 'Tax transparency 2014: Report on Progress'.
403. Global Forum (GF). 2020. 'Tax transparency and exchange of information in times of COVID-19', *2020 Global Forum Report*.

GF claimed that during these challenging times, transparency and exchange of information continue to deliver and generate much needed revenues.

Some EUR 107 billion in additional revenue arising from tax, interest, and penalties were identified worldwide via voluntary disclosure initiatives and offshore tax investigation, where some EUR 29 billion of these were reported by developing economies.[404] To ensure effective international cooperation constant improvements would be needed in the area of transparency and exchange of information for tax purposes for resolving any remaining and new challenges unfolding from accelerated developments in the digital economy. The GF to ensure the effective delivery of its mandate would set up a new Task Force On Risk empowered with the mandate to identify possible risks to the implementation of the transparency and exchange of information standards.[405]

The GF has now developed a process designed to quickly encourage the remaining jurisdictions to respond to the recommendations, failing which a rating of non-compliant would be issued. As of 2014, Australia, Belgium, Canada, China, Denmark, Finland, France, and thirteen others were rated as compliant. The largely compliant jurisdictions included the US, Malaysia, Hong Kong, Singapore, UK, the Cayman Islands, Guernsey, Saint Kitts and Nevis, Saint Vincent, the Bahamas, and twenty-eight others. Those partially compliant included Barbados, Turkey, Andorra, Anguilla, Indonesia, and three others. The non-compliant were the BVI, Cyprus, Luxembourg, and the Seychelles. Twelve jurisdictions, including Switzerland could not be rated because they could not migrate to Phase 2.

These evaluations in accordance with the OECD approach focused on one aspect of the features of tax havens. Since November 2015, ninety members committed to go beyond EOIR to implement the AETI, while seventy-four signed this framework agreement. This could go into effect only for each signatory after confirmation that specific steps have been implemented, like the enactments of national legislations.

Three themes dominated the work of GF in 2015. These included, first the AEI becoming the norm with ninety-six jurisdictions committed to its implementation over the next few years. Information on financial accounts held by non-residents would start flowing in from 2017. Residency country tax administrators would soon have access to their taxpayers' foreign bank and other financial account information automatically. This is expected to change the practice of international tax evasion forever, because the difficulty of hiding money offshore would be enhanced considerably. Second, 2015 saw the completion of the revised framework for reviewing the standard for EOIR. The contents of the Terms of Reference for reviewing jurisdictions had been strengthened, and information on the beneficial ownership of companies, trusts, and foundations would henceforth be required. This was targeted to reduce the risk of shell companies being misused to conceal financial flows.

Significant numbers of non-compliant jurisdictions migrated to largely compliant, reflecting the power of the peer-review process, and the determination of the jurisdictions concerned to quickly resolve deficiencies in their laws and practices.

404. *Supra* note [403]. GF. 2020.
405. *Supra* note [403]. GF. 2020.

Third, developing economies accounting for more than half of the GF's membership would be integrated fully into this process to ensure that the exchange of information enjoyed a worldwide reach. This was expected to be achieved with the assistance of observer organizations and national agencies. The international legal basis for exchange has also advanced with more focus on multilateral instruments. Indeed, more jurisdictions joined the multilateral Convention on Mutual Administrative Assistance in Tax Matters.

As at October 2015, eight-six jurisdictions received ratings after completion of their Phase 2 reviews. Of these, seventy-four were rated as compliant, or largely complaint. Overall, for 2015, twenty-two jurisdictions were rated as compliant, fifty-two as largely compliant, and twelve as partially compliant. There were eight jurisdictions that could not be rated, as they could not go on to Phase 2. These comprised Guatemala, Kazakhstan, Lebanon, Liberia, the Federated States of Micronesia, Nauru, Trinidad and Tobago, and Vanuatu. Following calls in April 2016 by the G20 Finance Ministers, a special fast track review procedure was implemented between April and June 2017. As a result, several jurisdictions were granted provisional upgrades to their ratings.[406]

The year 2016 marked the end of the first round of reviews.[407] The year also witnessed the first batch of financial account information by financial institutions, as preparation for the first AEI exchanges in 2017. The GF focused its attention to improve international tax transparency and international tax cooperation. Its work agenda included the rapid and effective implementation of the standard for EOIR; rapid and effective implementation of the standard for AEI; and supporting developing economies to implement the standards.

The GF finished its first round of peer reviews of the EOIR standard and the assignment of compliance ratings in November 2016. This indicated that the EOIR standard was already substantially implemented across the world, with ninety-nine out of one hundred and sixteen jurisdictions rated, as having achieved compliant, or largely compliant ratings. No less than sixty jurisdictions removed restrictions on exchanging bank information, and some thirty have eliminated, or immobilized bearer shares. An approach emerged in place to recognize jurisdictions that have less than satisfactory ratings, but which would have made adequate progress towards a satisfactory level of tax transparency standards by the G20 Summit in July 2017. The new rounds of the EOIR standard in the context of strengthened terms of reference included ensuring the availability of beneficial ownership has also been launched.[408]

The overall ratings indicated that twenty-two jurisdictions were rated compliant, seventy-seven as largely compliant, twelve as partially compliant, and five as non-compliant.[409] The non-compliant comprised Guatemala, the Federated States of Micronesia, and Trinidad and Tobago. The GF, with the steady progress thus made, argued

406. OECD. 2021. 'Compliance ratings following peer reviews against the standard of EOIR'; OECD. 2021. 'Frequently asked questions: Fast track review procedure'.
407. Global Forum. 2016. 'Tax transparency 2016: Report on Progress'.
408. *Supra* note [407]. Global Forum. 2016.
409. *Supra* note [407]. Global Forum. 2016.

that the solutions needed to combat tax evasion had been effectively launched. Further things to be done would include increasing the power and range of tools that are currently available for applications by all countries, and deployed effectively to counter international tax evasions.

§6.05 TAX TRANSPARENCY IN DIGITAL PLATFORMS

EU Member States in November 2020 agreed to put digital platforms under the EU's tax transparency rules, and formal adoption would follow, once the European Parliament (EP) and the Economic and Social Committee give their opinion to enable the application of the new rules as from 1 January 2023 onwards.[410] Under this EU tax transparency for digital platforms (DAC7) proposal [COM (2020) 314 final], EU Members States have to automatically exchange information concerning cross-border revenues generated by EU sellers on digital platforms, even if those platforms are not based in the EU. This is envisaged to be effective from 1 January 2023, when sellers would have to report income from the rental of immovable property; provision of personal services; sale of goods; rentals of any modes of transport; and investment and lending in digital platforms. The EU was also simultaneously reflecting a DAC8 addressing cryptocurrency and e-money transparency. This was prompted by considerations that national tax administrators lacked information on crypto assets and e-money usage, and could be missing out on potential key sources of revenues, as well as concerns over disparities in how sanctions would be applied across Member States.

These have to be viewed in the context of EU's agenda to simplify taxpayer compliance and subjecting cryptocurrency and e-money exchanges to exchange of information rules. As the details are being worked out, the EU has the option of either simply issuing crypto-linked guidelines for Member States, or issue a more formal DAC8.[411] The European Payments Institutions Federation (EPIF) and other stakeholders in response expressed concerns about the impacts on low-value users and importantly that economy and e-money institutions were already well regulated under existing laws and requirements and might not need to fall under DAC8. As such, the EPIF argued that the best approach for handling this would involve establishing clear reporting thresholds to demarcate between those accounts used for storing money and those for transactional purposes.[412]

Transparency of crypto assets is also on the OECD's agenda, as shown by its plan to release a crypto tax framework in 2021. This said new system would be premised under the OECD's CRS to enable the AEI.[413] Though the general reporting infrastructure has been finalized, technical matters needing resolutions, included considerations

410. Croner-i. 2020. 'EC welcomes tax transparency rules on digital platforms', *Croner-i 4/12/20*; *Council Directive (EU) 2018/822 of 25 May 2018 amending Directive 2011/16/EU pertaining to mandatory automatic exchange of information in the field of taxation in relation to reportable cross-border arrangements*.
411. N.A. Sarfo. 2021. 'Strengthening tax transparency in 2021', *Forbes 26/1/21*.
412. *Supra* note [411]. Sarfo. 2021.
413. OECD. 2020. 'OECD Secretary-General Tax Report to G20 Finance Ministers and Central Bank Governors-October 2020'.

as to whether other kinds of virtual assets should be onboarded in the scope; whether other intermediaries, like wallet providers, should be included; whether other income besides sales should be reported; and whether the values of crypto asset holdings should be reported.[414]

§6.06 BENEFICIAL OWNERSHIP TRANSPARENCY AND COUNTRY-BY-COUNTRY (CBC) REPORTING

Pertaining to beneficial ownership transparency, all UK-inhabited overseas territories agreed at the end of 2020 to implement public beneficial ownership registers.[415] These though would not be in operation until 2023, as considerable work is needed between now and then. For UK overseas territories, like the Cayman Islands and the BVI, the new rules would not be too burdensome, as these territories already share beneficial ownership and tax information with UK law enforcement owing to their robust offshore finance industries. Beneficial ownership for these registers would include direct and indirect control via shareholdings, voting rights, and the ability to appoint or remove a majority of directors. Overseas territories would be empowered to decide on what percentage of control to trigger reporting requirements, but would be unlikely to exceed a 25% maximum to align with international standards.[416] The UK Foreign, Commonwealth & Development Office would in future compile best practices for beneficial ownership registers to encourage other countries to launch their own public beneficial ownership registers.

EU lawmakers supported by the EP have urged the European Council to prioritize public CbC reporting. The EP had in 2019 approved a proposal requiring multinationals with at least EUR 750 million in worldwide revenue to disclose their earnings, profits, and the level of tax paid in the economies they do business.[417] The proposal lacking a qualified majority never made it in the European Council, but this was loudly supported by the European Free Alliance/EU Greens Coalition and others,[418] arguing that it was more important than ever, because of the economic impacts of COVID-19. Meanwhile, the EC would be prioritizing public CbC reporting for its 2021 action plan.[419]

The Extractive Industries Transparency Initiative (EITI), a global standard for good governance practices within the oil, gas, and mineral extractive sectors, adopted in 2016 new beneficial ownership disclosure requirements, known as the 2016 EITI

---

414. *Supra* note [413]. OECD. 2020.
415. *Supra* note [411]. Sarfo. 2021.
416. *Supra* note [411]. Sarfo. 2021.
417. European Parliament. (EP). 2019. 'Public country by country reporting proposal', *EP Briefing April 2019*.
418. F. Amaddeo. 2021. 'Eu agenda includes public country-by-country reporting', *MNE Tax 13/1/21*.
419. European Commission (EC). 2016. 'Introducing public country-by-country reporting for multinational enterprises', *EC 12/4/16*.

Standard.[420] This sets a timeline for member countries to design and set-up publicly available beneficial ownership registries in their extractive sectors, where thus far, fifty-three countries have signed up, and forty-two in compliance with its guidelines. The US withdrew in 2017 in line with Trump's general isolation policy. It remained unclear whether the new US administration would return, and what impact this would have on US extractives multinationals where some had been hesitant about publicly disclosing their tax information. Already, Exxon Mobil and Chevron, both obligated to do so, as EITI board members, had refused to publicly disclose their US tax payments in 2018.[421]

On the accounting perspective, the FASB in the process of updating income taxes disclosure framework has already received calls from US lawmakers to include CbC reporting requirements. In any case, US multinationals with over USD 850 million in annual revenues are required by the US IRS to file CbC reports. The FASB had yet to make its final decision, and is now engaged in more research and outreach on potential alternatives for disclosing some disaggregated income tax amendments.[422] Disaggregation concepts generally carry significant costs as reporting systems were not generally designed to keep pace with changes in tax law, as well as potential dissimilar processes of determination that could outweigh possible benefits for financial statements' users, thereby necessitating measurements against objectives formulated in the guiding principles.[423]

Thus far, developing economies and EMEs had gradually begun to apply the OECD's Common Reporting Standard (CRS) and AEI, but more developments are envisaged for 2021. There appeared to be considerable scope for further progress. The OECD has reported that there were still forty-three developing country members of the Global Forum on Transparency that had not been asked to commit to AEI and have yet to set a date for their first year of exchanges. Further, the OECD appeared to be tuning to the idea of tax transparency as a way where economies could restrengthen their economies post-COVID-19, especially with regard to the increasing of their capital taxations.[424]

In general, OECD's categorization of tax havens and overseas financial centres served as guidelines for those needing to use them for various purposes. There had, however, been suggestions that many jurisdictions were tax havens, or bore features of tax havens that were overlooked. These included major economies, like the US, the UK, the Netherlands, Denmark, Hungary, Israel, Portugal, and Canada. Particular attentions were drawn to Delaware, Nevada, and Wyoming in the US. Campione d'Italia, an Italian town within Switzerland, had also been cited. The Netherlands, often considered a tax haven in the corporate world, was also not included, even though it allowed

420. P.F. Villar. 2020. 'The Extractive Industries Transparency Initiative (EITI) and trust in politicians', *Resources Policy*, Vol. 68(2020): 1-13.
421. E. Cooks. 2018. 'Exxon Mobile and Chevron accused over tax secrecy: Refusal to disclose US tax payments undermines global transparency push, group says', *Financial Times 6/6/18.*
422. K. Brockman. 2020. 'FASB Income Tax Disclosure Framework-Part 2', *Bloomberg Tax 15/9/20.*
423. *Supra* note [422]. Brockman. 2020.
424. D. Allain-Dupre. 2020. 'The territorial impact of COVID-19: Managing the crisis across levels of government', *OECD 10/11/20.*

firms to reduce taxes on dividends and capital gains from subsidiaries, together with a wide range of treaties that reduced taxes.

The jurisdiction has also been said to be facilitating movements to tax havens via provisions known as 'Dutch sandwich'. The EC since 2014 had been examining whether certain arrangements in Ireland and Luxembourg constituted prohibited state aid. This enquiry has now been expanded to all Member States.[425] The EU has further agreed to insert an anti-abuse clause to its provision to discourage double taxation within EU Member States that could have important implications to these arrangements in the future.[426]

Questions have been raised over haven-like features of the US states of Delaware, Nevada, and Wyoming, especially over the lack of reporting requirements, failure to tax interest and other exempt passive incomes paid to foreign taxation, and the ease of incorporation.[427] There were mentions of three US practices that facilitated international evasions. These comprised: the failures to gather information on tax-exempt interest income paid to foreign entities; foreign institutions acting as qualified intermediaries without disclosures of their clientele; and people being allowed to conceal their identities as stockholders or depositors, including allowing corporations to have bearer shares to enable anonymous ownership.[428]

But recent US legislation appeared to require the disclosure of beneficial owners in the US.[429] The UK and its protected territories were also singled out for identification, as tax havens, on the particular allegation that non-domiciled UK laws allowed foreign nationals to live in the UK without paying taxes on their overseas incomes. Amendments to the UK Criminal Finance Act 2017 compelling British territories to follow the UK in making public their company ownership registers to the tax authorities by 2020 could nevertheless close this loophole.[430]

Part of this said legislation, included the offence of failure to prevent tax evasion that applied to corporates incorporated or formed in the UK, as well as corporates with business establishments in the UK and any corporate wherever located, where a step in the facilitation offence occurred in the UK. This rendered the extraterritorial effect of this provision wider than in the case of the Bribery Act 2010. As part of its drive to increase corporate transparency, the UK planned to extend the persons with significant control (PSC) rules to cover offshore vehicles holding UK real estate. In line with its push on transparency of ownership, the UK has also been planning to create a new

425. Ernst & Young (E&Y). 2014. 'EU, Ireland, Luxembourg and Netherland: State Aid-Commission investigates Transfer Pricing Arrangements on Corporate Taxation of Apple (Ireland), Starbucks (Netherlands), and Fiat Finance and Trade (Luxembourg)', *E&Y Tax Insights June 2014*.
426. Council of the EU. 2014. 'Parent-Subsidiary Directive: Council agrees to add anti-abuse clause against corporate tax avoidance', *Council of the EU 9/12/14*.
427. C. Gnaedinger. 2009. 'Luxembourg P.M. calls out U.S. states as tax havens', *Tax Notes 6/4/09*, p. 13; C. Gnaedinger. 2009a. 'U.S. Cayman Islands debate tax haven status', *Tax Notes 4/5/09*, pp. 548-545.
428. M. McIntyre. 2009. 'A Program for international tax reforms', *Tax Notes 23/2/09*, pp. 1021-1026.
429. *Supra* note [427]. Gnaedinger. 2009a; U. Lomas. 2009. 'Luxembourg PM calls for US "tax havens" to be blacklisted', *Tax News 3/4/09*.
430. A. Seely, S. Godec & T. Edmonds. 2017. 'Criminal Finances Bill: Lords amendments', *House of Commons Research Briefing 24/4/17*.

register of beneficial ownership information for overseas legal entities in certain circumstances.

§6.07 TAX HAVENS CLASSIFICATION REVIEWS

When big and influential economies in Europe and the US were called out as tax havens, general global controversies arose. But, the categorization of tax havens into four domains in research had already suggested this, before the open quarrels occurring between developing and advanced economies. Here, tax havens have argued to comprise continental European havens, like Switzerland and Luxembourg; a UK zone of influence that included the City of London, jurisdictions formally connected to the UK, like Jersey, Guernsey, the Isle of Man, Bermuda and many islands in the West Indies and the Caribbean; an US zone, that included some of its states along with the US Virgin Islands, the Marshall Islands, Liberia and the Panama; and other jurisdictions, like Mauritius.[431]

An even wider list was provided by the TJN that included the Americas and Caribbean, New York and Uruguay, as well as various cities and areas in Africa, the Middle East and Asia. For Europe, this included Belgium, the City of London, Dublin, and Frankfurt. Others covered those in the Indian and Pacific Oceans and the Marianas.[432] Yet another research suggested eleven different lists of tax havens.[433] While the TJN appeared to have the broadest list, it had also not included jurisdictions appearing in the others' lists.[434] Nevertheless, eight jurisdictions appeared on all the lists. These were the Bahamas, the Cayman Islands, Guernsey, Jersey, Malta, Belgium, the Netherlands, and Luxembourg. The US and the UK are argued for inclusions because of particular aspects of their rules. For the UK, things could change with inserting of new rules for the enhancing of corporate transparency and beneficial ownership, especially in real estate.

The failures to agree to a common understanding as which jurisdictions were tax havens, and which were not, presented a slight setback to international efforts to curb the key excesses of tax havens, like the concealing of beneficial ownerships, or the accommodations of extreme forms of tax shifting. Excessive financialization and harmful tax haven activities when allowed to persist could lead to the inevitable widening of income and wealth inequality between rich and poor economies, rich and poor businesses, and rich and poor individuals. These were what research insights have been telling the world.[435] Tax havens facilitated this process, but far worse. They

431. N. Shaxson. 2011. *Treasure islands: Tax havens and the men who stole the world*, London: The Bodley Head.
432. Tax Justice Network (TJN). 2005. 'Tax us if you can', *TJN September 2005*.
433. R. Palan. 2012. 'Tax havens and offshore financial centres', *Academic Foresights*, Vol. 4(April-June 2012): 1-15; *Supra* note [165]. Palan, Murphy & Chavagneux. 2010. 'Tax havens: How globalization really works', Ithaca: Cornell University Press.
434. *Supra* note [433]. Palan, Murphy & & Chavagneux. 2010.
435. S. Dalen. 2016. 'Tax havens. Secrecy jurisdictions and journalistic investigations: How to make it part of the global discussion', *Reuters Institute Fellowship Paper University of Oxford, July 2016;* J. Slater. 2016. '62 people own the same as half the world, reveals Oxfam Davos report',

facilitated corruption, frauds, and illegal trades with terror groups and blacklisted regimes. They did not just attract their clientele base with little or no tax, but as shelters from national laws and regulations that hid the identities of owners behind shell companies, bank accounts, trusts, and so on. These were all undertaken with the ultimate purpose of evading public scrutiny and criminal investigations, including the obstructions of free media. In short, tax havens operated as masters of opacity.[436]

§6.08 BASE EROSION PROFIT SHIFTING (BEPS)

Tax havens aside, businesses and individuals avoided taxes via various mechanisms. As US multinationals dominate the world, they attracted particular attention. US multinationals were not taxed on incomes earned by foreign subsidiaries, until these were repatriated to the US parents as dividends, though some passive and related corporate incomes that could be easily shifted are taxed currently under anti-abuse rules, referred to as Subpart F.[437] But, when businesses shifted profits to a low-tax jurisdiction from a high-tax locale, their taxes would be reduced without impacting other aspects of their businesses.

Tax avoidance pertained both to the US parent companies shifting profits abroad to low-tax jurisdictions, as well as the shifting of profits out of the US by foreign parents of US subsidiaries. These could happen, because US taxes all income earned in its borders, as well as imposing residual taxes on incomes earned abroad by US persons. Research suggested that around 50% difference between profitability in low-tax and high-tax jurisdictions could come about from artificial income shifting, and this has been mainly attributed to transfers of intellectual property or intangibles,[438] and the allocation of debts, to a lesser degree.

One way of shifting profits from high- to low-tax regimes was by borrowing more in the high-tax jurisdiction, and less in the low-tax jurisdiction, without altering the debt burden of the business. This could be achieved also by assets stripping, transfer pricing, contract manufacturing, use of hybrid entities and instruments, and so on.[439] Earnings stripping caught media attention, when several US MNCs 'inverted', meaning the transferring of their parent firms overseas so that US operations became subsidiaries of those parents.

Oxfam International 18/1/16; J.E. Stiglitz. 2014. 'Of the 1%, by the 1%, for the 1%', *Vanity Fair 29/4/14*; T. Piketty. 2014. *Capital in the twenty-first century*, Boston: Harvard College.

436. *Supra* note [435]. Dalen. 2016.
437. S. Beer, R. de Mooij & L. Liu. 2018. 'International corporate tax avoidance: A review of the channels, effect sizes, and blind spots', *IMF Working Paper WP/18/168 July 2018*.
438. H. Gruber. 2003. 'Intangible income, intercompany transactions, income shifting and the choice of locations: Part II', *National Tax Journal*, Vol. 56(March 2003): 221-242; S.J. Pak & J.S. Zdanowicz. 2002. 'U.S. trade with the world, an estimate of 2001 lost U.S. federal income tax revenues due to over-invoiced imports and under-invoiced exports', *Center for International Business, Education and Research 31/1/02*.
439. N. Omar & S. Zolkaflil. 2015. 'Profit shifting and earnings management through tax haven subsidiaries: An exploratory analysis of multinational companies', *Procedia Economics and Finance*, Vol. 28(2015): 53-58.

The US Treasury investigations were not able to find conclusive evidence about the shifting of profits out of US arising from high leverage rates for US subsidiaries of foreign firms, but found evidence of shifting for inverted businesses.[440] In response, regulatory changes were initiated to limit some of the benefits of inversion. These comprised the measures announced in 22 September 2014, 19 November 2015 and 4 April 2016.[441]

Transfer pricing is said to occur when prices of goods and services sold by parents and affiliates were lowered in high-tax situations and the price of purchases inflated.[442] This shifted income. When a patent developed in the US (or UK) is licensed to an affiliate in a low-tax jurisdiction, incomes could be shifted where the royalty or other payments were lower than the true value of the license. Intangibles like this presented particular problems for those involved in the monitoring and policing of transfer pricing. The problems pertaining to intellectual properties could be accentuated further, when cost-sharing agreements were in play, and where different affiliates contributed to the cost. Hence, tax-motivated transfer mispricing in real goods increased substantially under the circumstances: first, when taxation of foreign profits changed from a worldwide to a territorial approach in the UK, with multinationals shifting more profits into low-tax jurisdictions; second, with a firm's increased R&D intensity; and third such tax-motivated transfer mispricing was concentrated in countries that are not tax havens and had low-to-medium-level corporate taxes.[443]

Shifting profits to some tax havens could be tricky in those jurisdictions that might not have labour and other resources to undertake the activity. Methods and mechanisms could be available for exploiting the advantage of tax laws in other countries to achieve productive operations, even as profits were shifted to no-tax jurisdictions. Under the *Double Irish Dutch Sandwich* method, US firms transferred their intangible assets to Irish holding corporations. The latter had subsidiary sales companies that sold, say advertising, to Europe. Sandwiched between the Irish holding companies and the Irish sales subsidiaries could be Dutch subsidiaries collecting royalties from the sales subsidiaries and transferring them to the Irish holding companies. The Irish holding companies could claim corporate management and tax domicile in, say the Bermuda, with 0% tax rate for corporate tax purposes.

This option enabled the Irish operation to avoid even the low Irish tax of say 12.5%, and avoid Irish withholding taxes that were not due on payments to EU companies by employing the 'Dutch sandwich'.[444] These enabled US multinationals to delay paying US taxes on international earnings for years, as well as paying lower tax

440. US Treasury. 2007. *Taxation of the foreign profits of companies: A discussion document*, London: HM Treasury.
441. D.J. Marples & J.G. Gravelle. 2016. 'Corporate expatriation, inversions and mergers: Tax issues', *Congressional Research Service (CRS) 7-5700 R43568 Report 27/4/16.*
442. L. Li, T. Schmidt-Eisenlohr & D. Guo. 2017. 'International transfer pricing and tax avoidance: Evidence from linked trade-tax statistics in the UK', *International Finance Discussion Paper 1214.*
443. *Supra* note [442]. Li, Schmidt-Eisenlohr & Guo. 2017.
444. C.B. Murphy & K. Khartit. 2020. 'Double Irish with a Dutch Sandwich', *Investopedia 30/10/20*; A. Beebeejaun. 2020. 'The Double Irish and Dutch Sandwich strategies and tax avoidance in Mauritius', *Journal of Money Laundering Control.*

rates overseas. Various EU Member States have complained about these arrangements by MNCs like Apple, Google, Amazon, Facebook, and Starbucks. International tax authorities were pleasantly surprised by recent Google confirmation that the company would scrap its intellectual property licensing structure through which international profits were channelled through Ireland and on to Caribbean tax havens, putting them outside the reach of US tax authorities.[445] This would simplify Google's tax arrangements to be in alignment with the OECD's initiatives to limit international tax avoidance, following changes to the US and Irish Tax laws.

Indeed, it had been estimated that by the end of 2017, some of the most profitable US companies, including Apple, the biggest by market capitalization, had squirreled more than USD 1 trillion offshore, using the 'double Irish' to sequestered billions in 'ghost entities'. The PRP revealed that Apple, for instance, had designed a new tax structure to exploit, routing international profits through Jersey. Indeed, US multinationals have been perceived as the global grandmasters of tax avoidance schemes that had not only considerably reduced US tax collections but also the tax collections of almost every large economy in the world, according to the late Ed Kleinbarb, Tax Law Professor at the University of Southern California.[446]

Setting-up subsidiaries in low-tax economies to shift profits might not always be feasible, especially when these had not been desirable places to actually manufacture and sell the products. For instance, an Irish subsidiary's market could be in Germany, but to obtain profits in high tax, Germany would not minimize tax, and so the Irish business might contract with a German outfit for contract manufacturing. The latter would then produce the item for cost including a fixed markup. Arrangements could then be structured to get exemption from Subpart F taxes.[447] Also, *check-the-box provisions* when employed to foreign situations via the disregarded entity rules led to the expansion of hybrid entities, where an entity could be recognized as a corporation by one jurisdiction, but not by another.

A US parent's subsidiary in a low-tax economy could also lend to its subsidiary in a high-tax economy with interest deductible, because the latter economy recognized the firm as a separate corporation. Such check-the-box and similar hybrid entity operations could also be applied to avoid other kinds of Subpart F income, for instance, from contract manufacturing arrangements. Aside from these, there could also be other hybrid instruments that could avoid taxation by being treated as debts in one jurisdiction and equities in another.[448]

---

445. E. Helmore. 2020. 'Google says it will no longer use "Double Irish, Dutch sandwich" tax loophole', *The Guardian 1/1/20.*
446. *Supra* note [445]. Helmore. 2020; S. Alecci. 2021. 'Multinationals shifted $1 trillion offshore, stripping countries of billions in tax revenues, study say', *ICIJ 1 April 2021*; J. Garcia-Bernardo & P. Jansky. 2021. 'Profit shifting of multinational corporations worldwide', *ICTD Working Paper 119 March 2021.*
447. J. Silbering-Meyer. 2018. 'Should companies plan into Subpart F following US tax reforms?', *Thomson Reuters Paper.*
448. S. Foley. 2007. 'U.S. outbound: Cross border hybrid instrument transactions to gain increased scrutiny during IRS audit', *International Tax Review*, Vol. 18(9): 9; A. Kraymal. 2005. 'International hybrid instruments: Jurisdiction dependent characterization', *Houston Business and Tax Law Journal*, Vol. 5(2005): 98-107.

Receipts of incomes in the US from low-tax jurisdictions could avoid taxes due to cross-crediting. This would involve the application of excess foreign taxes paid in one jurisdiction, or on one kind of income, to offset US tax that would be due on other incomes. Businesses that originated from jurisdictions with taxes in excess of US taxes could also opt to realize income from jurisdictions with low taxes and apply the excess credits to offset US tax on that income. Research suggested that between cross-crediting and deferral, US multinationals usually paid virtually no US tax on foreign-source incomes.[449]

The ability to lower US taxes due to cross-crediting could be enhanced, when income that should be viewed as US source income is treated as foreign-source income thereby raising the foreign tax credit limit. Included in this could be US exports that qualify as a US source income, as the title passage rule provision allows half of export income to be allocated to the country in which the title passed. Royalty income from active business could be another kind of income that could be considered foreign source and thus shielded with foreign tax credits. Such a benefit occurring in high-tax jurisdictions as royalties could be generally deductible from income. But as all such incomes were yields from investments in the US, these would arguably be US source incomes, or at least lumped into a different foreign tax credit receptacle, so that credits generated by dividends could not be employed to offset such incomes.

Corporate profits shifting through the above methods and more were suggested in various sources.[450] These research insights suggested that profits appeared in economies inconsistent with economic motivations.[451] It had also been reported that, for instance, profits of controlled foreign companies (CFCs) in manufacturing relative to sales in Ireland appeared relatively very large.[452] There were also reported higher share of US pre-tax profits of US multinationals than of value-added, tangible assets, sales, compensation, or employees in low-tax jurisdictions like Switzerland, UK Caribbean, Ireland, and Bermuda.[453] Other research findings provided similar and related suggestions.[454]

Growing international financial globalization and ease of transacting on the Internet have facilitated individual evasion of taxes that have assumed many different

449. M. Costa & J. Gravelle. 2012. 'Taxing multinational corporations: Average tax rates', *Tax Law Review*, Vol. 65(3): 391-414; Government Accountability Office (GAO). 2008. 'US multinational corporations: Effective tax rates are correlated with where income is reported', *GAO Paper GAO-08-950.*
450. K.A. Clausing. 2016. 'Policy shifting and U.S. tax policy reform', *Washington Centre for Equitable Growth Paper May 2016*; B. Salvador & A. Diego. 2016. 'Estimating corporate profit shifting with firm-level panel date: Time trends and industrial heterogeneity', *JRC Working Papers on Taxation and Structural Reforms No. 7/2016.*
451. J.G. Gravelle. 2015. *Tax havens: International tax avoidance and evasion*, Washington, DC: Congressional Research Service.
452. H. Grubert & R. Altshuler. 2008. 'Corporate taxes in a world economy: Reforming the taxation of cross-border income', in W.J. Diamond & G. Zodrow (eds.), *Fundamental tax reform: Issues, choices and implications*, Cambridge: MIT Press.
453. Government Accountability Office. GAO. 2008. 'U.S. multinational corporations: Effective tax rates are correlated with where income is reported', *GAO Paper GAO-08-950.*
454. M. Sullivan. 2008. 'Extraordinary profitability in low-tax countries', *Tax Notes 25/8/08*: 724-727.

forms.[455] Individuals could acquire foreign investments directly in various places likes shares and bonds, or place money in foreign bank accounts and simply not reporting the incomes even when these were subject to tax as there had been little or no withholding information on individual taxpayers for this kind of action. Individuals could also employ structures, like trusts or shell corporations to evade tax on investments by arbitraging on different tax laws.

However, especially in the case of the US, FATCA could alter matters. Also, no less than fifty economies have, as mentioned earlier, signed into a multilateral information exchange initiative that formulated reporting standards contributing to fuller exchange of tax information by most economies. This would be important, as research suggested that of the USD 1.2 trillion in overseas profits US businesses reported in 2012, USD 600 billion could be attributed to tax havens in Bermuda, Ireland, Luxembourg, the Netherlands, Switzerland, and the UK Caribbean Islands. The Netherlands appeared to be the most popular destination, accounting for something like 14.1% of all overseas earnings of US businesses.[456]

Indeed, the OECD did not idle by, where international tax avoidance and tax evasion were concerned. It had the most advance initiative to contain corporate and related tax avoidance and evasion policy measures. This grew to be referred to as *BEPS*. This pertained to tax avoidance strategies that exploited gaps and mismatches in tax rules to artificially shift profits to low or no-tax situations. Although some of the schemes used could be illegal, most were not. Nevertheless, they undermined the fairness and integrity of tax systems. When businesses operated beyond national borders, they could employ BEPS to achieve competitive advantages over enterprises that do not. There could also be a signalling effect, when taxpayers witnessed multinationals legally avoiding income tax. This could have the effect of undermining voluntary compliance by all other taxpayers.[457]

The OECD/G20 BEPS package provided fifteen Actions to equip governments with the domestic and international instruments needed to deal with BEPS.[458] Participating economies now had access to mechanisms to ensure that profits were taxed where economic activities generating the profits were performed, and where values were generated. Businesses also benefited from enhanced certainty by reducing disputes pertaining to the application of international tax rules, as well as, from the standardizing of compliance requirements. The OECD identified fifteen actions to address BEPS in a comprehensive way. The G20 Finance Ministers in October 2015 endorsed the BEPS package.

The 15 Actions were depicted as follows:[459]

> Action 1 addressed the tax challenges of the digital economy and identified the principal difficulties that the digital economy poses for the application of

455. *Supra* note [451]. Gravelle. 2015.
456. M.P. Knightley & J. M. Stupak. 2015. 'Corporate tax base erosion and profit shifting (BEPS): An examination of the data', *Congressional Research Service (CRS) Report 7-5700 R44013* 30/4/15.
457. OECD. 2017. 'Base erosion and profit sharing', *OECD*.
458. OECD. 2013. *Action plan on Base Erosion and Profit Shifting*, Paris: OECD.
459. *Supra* note [458]. OECD. 2013.

existing international tax rules.[460] The digital economy was the outcome of a transformative process induced by information and communication technology (ICT) that made technologies cheaper, more powerful, and widely standardized thereby improving businesses processes and bolstering innovations across all parts of the economy. It would be generally impossible to ring-fence the digital economy from the rest of the economy for tax purposes.

Some key features of the digital economy and its business models could be of potential tax implications. Such features included mobility, data reliance, network effects, spread of multisided business models and a tendency towards monopoly/oligopoly and volatility. Business models in play included several kinds of e-commerce, app stores, online advertising, cloud computing, participative networked platforms, high speed trading, and online payment services. The digital economy also accelerated and altered the spread of global value chains, where MNCs could integrate their worldwide operations. These BEPS risks were identified, while the relevant actions of the BEPS project were informed by these findings to ensure that the proposed solutions fully addressed BEPS in the digital economy.

It was accordingly agreed to modify the list of exceptions to the definitions of Permanent Establishment (PE). This was to ensure that each of the exceptions included therein was confined to activities that were otherwise of a 'preparatory or auxiliary' character, while introducing a new anti-fragmentation rule to ensure that it would not be possible to benefit from these exceptions through the fragmentation of business activities among closely related enterprises. The definition of PE was also modified, to address circumstances, in which artificial arrangements relating to the sales of goods and services of one company in a multinational group effectively led to contractual arrangements, where sales could be treated as if they had been made by the company.

Pertaining to the transfer pricing guidance, it had been revised to make it clear that legal ownership alone did not necessarily generate a right to all of the returns that were generated by leveraging intangibles; but that the group companies undertaking important functions, like contributing important assets and controlling economically important risks as determined via the accurate delineation of the actual transaction would be entitled to the appropriate returns. The basis for effective CFC now included definitions of CFC income that would subject income that is typically earned in the digital economy to taxation in the jurisdiction of the ultimate parent company.

It is envisaged that implementation of the above measures, together with other measures, like the minimum standard to address treaty shopping arrangements, best practices in the design of domestic rules on interest and other deductible financial payments, including insertion of the substantial activity requirement in Internet Protocol (IP) regimes, would significantly

460. OECD. 2015. *OECD/G20 Base Erosion and Profit-Sharing Project: Addressing the tax challenges of the digital economy*, Paris: OECD.

address the BEPS issues accentuated by the digital economy, at the levels of market jurisdiction and jurisdiction of the ultimate parent company. This would have the objective of ending the stateless income phenomenon.

Incidentally, the digital economy posed wide tax challenges for policy-makers. These pertained in particular to nexus, data, and characterization for direct tax purposes that would frequently overlap with each other. There were also particular challenges for VAT collection, especially where goods, services, and intangibles were acquired by private consumers from suppliers abroad.

The Task Force on Digital Economy (TFDE) made several key observations.[461] First, it suggested the option to modify the exceptions to PE status to ensure that they were available only for activities that could be preparatory, or auxiliary in nature. This was envisaged to be implemented across the existing tax treaty network in a synchronized and efficient manner via the conclusion of the multilateral instrument that modified bilateral tax treaties under Action 15.

Second, participating economies were recommended to apply the principles of the International VAT/GST Guidelines, and to also consider introducing the collection mechanisms included therein. Third, participating economies could introduce the three options of having a new nexus of a significant economic presence, withholding tax on particular digital transactions, and an equalization levy in their domestic laws, as additional safeguards against BEPS, provided they respected existing treaty obligations, or in their bilateral tax treaties.

Action 2 sought to neutralize the impacts of hybrid mismatch arrangements. It developed model treaty provisions and recommendations pertaining to the formulation of domestic rules to neutralize the effects of hybrid instruments and entities, as exemplified by double non-taxation, double deduction, and long-term deferral.[462]

Action 3 made recommendations to strengthen the rules for the taxation of CFCs.[463]

Action 4 provided a common approach drawn from best practices for preventing base erosion, via the application of interest expense, like via the employment of related-party and third-party debt to realize excessive interest deductions, or to finance the production of exempt or deferred income.[464]

Action 5 revamped the work on harmful tax practices focusing on improving transparency. These included compulsory spontaneous exchange

461. OECD. 2014. 'Introduction to tax challenges of the digital economy', in *Addressing the tax challenges of the digital economy*, Paris: OECD.
462. OECD. 2016. 'OECD releases discussion draft on branch mismatch structures under Action 2 of the BEPS Action Plan', *OECD 22/8/16*.
463. OECD. 2015. *Designing effective controlled foreign company rules, Action 3 – 2015 Final Report*, Paris: OECD.
464. OECD. 2016. *Limiting base erosion involving interest deductions and other financial payments, Action 4 – 2016 update*, Paris: OECD.

on ruling pertaining to preferential regimes, and on the insisting of substantial activities for preferential regimes, like the IP regimes.[465]

Action 6 formulated model treaty provisions and recommendations pertaining to the design of domestic rules to deter treaty abuses.[466]

Action 7 provided changes to the definition of PE. This was to prevent its artificial circumvention by the application of commissionaire structures and similar equivalents.[467]

Actions 8-10 provided transfer pricing guidance to assure that transfer pricing outcomes align with value creation pertaining to intangibles, including hard-to-value kinds, risks and capital, and other high-risk transactions.[468]

Action 11 offered methodologies to gather and analyse data on BEPS, and the actions to address it. Here, it developed recommendations regarding indicators of the scale and economic impact of BEPS and to ensure that instruments were available for monitoring and evaluating the effectiveness and economic impacts of the actions taken to address BEPS on an ongoing basis.[469]

Action 12 provided recommendations regarding the formulation of mandatory disclosure rules for aggressive tax planning schemes, taking into account the administrative costs for tax administrations and business, and tapping on the experiences of the increasing number of economies with such rules.[470]

Action 13 provided revised guidance on transfer pricing documentation, including the template for CbC reporting for enhancing transparency, as well as accounting for compliance costs.[471]

Action 14 offered solutions to address obstacles that prevented nations from solving treaty-related disputes under Mutual Agreement Procedures (MAP) through a minimum standard in this area, including various number of best practices, as well as arbitration as options for willing economies.[472]

Action 15 contained an analysis of the legal issues relating to the development of multilateral instruments to help economies streamline the implementation of the BEPS treaty measures, including the mandate to

465. OECD. 2017. *BEPS Action 5 on harmful tax practices: Transparency framework*, Paris: OECD; OECD. 2015. *Countering harmful tax practices more effectively, taking into account transparency and substance, Action 5 – 2015 Final Report*, Paris: OECD.
466. OECD. 2015. *Preventing the granting of treaty benefits in inappropriate circumstances, Action 6 –2015 Final Report*, Paris: OECD.
467. OECD. 2015. *Preventing the artificial avoidance of permanent establishment status, Action 7 – 2015 Final Report*, Paris: OECD.
468. OECD. 2015. *Aligning transfer pricing outcomes with value creation, Actions 8-10 – 2015 Final Reports*, Paris: OECD.
469. OECD. 2015. *Measuring and monitoring BEPS, Action 11 –2015 Final Report*, Paris: OECD.
470. OECD. 2015. *Mandatory disclosure rules, Action 12 – 2015 Final Report*, Paris: OECD.
471. OECD. 2015. *Transfer pricing document and country-by-country reporting, Action 13 – 2015 Final Report*, Paris: OECD.
472. OECD. 2015. *Making dispute resolution mechanisms more effective, Action 14 – 2015 Final Report*, Paris: OECD; OECD. 2017. *Manual on effective mutual agreement procedures (MEMAP)*, Paris: OECD.

implement the work in 2016.[473] The ad hoc group for completing the work under Action 15 was set up with more than ninety jurisdictions participating.

The BEPS report therefore outlined options to resolve various difficulties, while adopting a holistic approach and accounting for both direct and indirect taxation. BEPS implementation took a step further, when some fifty delegates from fourteen countries and seven organization met in Tbilisi Georgia on 7 April 2017 to participate in the new series of regional meetings. Such meetings were expected to offer the opportunities to provide views and inputs to the Inclusive Framework on BEPS.[474]

A new era in international tax was launched earlier in 30 June-1 July 2016 in Kyoto, Japan with the participation of more than eighty jurisdictions. This was the first time that a wide range of economies representing varying levels of development gathered on equal footing in OECD's Committee on Fiscal Affairs. They came together to inaugurate the new inclusive framework on BEPS implementation.[475] The BEPS Project sought to deliver solutions for governments to close the gaps. Over 100 economies had since been collaborating to implement the BEPS measures and inserting these in existing international rules that had hitherto enabled corporate profits to evaporate, or artificially shifted to low/no tax jurisdictions, when such corporations there had little, or no economic activities.

Revenue losses from BEPS were conservatively estimated at USD 100-240 billion annually, or some 4%-10% of global CIT revenues.[476] The impacts of these on developing countries were of particular concerns, as they usually relied substantially on this for funding their developments. Thus far, since its establishment in 2016, ninety-five jurisdictions[477] have formally joined the new inclusive BEPS framework including the US, UK, Hong Kong (China), Indonesia, Finland, and Germany.

BEPS gatherings had proceeded with standard-settings for various remaining issues, including transfer pricing and interest deductibility, as well as the development of practical guidance to support consistent global implementation of participating economies' commitments to the BEPS package. The focus in particular was on ensuring implementation of the four minimum standards arising from the BEPS initiative. These comprised harmful tax practices, tax treaty abuse, CbC reporting, and dispute resolution mechanisms. These areas would be subject to peer-review process, together with ongoing monitoring of the other elements of the package. International organizations and regional tax entities also participated to ensure economies in particular developing economies were well resourced to deal with BEPS.

As mentioned earlier, state revenue losses, first arose from illegal tax evasion by highly affluent individuals placing their undeclared funds in overseas banks, tax haven

473. OECD. 2015. *Developing a multilateral instrument to modify bilateral tax treaties, Action 15 – 2015 Final Report*, Paris: OECD.
474. OECD. 2017. 'OECD and tax administrations discuss BEPS implementation at regional meeting in Georgia', *OECD 7/4/17*.
475. OECD. 2016. 'First meeting of the new inclusive framework to tackle Base Erosion and Profit Shifting marks a new era in international tax co-operation', *OECD 30/6/16*.
476. OECD. 2017. 'Base erosion and profit shifting'.
477. A. Gurria. 2021. 'Remarks by Angel Gurria, Secretary-General, OECD at 11th Meeting of the Inclusive Framework on BEPS', *OECD Paris 27/1/21*.

companies, trusts, and other structures. Second, they arose from legal tax avoidance by many MNCs and big businesses via aggressively structuring their operations to engage in operations frequently lacking in economic reality. These enabled the MNCs to earn profits that became subjected to zero, or low taxation. While technically legal, the tax avoidance practices were usually inconsistent with the purposes and intentions of the applicable tax laws and tax treaties. There were initiatives launched at national and international levels to deal with tax evasions. The BEPS on the other hand focused on MNC tax avoidance.

Despite the growing attention on BEPS activities, since the OECD got involved, there continued to be some key areas of disagreements among leading tax scholars, practitioners, and policy experts.[478] These had been, as follows:[479]

(i) A uniform definition of profit shifting was still being awaited. The issues were whether the notion included corporate real responses in terms of movement of jobs and investments (something not favoured by the previous Trump administration), or narrowly covered only the MNCs' tax-motivated responses that were strictly financial in nature. This led to the difficulties of deciding which corporate behaviours could be labelled as shifting profits, as tax reasons comprised only a constituent of the underlying rationale in MNC decision-making.

(ii) The capacity and desire to shift profits, as well as the costs and benefits of profit shifting varied among and between MNCs. Not all MNCs have tax haven affiliates, even though this was an attractive cost-effective way to facilitate profit shifting.

(iii) The real extent or magnitude of profit shifting was shown by crude estimates based on anecdotal evidence, and consequently highly unstable. The BEPS project was launched, before more extensive formal analysis such as Action 11 of the BEPS project had been undertaken. In this sense, the BEPS project drew from anecdotal and political convictions, instead of more scientific evidence. Insufficient attention paid to benefit-cost outcomes could lead to increased administrative and regulatory burdens. Recent reviews of empirical estimates of profit shifting suggested that estimates ranged from around 2%-30% of corporate profits being shifted out of high-tax jurisdictions. The wide range supported the uncertainty argument pertaining to the magnitude of profit shifting.[480] However, there would be no big surprises for US MNCs to become more responsive to tax rate differentials between the US and other OECD countries, given the

478. E. Cederwell. 2015. 'Tax Foundation Forum: Making sense of profit shifting', *Tax Foundation 12/5/15*.

479. E. Cederwell. 2016. 'Reconciling the profit-shifting debate', *Tax Notes*, Vol. 50(6): 713-718.

480. K.A. Clausing. 2016. 'The effect of profit shifting on the corporate tax base', *Tax Notes 25/1/16*: 427; M.J. Mazur. 2013. 'Testimony of Assistant Secretary for Tax Policy Mark Mazur before The U.S. Senate Homeland Security and Government Affairs Permanent Subcommittee on Investigations on "The shifting of profits offshore by U.S. multinationals 21/05/13"'.

significant and increasing tax rates between them, as well as other economies.

(iv) The premise that MNCs and governments could geographically pinpoint the source of income is flawed. Both find difficulties in achieving this, because MNCs derived significant level of their incomes from intellectual property (IP). In a global and tightly integrated economy, IP did not really have a clear and explicitly defined home. This has been a growing trend, since the late 1990s, and in recent years, some 75% of the market capitalization of Fortune 500 corporations was accounted for by IP.[481] The ambiguity gave rise to multiple governments laying claims on the right to tax income, while simultaneously asserting profit shifting where their initiatives to tax income failed. On the other hand, the ambiguity facilitated corporate tax planning, as MNCs could select the most economically efficient location for their IP assets.[482]

(v) Irrespective of how widely profit shifting is defined, it undoubtedly impacted decision-making and could lead to the undertaking of economically distortive actions. There could also be significant implications for jobs and product market competitions in domestic markets, comprising both MNCs and domestic businesses.

(vi) The US Government and the US citizens have appeared to gain from profits shifting, as US MNCs pay less tax to foreign governments, implying the US Treasury paid less in tax credits to US MNCs. US MNCs paying less taxes to the US Treasury, together with less taxes paid to foreign governments, would likely contribute to higher corporate valuations. This in turn would lead to higher capital gains tax paid by shareholders over time. Additionally, it has been claimed that corporate tax has the disadvantage of discouraging investments badly needed in the twenty-first century. These could have serious implications for innovations and international competitiveness for MNCs. and in particular US MNCs. This merited the claim that rather than focusing merely on profit shifting, it might be better to align US corporate tax rates with US major trading partners.

Thus, review of research insights on the profit-shifting debate suggested the following major disagreement areas:[483]

- non-uniform definitions of profit shifting;
- significant heterogeneity among MNCs;
- issues and discrepancies pertaining to the direction and magnitude of profit shifting;

481. S. Violaris & A. Iosif. 2015. 'Cyprus coming to the forefront on intellectual property tax planning', *PwC 5/11/15*.
482. E. Cederwell. 2015. 'Tax Foundation Forum: Making sense of profit shifting', *Tax Foundation 12/5/15*.
483. E. Cederwell. 2016. 'Reconciling the profit-shifting debate', *Tax Notes*, Vol. 150 (6): 713-718.

- the argument that value-added could be geographically pinpointed by governments and MNCs is flawed;
- the implications of profit shifting for distortions of real economic activity were not well known;
- the notion of profit shifting being altogether misconceived by lawmakers and the public, and;
- hence the debate could be misdirected.

Public conversations on profit shifting have therefore misrepresented the reality, the effect, as well as the underlying dynamics of profit shifting. This could be attributed to politics, and an incomplete or even sloppy analysis of the economic impacts of profit shifting. Profit shifting, although highly heterogeneous among US MNCs, has supported the US economy in its recovery from the 2007 GFC, and also directly and indirectly generated revenues for the US Treasury. Instead of this, it had been argued then that a much better alternative would be to make US corporate tax rate and treatment of income significantly more competitive than those of major US trading partners, more so other OECD members. This would then lead to profits and corporations returning to the US to induce more human capital to be directed to pursuits more economically productive than tax engineering. The Trump administration did that in 2017,[484] but somehow the desired outcomes appeared to be disrupted by factors not seriously accounted for, such as geopolitical tensions arising from economic isolation policies and importantly incomes of US MNCs shifting to seven major global tax havens in 2017, but flattening in 2018 and 2019.[485]

Allegations of profit shifting spawned the ethical tensions between those MNCs that viewed legitimate minimization of tax obligations as acceptable corporate behaviour, and those other MNCs that took the positions that every business had the responsibility to pay its fair share of taxes as a way of funding governments in locations where the MNCs earned their revenues.[486] Back in 1935, the judiciary had ruled taxpayers were free to arrange their financial affairs to attract less taxes.[487]

Still, subjective tests involving the notions of business purpose and substance over form began making the rounds thereafter. US tax history as such was littered with cases where the government was seen using the judicial concepts against taxpayers who engaged in every kind of transaction conceivable. The subjectivity test meant both wins and losses for the state. There was paltry evidence that these judicial ideas were intended to constrain taxpayers' behaviours to generate the desired impacts.[488]

On the contrary, this instead was argued to be providing a façade of legitimacy for the emergence of many abusive tax structures perceived to be linked to aggressive profit-shifting arrangements that helped US MNCs to stockpile more than USD 2

484. *The Tax Cuts and Jobs Act of 2017.*
485. L. O'Neal. 2021. 'The Trump tax cuts: Promises made, promises kept', *Bloomberg Tax 26/1/21.*
486. D. Narotzki. 2016. 'Corporate social responsibility and taxation: An evolving theory', *Tax Notes 25/1/16*: 455.
487. L. Hand. 1935. Citing *Gregory v. Helvering, 293 U.S. 465 (1935), aff'g 69 F.2d 809 (2d Cir. 1934).*
488. J.M. Kadet & D.L. Koontz. 2016. 'Profit-shifting structures: Making ethical judgments objectively', *Tax Notes*, Vol. 151(13): 1831-1843; J.M. Kadet & D.L. Koontz. 2016. 'Profit-shifting structures: Making ethical judgments objectively, Part 2', *Tax Notes*, Vol. 152(1): 85-95.

trillion, on which no US tax had been paid.[489] Relative to this, global revenue losses arising from profit-shifting activities from underpaid CITs could be around USD 240 billion annually.[490] This triggered growing criticisms whether some MNCs could have stepped beyond some ethical lines when devising and implementing such schemes. This was viewed as a serious affront and challenge to the reasonable collection of taxes in many economies. A case in point involved the Luxembourg leaks,[491] that suggested private tax rulings granting special privileges to hundreds of MNCs.

Here, instead of slowing down, more than 170 new secret tax agreements or sweetheart deals were seen some twelve months subsequent to the leaks.[492] Luxembourg came under intense EC scrutiny thereafter, but so were other EU Members States like the Netherlands, Ireland, and Belgium. The jurisdiction reformed its tax laws in December 2016, ushering in penalties for fraud and making aggravated tax evasion, a criminal offence, in addition to reviewing the way its tax agency works.[493]

Indeed, MNCs positioned themselves as model corporate citizens and role models when funding large numbers of CSR-based or charity-based activities.[494] Left unsaid were profit-shifting activities relying on strained interpretations of the tax laws, unintended benefits from these and tax treaties, inconsistent positions in different economies, hidden concessions from tax havens, and in some situations, ignorance of how the corporations actually ran their businesses. These have been depicted as mere ordinary and benign corporate planning fully compliant with the laws.[495] Questions have arisen over whether these conflicting behaviours implied that the ethics of paying taxes vary considerably with the identity and values of people driving the big corporations. The idea that minimization of tax burdens to the extent legally possible constituted a part of director's fiduciary duty did not appear to be supported by case laws especially in the US.[496] There appeared to be a distinction between right and legal obligation/duty. Others took the view that taxpayers ought to pay their fair share to help fund legitimate governmental and societal needs.[497]

It has been further claimed that the very complexity and overly technical US tax laws might actually provide in some cases the cover for those failing to conscientiously discharge their ethical obligations to employers, stakeholders, and society at large.

489. R. Rubin. 2015. 'U.S. companies are stashing $2.1 trillion overseas to avoid taxes', *Bloomberg Business 4/3/15*.
490. OECD. 2015. *Measuring and monitoring BEPS, Action 11- 2015 Final Report*, Paris: OECD.
491. V. Houlder. 2014. ' Leak reveals scale of corporate tax deals with Luxembourg', *Financial Times 6/11/14*.
492. Eurodad. 2016. *Survival of the richest: Europe's role in supporting an unjust global tax system in 2016*, Brussels: Eurodad.
493. J. Brunsden. 2017. 'LuxLeaks: Luxembourg's response to an international tax scandal', *Financial Times 23/6/17*.
494. B.C. Chaffin, H. Gosnell & B.A. Cosens. 2014. 'A decade of adaptive governance scholarship: synthesis and future directions', *Ecology and Society*, Vol. 19(3): 56-76.
495. C. Arthur. 2013. 'Google Chairman Eric Schmidt defends tax avoidance policies', *The Guardian 22/4/13*.
496. D. Hemel. 2015. 'A "duty" to minimize taxes?', *The University of Chicago Law School Faculty Blog 22/12/15*.
497. J. McCain. 2013. 'Opening statement by Senator John McCain at PSI hearing on JP Morgan Chase Whale Trades'.

Corporate board members and management therefore would need to employ an objective approach to ascertain corporate taxpaying behaviours.[498] This could satisfy themselves and others that all significant tax planning complied with both the spirit and language of the law. This would then enable the MNCs to reclaim the moral high ground in facing queries about their tax structures.

Where these breached ethical tax norms, or the US International Revenue Code (IRC), considerations could be given to change or unwound the structures. Thus, when examinations of MNCs show that all or a portion of a foreign group member's income could be currently taxable as Effectively Connected Income (ECI), but that member failed to submit US tax returns and pay tax, that member could be said to have acted contrary to congressional intent and the law. Many MNCs could, as such, be said to be in this position.[499]

The objective ECI approach could realistically open the path for MNCs to assess their tax risks and achieve good corporate tax citizenship.[500] The ECI approach could be employed, both internally and externally, but regardless of this, outside auditors must independently scrutinized the factual situations for possible ECI for each of their MNC clients to get the data fully accepted and trusted. Further steps could also be taken to simultaneously lift the ethical standards of MNCs and more effectively apply the tax laws to generate in consequence a more level playing field for all taxpayers.[501]

As discussed earlier, MNCs' BEPS activities, as perceived broadly, could include one or more combinations of the following:[502]

(i) Using supply chain models that would divert the greater portion of their profits to a zero or low-tax subsidiary that owned or held the rights to valuable intangibles.
(ii) Transferring of hard-to-value intangible properties, like patents, copyrights, and trademarks between group members via sale, licence, or cost distribution agreement instruments at artificially low prices to allow relatively higher profits from the intangibles to be earned within zero or low-taxed groups members.
(iii) Group activities among group members in different countries with different taxation features could be structured to effect transfer pricing between them to maximize income in low-/no-tax jurisdictions.
(iv) MNCs could structure local sales, product support, warehousing, and other distribution functions through service companies to avoid taxation on sales incomes in the jurisdictions where customers were located.

498. J.M. Kadet & D.L. Koontz. 2016. 'Profit-shifting structures: Making ethical judgments objectively', *Tax Notes*, Vol. 151(13): 1831-1843.
499. R. Philips, M. Gardner, K. Kitson, A. Robins & M. Surka. 2016. 'Offshore shell games 2016: The use of offshore tax havens by Fortune 500 companies', *Citizens for Tax Justice, Institute on Taxation and Economic Policy and U.S. PIRG Education Fund Paper* 4/10/16.
500. *Supra* note [498]. Kadet & Koontz. 2016.
501. J.M. Kadet & D.L. Koontz. 2016. 'Profit-shifting structures: Making ethical judgments objectively, Part 2', *Tax Notes*, Vol. 152(1): 85-95.
502. *Supra* note [498]. Kadet & Koontz. 2016; J.M. Kadet. 2013. 'Worldwide tax reform: Reversing the race to the bottom', *Tax Notes 11/3/10* 23: 1245.

(v) Digital transactions could be structured, such that profits were earned by a group member in a zero/low tax location to avoid any tax in the MNC's home country, or in jurisdictions where other parties would use or access the digital platforms.
(vi) Group members and their transactions could be structured to exploit benefits offered by some jurisdictions that would have the spill over effect of undermining tax bases of other countries.
(vii) Contractual arrangements could be made to structure interest, royalty, management fees, and other intercompany charges with the aim of reducing income in jurisdictions where the activities were conducted.
(viii) MNCs could capitalize subsidiaries to maximize interest-bearing debts and minimize equity capital to achieve significantly more tax-deductible debts than the total debts owed by the group to third-party creditors and lenders.
(ix) Hybrid entities and instruments could be used to achieve tax savings by exploiting multiple jurisdictions by varying characterizations of particular entities, transactions, or items of income.
(x) MNCs could structure transactions indirectly via one or more intermediary jurisdictions to realize lower withholding taxes available under tax treaties for some outbound payments.

The apparent success of MNCs in using any, or combinations of the above measures, in reducing effective tax rates irrespective of where the groups were headquartered has enhanced pressures on governments around the world to respond appropriately. Meantime, the OECD BEPS project undertaken since 2013 noted the high significance of the financial leakages, with global CIT revenue losses of between 4-10% of global CIT, or some USD 100-240 billion annually. This was the main reason why the G20 endorsed and gave support to the OECD BEPS project.

A very interesting case in connection with the OECD BEPS project pertained to the investigations by the EU Commission (EC) into Ireland's tax ruling practices pertaining to the prohibited subsidy of Apple. This came to be known as fiscal state aid and was in contravention of EU law. The outcome of this investigation could go beyond Europe. This was an investigation into whether Ireland gave Apple unfair benefits, and what governments could do to stop the strategic employment of national tax systems to lure international trade and investments. The legal basis for the EC's ruling was provided by Article 107.1 of the Treaty on the Functioning of the EU.[503] This provision prohibited state aid granted by a Member State or through state resources in any form that distorted or threatened to distort competition by favouring certain undertakings.

The EC in this case ruled that by effectively employing a corporate tax law of less than 2%, instead of 12.5% to Irish Sub's income, Ireland violated Article 107.1 by providing state aid to Apple giving thereby the company significant advantage over businesses subject to the regular 12.5% Irish rate. For violation of this provision, offending member governments could be required to recover ten years' equivalent of

503. J.C. Fleming Jr. 2017. 'The EU Apple case: Who has a dog in the fight', *Tax Notes*, Vol. 154(2017): 251-256.

illegal state aid, plus interest. The EC calculated that the tax portion of the recovery could be around EUR 13 billion. Ireland and Apple have appealed to the EU judiciary against the EC ruling.[504]

No matter the eventual circumstances, Apple faced at the time a potential 35% tax that could either be paid entirely to the US, or pay 12.5% to Ireland and 22.5% to the US.[505] It was likely that Apple would find it more beneficial to defer tax until income was repatriated to the US, instead of paying tax currently to Ireland. Hence, Apple's appeal was likely about the resulting loss of the opportunity to defer 12.5% of tax, or to avoid that amount of tax to the extent that there would be no income repatriation to the US. This option could be available to Apple because of the deferral feature of the US international income tax regime.[506] Fast forward to 2021, the EC has filed an appeal with the Official Journal of the EU over the General Court's decision to annul a decision to impose EUR 13 billion (USD 14.9 billion) in Irish back taxes against Apple Inc.[507]

§6.09 ADVANCED TAX AGREEMENTS

The EC's case against Ireland upped the stakes for European tax planning by MNCs. Doubts have arisen as to whether privately arranged deals between EU Member States and multinationals could survive scrutiny by EU authorities. The case sent a clear message about the disclosure ramifications for even well-designed fully documented tax structures upon which MNCs based their earnings reports. This could pose risk of shareholder litigations. Others on the radar then included Amazon in Luxembourg and Starbucks in the Netherlands.[508]

The ICIJ published in November 2014 hundreds of privately negotiated ATAs granted by tax authorities in Luxembourg.[509] This came to be known as the '*LuxLeaks*'. They contained secret tax agreements extending tax-reliefs for more than 350 companies across the world from 2003 to 2011 and supported evidence that these were indeed approved by Luxembourg authorities.[510]

The revelations meant that many brand-name corporations and 340 other international companies appeared to secure tax deals from the Luxembourg authorities thereby enabling them to slash their global tax obligations, while maintaining little presence in the tiny European jurisdiction.[511] Such tax savings were said to be achieved by creating complicated accounting and legal structures that moved profits to low-tax Luxembourg from higher-tax economies where they were headquartered, or undertook lot of businesses.

504. S. Schechner. 2016. 'Apple, EU trade jabs in tax case', *The Wall Street Journal 20/12/16*, B1.
505. *Supra* note [503]. Fleming Jr. 2017.
506. *Supra* note [503]. Fleming Jr. 2017.
507. P. Magdirila. 2021. 'EC appeals against ruling in Apple's Irish tax case', *S&P Global 2/2/21*.
508. A. Christians. 2015. 'Friends with tax benefits: Apple's cautionary tale', *Tax Notes International*, Vol. 78(11): 1031-1034.
509. ICIJ. 2014. 'Luxembourg leaks: Global companies' secrets exposed', *ICIJ 5/11/14*.
510. M.C. Galizia, M. Cabra, M. Williams, E. Diza-Struck & H.B. Rudder. 2014. 'Explore the documents: Luxembourg leaks database', *ICIJ 9/12/14*.
511. *Supra* note [510]. Galizia et al. 2014.

The leaked documents further suggested these companies enjoyed tax rates of less than 1% on the profits they shuffled into Luxembourg. It has been further claimed that the private deals though legal in Luxembourg could be subject to legal challenge outside the country, where such deals could be interpreted as improper. Those associated with the structuring of such schemes have, however, counterclaimed that such structures were generally within applicable local, European, and international tax laws and agreements, and also guided by best practice global tax code of conduct.

The revelations, nevertheless, generated a major uproar.[512] The EU and Luxembourg became embroiled in serious negotiations over the latter's reluctance to provide a larger set of documents relating to its tax rulings. MNCs were criticized for channelling hundreds of billions of dollars via Luxembourg to achieve large-scale tax savings.[513] This outcome was argued to be facilitated by Luxembourg's tax authorities who were alleged to have engaged in rubber-stamping tax avoidance on an industrial scale.[514] The alleged facilitated tax rulings in Luxembourg thus helped to enable MNCs avoid high-tax obligations in jurisdictions where they engaged in real economic activities, and instead enjoyed paying less taxes to Luxembourg, where they undertake little or no activity.

While public attention focused on the substance of the Luxembourg ATAs, the process as to how these ATAs were issued deserved some attention too. This was because the process exposed in the *LuxLeaks* did not appear to meet the standards generally associated with those of developed democracies. Evidence suggested that the jurisdiction issued ATAs without seriously reviewing taxpayers' submissions, receiving, or asking necessary information. The jurisdiction appeared to have ignored a previous EC decision, as well as its own administrative guidance. Thus, there were no insights of the legal and institutional environment that facilitated an almost completely unchecked administrative process. There was no information as to who instituted the process, who directed it, the reasons for doing this, and importantly the legal basis. While Luxembourg continued to insist that the process complied with the law, mounting evidence suggested the contrary.[515]

The *LuxLeaks* induced several official investigations. A Special Committee on Tax Rulings and Other Measures Similar in Nature or Effect otherwise known as 'TAXE I' was set up in the EP to investigate private tax ruling practices by all EU Member States. Consequently, TAXE I[516] and TAXE II[517] were respectively published in November 2015 and June 2016. Tax rulings constituted the umbrella term for all types of tax

512. S. Bowers. 2019. 'Why has the European Commission not investigated Lux Leaks tax deals?', *ICIJ 12/2/19*.
513. J. Kanter. 2014. 'Hundreds of companies seen cutting tax bills by sending money through Luxembourg', *The New York Times* 5/11/14.
514. S. Bowers. 2014. 'Luxembourg tax files: How tiny state rubber-stamped tax avoidance on an industrial scale', *The Guardian 5/11/14*.
515. O. Marian. 2016. 'Is something rotten in the Grand Duchy of Luxembourg?', *Tax Notes International 17/10/16*: 281-293.
516. E.V. De Velde. 2015. 'Tax rulings in the EU member states: Study for the ECON Committee', *IP/A/ECON/2015-08 PE 563.447* November 2015.

arrangements. Tax rulings have been made around the world and have progressed as a result of changing approaches within tax agencies as they sought higher extent of tax compliance and economic investments and also as outcomes of taxpayers' pursuits of legal certainty.

They were also instruments moving towards more reciprocal relationships between taxpayers and tax authorities. They were usually made in accordance with OECD, EU and national legal and policy boundaries. There were international limitations on tax rulings, as the OECD would ask for more transparency and equal treatment of all taxpayers through publications of the conditions for granting, refusing, and revoking tax decisions.[518] The EU too has asked for more transparency of tax rulings, as reflected by its Proposal for a Council Directive amending Directive 2011/16/EU.

The TAXE II report articulated concerns that thirteen Member States did not have proper rules to counter aggressive tax planning based on tax-free flow through of dividends, thirteen Member States did not apply any beneficial owner tests, when accepting claims for reduction of or exemptions from withholding tax, fourteen Member States did not have controlled company rules to prevent aggressive tax planning, and twenty-five others had no rules to counter the mismatching tax qualification of a local company by another state. Significantly, no Member States had called for a ban on aggressive tax structures. Very interestingly, TAXE II highlighted that with regard to uncooperative jurisdictions, including overseas territories, the only concrete measures taken by the EC had been the External Strategy for Effective Taxation.

It was further noted that the criteria for listing of uncooperative jurisdictions by the OECD have not proved efficient in resolving this issue, or in serving as a deterrent, and that there were still third countries protecting illegally obtained assets making recovery by the EU authorities almost impossible. As such, the EP called for a concrete EU regulatory framework for sanctions against the blacklisted uncooperative jurisdictions, including the possibility of reviewing and in the last resort suspending free trade agreements, suspending double taxation agreements, or prohibiting access to EU funds.

It further stressed that the purpose of sanctions was to stimulate changes in the legislation of the jurisdictions in question. This incorporated the need for these sanctions to apply to companies, banks, accountancy and law firms, and tax advisors proven to have been associated with illegal, harmful, or wrongful activities with those jurisdictions. Those others proven to have facilitated illegal, harmful, or wrongful corporate tax arrangements involving legal vehicles in those jurisdictions were also included.

Tax rulings could occur in the form of an advance tax ruling, an advance pricing arrangement, or any other tax arrangements of formal or informal basis. Advanced tax rulings were statements provided by tax authorities pertaining to the tax treatment of

---

517. European Parliament. 2016. 'Tax rulings and other measures similar in nature or effect (TAXE 2): EP resolution of 6 July on tax rulings and other measures similar in nature or effect (2016)/2038 (INI)', *P8 _TA (2016))0310, EP 2014-2019*, 6/7/16.
518. *Supra* note [516]. De Velde. 2015.

taxpayers with respect to their future transactions and on which they were entitled to rely on. Advance pricing agreements were ascertained in accordance with the law and OECD Guidelines in advance, as to whether transfer prices between two related parties within a group were at arms' lengths, compared to the transfer price with unrelated parties.

Many tax arrangements in practice are done in the absence of any framework between taxpayers and local tax inspectors before specific transactions taking place, or before the filing of tax returns; after a tax mediation process, in court, within a horizontal monitoring process, or within the context of a tax audit. The EC's intention appeared to include the administrative practice of advance tax rulings, advance pricing arrangements, and all other advance tax arrangements even within the context of a tax audit. Important questions arose as to whether Member States would qualify their country-specific statements, opinions, decisions, clearances and so on as tax rulings in the context of the EC proposal on AEI.

At the time of the *LuxLeaks*, the EC was already investigating whether several tax rulings granted by EU Member States fell within EU's forbidden state aid. The *LuxLeaks* extended the scope of the investigation to include tax ruling practices of all EU Member States.[519] Several decisions characterizing ATAs by Luxembourg, the Netherlands, Ireland, and Belgium's illegal state aid came about as result of these investigations. The UK Parliament, for instance, launched an investigation into the role of accountancy firms in marketing the Luxembourg schemes.[520]

The four large global accounting firms, namely PwC, Deloitte, E&Y, and KPMG achieved USD 24.7 billion in global revenue from tax practice 2011-2012, with their UK operations accounting for some 22% of this and employing some 9,000 people.[521] While these four firms maintained that they did not provide advice that would help tax evasion, they conceded that some schemes on which they advised were ruled against by tribunals and would be unlawful to run again. They recognized also that the distinction between tax planning and tax avoidance using law to gain advantage never intended by legislations had been difficult to define and persisted as a grey area. Nevertheless, they have developed guiding principles or codes of conduct to define what advice could be acceptable, especially those supportable in law. They would also explain fully to clients the tax, reputational, and commercial risks of suggested options.

The 2015 House of Commons report recommended five courses of actions.[522] First, it concluded that the UK tax system was too complex and therefore required a more radical simplified approach. Second, there appeared to be no clarity over where firms could draw the line between acceptable tax planning and aggressive tax avoidance. As such, the UK Treasury has been urged to introduce a code of conduct for tax advisors setting out what it would consider as acceptable in terms of tax planning. Compliance with the code should decide whether or not these firms could access both

519. European Commission (EC). 2014. 'State aid: Commission extends information enquiry on tax ruling practice to all Member States', *EC Release IP/14/2742* 17/12/14.
520. House of Commons (HC). 2015. 'Tax Avoidance: The role of large accountancy firms', *House of Commons Committee of Public Accounts 44th Report of Session 2012-13* 28/1/15.
521. *Supra* note [520]. HC. 2015.
522. *Supra* note [520]. HC. 2015.

government and the wider public sector work. Third, it would be considered inappropriate for individuals from firms to advise the Treasury on tax law and then devised ways to circumvent it. As such, the proposed code of conduct alluded to earlier should set out how conflicts of interest should be managed when firms engaged in advising the government on the formulation of tax laws, but subsequently provided tax advice to clients in related areas.

Fourth, as tax laws could come quickly out of date and needed regular updating or revising, the UK has been urged to take the lead in demanding urgent reforms of international tax laws. Fifth, enhanced transparency over companies' tax affairs would enhance the pressure on MNCs to pay a fair share of tax in the jurisdictions where they operated. As such, the UK has been urged to push for an international commitment to improve transparency, including developing specific proposals to improve the quality and credibility of public information about companies' tax affairs.

As for Luxembourg, it strongly defended its administrative tax ruling practices as legal from both domestic and EU perspectives. It further claimed that the legality of its practices had been uncontested, but this had since been disputed.[523] There have been no suggestions that Luxembourg engages in illegal behaviour, but rather serious questions arose as to the legality of the process involved. There were, first, the suggestions that there could be possible violations of EU law in terms of state aid in general, and the failures to spontaneously exchange information.

Further, the process of granting ATAs did not commensurate with the standards of a developed democracy, like Luxembourg. This was because Luxembourg's standard of review is likely to have not been adhered to. These included[524] indications suggesting that submissions were approved with little or no review, approval of submissions lacking in relevant information, and self-contradicting rulings.[525] These were serious questions needing answers, but thus far the jurisdiction appeared unwilling to provide comprehensive answers. The only possible way forward would be through an international investigative fact-finding committee with real investigatory powers, but Luxembourg for some reasons fell below EU's regulatory radar.[526]

Instead, Luxembourg focused on the prosecutions of the *LuxLeaks* whistle-blowers, namely, Antoine Deltour and Raphael Halet both of whom were convicted by the Luxembourg court in June 2016 with relatively short deferred sentences. The Court of Appeal upheld the first verdict, but with reduced sentences. This was greeted with disapprovals by CSOs, as they argue that whistle-blowers who exposed tax dodging should be praised and not punished, as they acted in the public interest in exposing tax cheats who deprived countries across Europe and globally of millions in tax revenue that were badly needed to shore up state coffers. Additionally, they called upon governments to provide protections for whistle-blowers and not to rely on them to police the tax systems, while simultaneously appealing to governments to insist that all

523. O. Marian. 2017. 'The state administration of international tax avoidance', *Harvard Business Law Review*, Vol. 7(1): 1-65.
524. M. Pruce. 2017. 'LuxLeaks whistleblowers verdict-Oxfam reaction', *Oxfam 15/3/17*.
525. *Supra* note [523]. Marian. 2017.
526. N. Fowler. 2019. 'Why has the European Commission not investigated #LuxLeaks tax deals?', *Tax Justice Network 13/2/19*.

MNCs publish financial information for every jurisdiction they operated in, so as to indicate whether they could be paying their fair share of taxes.

Finally, after years of hearings the two mentioned whistle-blowers were finally acquitted. The CSOs have called for further investigations on the *LuxLeaks* cases, and some thoughtful response in disciplining global auditors implicated, considering that the EU Competition Commissioner is only empowered to investigate Member States, but not companies.[527] Pressures from this and earlier scrutiny by the EC, including several investigations on possible state-aid foul practices finally culminated in meaningful reforms in Luxembourg tax laws. These though were targeted initiatives, as what would be lacking is the attempt to systematically resolve the issue of arbitrage manufacturing, and the generation of global standards in controlling the issuance of private tax rulings.[528]

Though the EC is not in charge of setting global tax standards, it has played a useful supporting role in OECD's tax policy work. The EC has been continuing with this in the Apple case. At the very least, the EC's contribution at the very minimum could lead to more dialogues on whether using the tax system to deliver subsidy is consistent with a level playing field doctrine for international trade and investments. The impact of this and other cases on the tax practices of MNCs certainly went beyond the borders of the EU.[529]

In any case, on 30 August 2016, the EC ruled that because Irish Sub's non-Irish headquarters did less to generate Irish's Sub income than did Irish Sub's Irish operations, the income allocation endorsed by the Irish tax rulings deviated from a market-based outcome in line with the arm's length principle. As such, the EC concluded that Ireland's favourable treatment of Apple violated EU law and that more than USD 100 billion of income would have to be reallocated from Irish Sub's non-Irish headquarters to Ireland.[530] This meant that Ireland needed to collect about EUR 13 billion of tax from the MNC.

On the state aid phenomenon, there were conditional elements attached to it.[531] There must be an advantage, granted by a Member State to an undertaking, and that the advantage must be granted selectively, and it must distort trade or competition in the internal markets. Hence, under existing EU law, tax subsidies easily satisfied all these elements, other than the advantage and selectivity attributes that became main issues in the Apple appeals.[532] The question appeared to rest on whether the Irish rulings properly allocated profits to the Irish branches of Apple's Irish-incorporated subsidiaries. Where Ireland approved tax treatments in its rulings that were better than what were available under the reference baseline, Ireland could then be said to confer

527. *Supra* note [526]. Fowler. 2019.
528. *Supra* note [523]. Marian. 2017.
529. A. Christians. 2015. 'Friends with tax benefits: Apple's cautionary tale', *Tax Notes International*, Vol. 78(11): 1031-1034.
530. EC. 2016. 'State aid: Ireland gave illegal tax benefits to Apple worth up to 13 billion euros', *EC Press Release 30/8/16*; C.F. Fleming Jr. 2017. 'The Apple case: Who has a dog in the fight', *Tax Notes 9/1/17*: 251.
531. R. Mason. 2017. 'Tax rulings on state aid', *Tax Notes 23/1/17*: 451.
532. J. Fioretti. 2017. 'Apple appeals against EU tax ruling, Brussels says no cause for low tax bill', *Reuters 19/12/16*.

an advantage to Apple. The test for selectivity fluctuated, depending on whether the contested measure represented an individual aid targeted to only one enterprise, or general aid targeted more generally.

In brief, as a matter of domestic law, Apple's tax plan appeared to comply with the applicable rules. The MNC shifted income out of the European consumer states into Ireland without the payment of source taxes or withholding tax largely due to massive deductible intercompany royalty payments that escaped withholding tax provided by the EU Interest and Royalty Directive[533] (Mason, 2017a). It then shifts the income out of Ireland to nowhere using the soon-defunct Irish tax-residence rules. None of this gets retrieved by Subpart F because of the check-the-box and look-through rules. The tax in the US gets deferred, but Apple picks the tax due date by keeping profits offshore. None of these procedures violates domestic law, not in the consumer states, not in Ireland and not in the US.

In response, the EC sought to undo part of the above outcome pertaining to the shifting of profit from Ireland to nowhere, by applying state aid rules. The latter had been employed to erode the Irish ruling that approved allocation of only a small portion of the Apple group's foreign profits to the Irish branches. In insisting that more profits have be allocated to the Irish branches, the EC shifted income from nowhere to Ireland. In response, Ireland and Apple contended with justifications, that the income at the heart of the controversy substantively was not Irish.

They argued that the substance was in Cupertino USA, where the engineers were located; in France, Germany, and Italy where the iPhone consumers were located; and in China where the factories were located. This suggested that in aggregate, the EC's allocation of Apple Sales International (ASI) to its Irish branches generated a result in conflict with economic substance. The EC's decision that half the profits of the Apple group belong to Ireland was argued to be hardly logical. It concluded this way, because it commenced with the formal result of Apple's careful tax planning, namely the enormous booked profit in ASI. The EC concluded that this profit could not be properly allocated to ASI's head office, as it existed solely on papers, and that the profit could be allocated only to ASI's Irish branch, because the Irish branch was the only part of the ASI with substance.[534]

Under pressure from US officials and unhappy over this result, the EC suggested various ways to get the income out of Ireland and into states where there was substance.[535] The EC argued that income could then be relocated to the US via retroactive amendments to ASI's cost-sharing agreements with Apple, while income could be reallocated to the European consumer states based on information disclosed in the EC's investigation that ASI had taxable PEs in their territory. The uncertainty of this result reflected both the malleability of international tax rules and the fundamental uncertainty about the correct application of EU's prohibition on state aid.[536]

533. R. Mason. 2017. 'Special report on state aid-Part 3: Apple', *Tax Notes*, Vol. 154(2017): 735-751.
534. *Supra* note [533]. Mason. 2017.
535. *Supra* note [533]. Mason. 2017.
536. *Supra* note [533]. Mason. 2017.

The EC's decision was seen in some quarters as legally contentious. Put differently, there was no EU income tax legislation imposing any restrictions on the multinational structure that led to profits from the sales of Apple products outside the Americas being allocated away from Irish Sub.[537] Possible tax law provisions and revisions would have to come from the national laws of Member States. Apple consistently maintained that its multinational structure fully complied with those laws, and these had not been seriously challenged over some time.[538]

Those above cases and others aside, BEPS behaviour is argued to be motivated by systemic issues and various particular developments over the past few decades. These could arise from the following:[539]

(i) Under worldwide tax systems and hybrid territorial tax systems, profits achieved within specified legal entities established outside a MNC's home jurisdiction would either not be currently taxed or would never be taxed by that home jurisdiction.
(ii) In general, courts and tax agencies around the world accept corporations and other entities as separate and independent legal persons, no matter where they were established, or who owned them.
(iii) Use of tax-motivated intragroup structuring with no economic significance.
(iv) In general, tax agencies and courts internationally accepted intercompany related-party contracts that have been structured mainly to realize profit-shifting and other taxation goals, as long as they showed some degree of commercial reasonableness. These were legally enforceable agreements respected within the MNC community.
(v) Resourced-constrained tax agencies found it hard to audit the subjective arm's length standard used in transfer pricing.
(vi) In general, international accounting standards have not been strict on profit-shifting activities that lowered financial statement effective tax rates and increased reported earnings. This was pursued by MNCs that were usually listed on stock exchanges around the world to induce higher share prices.
(vii) As most MNC compensation plans were related to higher share prices, MNC management became attracted to the strategic option of minimization of effective tax rates that BEPS activities could enable.

The above systemic factors would unlikely change in the short term, and hence, the continued running of BEPS activities. These aside, various developments over the last few decades had also helped to sustain BEPS activities. These included the proliferations of hybrid territorial tax systems, competitive reduction in corporate taxes

537. J.C. Fleming Jr. 2017. 'The EU Apple case: Who has a dog in the fight', *Tax Notes*, Vol. 154(2017): 251-256.
538. *Supra* note [537]. Fleming Jr. 2017.
539. J.M. Kadet. 2013. 'Worldwide tax reform: Reversing the race to the bottom', *Tax Notes 11/3/10* 23: 1245.

across the world when fighting for FDIs, elimination of restrictions on cash movements, developments of supply chains, and other new business models, together with advances in ICT, and the peddling of tax structures and techniques by large professional support service firms.[540] Also, US repatriation holidays that strongly encouraged US MNCs to shift profits even more aggressively in the hope that this holiday would be repeated.

BEPS behaviours could be reduced in two ways.[541]The first would involve identifying taxpayers employing BEPS structures and reversing their beneficial tax effects via the imposition of additional taxes. The effectiveness of this would second depend on the capacity to identify such BEPS structures, how to prioritize on which to probe deeper, and the ability of those in charge to ask the right questions.

Most economies would be likely to have sufficient capacity and skills to examine a small percentage of those MNCs that appeared to have high BEPS risk. Concerns are raised as to whether the tax authorities could be overwhelmed by too much information, especially when CbC reports of several MNC groups became accessible. This should no longer pose a major problem, as the PP have shown how more affordable big data analysis technology could be brought to use. Second, there have been concerns over whether the new OECD BEPS rules could sufficiently scare the management of MNCs into changing their attitude towards the risk of BEPS activities.

Two other approaches could change the environment and significantly reduce the strong motivations to continue with BEPS activities.[542] These are the unitary/formulary and the full-inclusion/worldwide consolidation taxation systems. The unitary approach would treat the MNCs as one centrally managed taxpayer. This approach involved a lengthy process and required considerable efforts to gain consensus of all participating countries and their agreements pertaining to methods of calculating and apportioning taxable income. It was rejected by the OECD in 2013, as it was felt that rather than seeking to replace the current transfer pricing system, the better option was to directly address the flaws in the existing system.

The full inclusion approach also ignored by the OECD involved the home jurisdictions of MNCs imposing the home-country tax at the home-country tax rate on the combined incomes of all group members, irrespective of the place of incorporation, or the location of tax residency. Still, both methods would significantly reduce or eliminate BEPS motivation, because the entire income of an MNC's income, no matter where earned would be subjected to tax, with the level of tax being unaffected by any intragroup contractual or structural arrangements.[543]

In excluding the two above suggestions, the OECD has been criticized for having limited the scope of the BEPS project. OECD officials claimed that the BEPS project would spell the end of double non-taxation and a change of paradigm that would help make tax planning marginal, rather than a core constituent of business models. In

540. J.M. Kadet & D.L. Koontz. 2016. 'Profit-shifting structures: Making ethical judgments objectively', *Tax Notes*, Vol. 151(13): 1831-1843; 'Part II', *Tax Notes*, Vol. 152(1): 85-95.
541. *Supra* note [540]. Kadet & Koontz. 2016.
542. *Supra* note [540]. Kadet & Koontz. 2016.
543. J.M. Kadet. 2013. 'Worldwide tax reform: Reversing the race to the bottom', *Tax Notes 11/3/10* 23: 1245.

reality, the project was argued to be flawed, as it was almost impossible to achieve consensus in favour of the radical overhaul required. The end result was argued to be a patch-up job offering improvements in particular areas, but failing to deal effectively with the core problems.[544] This was said to be further aggravated by OECD's stance on the flawed independent entity principle that was underpinned by the fictitious assumption that the various parent and subsidiary companies in a corporate group operated like separate legal persons transacting with each other at arm's length.

Participating countries in the BEPS project have been said to enjoy varying decision-making weights. This complicated matters, because of varying national interests and priorities. It is thus claimed that some BEPS measures could contradict the overall objective of eliminating BEPS structuring and instead encouraging it in the future. These included the continuation of harmful tax practices like patent boxes, limited changes to PE definition, lack of agreements on strong CFC rules, and the seemingly overly restrictive approach to distributing the new CbC reports.[545] The OECD has also prohibited any discussions that might change current source and residence taxation concepts in the OECD model treaty. This restriction severely limited any ability to consider how to engage the PE concept in the digital era.

OECD claimed that it has gone from enabler to quasi-enforcer and putative saviour of the international consensus with the GFC financial meltdown and Lichtenstein disclosures as catalysts. It has though failed to mention the contributions of NGOs and citizens' protests.[546] The BEPS project from conceptualization to implementation has been marked by the following features:[547]

(i) The various BEPS final reports would be guidelines for future actions and would not constitute authoritative documents that could be enforced by any government on any taxpayers.

(ii) The various minimum standards and recommendations in the reports would require implementation. For some, it meant local enactments via local legislations and administrative practices. For others, it could imply a successful conclusion of the multilateral agreements and ratification of all portions of those agreements by jurisdictions around the world. Only in this way, could the various changes to the OECD model treaty and commentary arising from the BEPS project become effective for the huge numbers of existing tax treaties. There would likely to be pushbacks and lobbying by MNCs in many jurisdictions, especially when legislations were required for implementation. To be noted is the likely nullification of much of Action 13's effect in the US, where lobbying had already begun to ensure that the US Treasury only provided CbC reports to a country only if US MNCs or subsidiaries were not required to provide master file information to that foreign country.

544. The Economist. 2015. 'New rules, same old paradigm: A plan to curb multinational's tax avoidance is an opportunity missed', *The Economist 10/10/15.*

545. *Supra* note [540]. Kadet & Koontz. 2016.

546. L.A. Sheppard. 2015. 'OECD head takes a BEPS victory lap', *Tax Notes 19/10/15*: 340.

547. *Supra* note [540]. Kadet & Koontz. 2016.

(iii) The OECD, its members, and non-member countries were expected to continue examining specific defined areas and to monitor other areas for further changes. Some peer-to-peer review monitoring of the manners in which particular countries implemented BEPS deterrents would be undertaken.

(iv) Considerable resources would be needed to implement BEPS at all levels. It remained to be seen, whether the BEPS project could be sustained. This could be clearly gauged when the participating countries showed efforts and commitments to develop the Action 15 multilateral agreement.

(v) The EC and the EP have been active in reviewing BEPS structures in light of the European State Aid rules. Several European internal approaches mooted to combat tax avoidance have suggested consideration of a common consolidated corporate tax base. This would represent an important area for future development.

(vi) Time would tell whether non-members, and in particular, the developing economies would become full participants, or develop their own particular solutions, because of perceived inadequate attention to their plights.

(vii) The UK and Australia could be examples of countries that have taken unilateral actions against some forms of BEPS behaviour to protect their tax base. It remained to be seen, whether more countries would follow suit, and if such would be the case, then confidence on the BEPS project could be shaken.

(viii) Some MNCs could continue to push the envelope, despite the presence of the BEPS project, but others, like Amazon, has been reported to be mooting taxable presence in various countries of sales.

It might appear that when the OECD/G20 opted to address all these fifteen issues simultaneously, it was being far too ambitious, as previously each respective item has proven so difficult to deal with. However, where the reason for such difficulties have been their linkages, addressing them as part of a comprehensive overhaul would make sense, and could also determine the ultimate success of the BEPS project.

From this position, the BEPS would present an opportunity to reform particular doctrines in the international tax regime, while simultaneously rethinking the fundamental policies underpinning the regime itself.[548] There were concerns that interest group politics could impact the progress of BEPS implementation. However, the various milestones reached by the BEPS project appeared to suggest that this matter had not significantly impacted its progress. Nevertheless, a suggestion has been made for a new intellectual framework for the international tax regimes for BEPS to be a success. To integrate the disparate goals of BEPS into a single coherent framework, four principles have been proposed to underpin the post-BEPS regime. These were as follows:[549]

548. A.H. Rosenzweig. 2014. 'News analysis: Building a Framework for a post-BEPS world', *Tax Notes International*, Vol. 74(12): 1077-1083.

549. *Supra* note [548]. Rosenzweig. 2014.

(1) The need to distinguish clearly between enforcements and divisions of tax base.
(2) The need to incorporate both distortions to taxpayer behaviour and the provision of public goods in tax efficiency analysis.
(3) The need to understand the balance between designing ideal rules and maximizing the number of participants.
(4) The need to build an institution to incorporate the interests of competing state actors.

The above four principles could merit reflections by the OECD together with all participating economies. Meanwhile, the BEPS project has been said to be different from any previous multilateral efforts on international taxation. It was unique and historic, as it was generated, promoted, received, and largely applauded at the Prime Minister or Head of State levels of the G20.[550] This had also never happened to an OECD international tax project. The implications of the OECD/G20 initiative to curb MNC's ability to avoid corporate tax and its association with Brexit and US Presidential races would need to be stressed. Tax avoidance by MNCs has come to be perceived by the public in the US and throughout Europe as a prime symptom of the unfairness of the current global and technologically sophisticated economy. It could be viewed as an important barometer of a global economy gone awry.

Middle-income Americans and Europeans (in particular the British) have been increasingly intolerant over the various allegations concerning profits shifting by global MNCs, as they struggled to face the impact of austerity measures in much of Europe and stagnating income in the rural hinterlands of the US. Political leaders and legislators in the US and the UK and most parts of Europe have conveniently found it easier to flow along with the tide, rather than striving harder to find solutions. Of implications, for those in Asia and elsewhere, had been the widely held perceptions of people in the US and Europe that their jobs and incomes had being outsourced to Asia without sufficient compensatory responses. They increasingly supported measures to put up barriers against cheap labour from abroad. International tax policy would now need to revolve around these contextual political whirlwinds.

When making international tax policy, individual nations would have to take note of what other economies could be doing and anticipate how they might react to changes. Declines in corporate taxes around the world and the mushrooming of patent boxes, or special tax regimes for intellectual property revenues, would suggest that nations have been competing more, than cooperating. The BEPS initiative could reduce that trend with regard to information production and sharing, but not with respect to the fundamental rules governing international income taxation.[551] With new facts and new laws unfolding, businesses and governments choices to be made while important are often temporarily done. Still, even with the turmoil in global economics and

550. M.J. Graetz. 2016. 'Follow the money: Essays on international taxation-Introduction', *Columbia Law & Economics Working Paper No. 538 (2016).*
551. *Supra* note [550]. Graetz. 2016.

politics, the fundamental notions of international taxation employed more than a century ago retained their relevance.

Indeed, today's twenty-first century high-tech integrated global economy has been still served by a twentieth century international tax system.[552] The BEPS project hardly challenged any of those key concepts. These modernizing initiatives instead attracted controversies. There were clashes of perspectives. As European economies strategized for the strengthening of their source-based taxation, the US administration was targeting to strengthening the residence-based taxation of US multinationals. Back then in the first half of the twentieth century that generated the key concepts, the global economy was a much simpler place in the absence of innovative financial instruments, and so on.

Back then, corporate residence was generally fixed, while the sources of income were also usually clear. Importantly, nations were, either capital exporters, like the US and the UK, or capital importers like France, Italy, and Spain, with clear interests. The global incomes of multinationals of today have undermined the notion of sources. Allocation of this income among nations, entities, and so on were inevitably contested and controversial. Virtually every economy today could be both importers and exporters of capital thereby seriously complicating their interests. Still despite such changes, the 1920 rules remained in play.

The US at the beginning of the 1960s ushered in the CFC rules that came to spread throughout the OECD.[553] This importantly signalled in the US a strong direction towards the taxation of business income, based on residence, reversing the previous US notion that had regarded source-based taxation, as superior at least for business income. Then somewhere in the late 1980s, economies across the world began widening their income tax bases and lowering rates.

This led to international competition and sophisticated tax planning by MNCs. Simultaneously, the technology revolution enabled information, money, products and services to be easily moved around the world. Financial innovations and engineering broke down the lines between debt and equity. The new aggressiveness in tax minimization by large businesses lowered transportation costs phenomenally to help spawn the emergence of important new economies in Eastern Europe and Asia.[554]

§6.10 SPECIAL PURPOSE ACQUISITION COMPANIES

Huge growth and globalization of global portfolio investment programmes followed. Large business entities became able to amass large pools of capital without having to go through the public capital markets via endowment funds, private equity, sovereign wealth funds, and these days, via the controversial use of SPACs. SPACs would be essentially shell companies set up by investors with the sole aim of raising funds via

552. *Supra* note [550]. Graetz. 2016.
553. *Supra* note [550]. Graetz. 2016.
554. *Supra* note [550]. Graetz. 2016.

IPOs to eventually acquire another company.[555] About 200 SPACs went public in 2020, raising about USD 64 billion in total funding, nearly as much as all 2019's IPOs combined.

SPACs therefore have no commercial operations, making no products and do not sell anything, with money raised in their IPOs typically as their only assets. Commonly, SPACs would be created or sponsored by teams of institutional investors, Wall Street professionals from the world of private equity, and high-profile CEOs, like Richard Branson and billionaires, like Tilman Fertitta; and for 2021, this could include Bill-Gates-backed portable ultrasound start-up, like Butterfly Network, valued at USD 1.5 billion, and digital media companies, like Bustle Media group, Vice Media, and Buzzfeed.

Importantly, when SPACs raised funds, investors buying into them would not know what the eventual acquisition target company could be. SPAC sponsors normally would have deadlines to locate suitable deals, usually around two years of the IPOs, or else the SPACs would be liquidated and money raised would be returned to investors with interest. Critics claimed that due diligence of the SPAC process could be relatively less rigorous than conventional IPOs, and that SPACs' sponsors under deadline pressures for completing these within two years would not necessarily seek out the best possible deal, and importantly not incentivized to avoid overpaying for target companies.[556] SPACS had been around for decades and had existed as last resorts for small companies facing difficulties raising funds on the open markets. However, because of extreme market volatility, in part contributed by the global COVID-19 pandemic, SPACs had lately become more prevalent and prominent.[557]

These later developments badly blurred the distinctions between pass-through entities, like limited liability companies and partnerships that would not be taxed at the entry levels, and taxable corporations. In the US, for example, in 2012 only 54% of total US business income were reported on CIT returns, while 46% was reported in individual returns with most flowing through from partnerships, including very large partnerships. This development significantly complicated the ability to reform business income taxation in the US.

§6.11 US INFLUENCE ON GLOBAL TAX SYSTEMS

Towards the end of the last century and continuing now, European treaties in Europe contributed significantly to the shaping of international tax policies especially in the CFC domains, thin capitalization rules, and in the dismantling of the European imputation system. The US, thus far, had done little to reform its corporate rate tax policy, while other economies have revamped their tax systems to attract global capital, or more specifically to exploit the vulnerabilities of the US tax system. The US consequently could be differentiated for its high tax rate and its worldwide tax system,

555. T. Huddleston Jr. 2021. 'What is a SPAC? Explaining one of Wall Street's hottest trends?', *CNBC 30/1/21*.
556. *Supra* note [555]. Huddleston Jr. 2021.
557. *Supra* note [555]. Huddleston Jr. 2021.

that allowed deferrals of taxation of foreign earnings, until repatriations. These two distinctive features came to define the vulnerabilities of the US system.[558]

One would involve the loss of its tax base associated with transfer pricing. In the increasingly digital and digitized global economy, intangible assets like patents, copyrights, and brands would be vital to economic growths. The US would be associated with these extraordinary transfer pricing vulnerabilities, because its MNCs had leeway to locate these intangible assets and price their uses. This led to substantial erosion of the US tax base associated with both shifting income outside of its boundary and indefinitely deferring the repatriation of that income. As a result, more than USD 2 trillion in foreign earnings of US-domiciled MNCs have been retained abroad.[559] Interestingly, as this had not been taxed by the US corporate tax system, a suggestion has been made to tax this, regardless of whether it had been distributed to US parent companies.[560]

Also, while other economies reduced tax rates to achieve more competitive postures to attract and retain capital, the US has maintained its tax rate resulting in its tax rate being significantly higher than the tax rates of other developed economies that was until its significant lowering under the Trump administration in 2017 as mentioned earlier. The tax rate gap hitherto enhanced the incentive to apply transfer pricing strategies to move US earnings offshore and thereby increasing the transaction costs to repatriate earnings shifted or earned offshore. It would appear that reform proposals that could attract bipartisan political support in the US legislatures could include expanding the tax base and lowering tax rates, tax code simplification, and increasing the perception of fairness.[561]

In this connection and in the context of research findings, this would point towards burden-neutral worldwide tax systems to reform the US international tax system. The burden-neutral worldwide tax system relative to the territorial system could provide better opportunities to eliminate the tax incentive to shift income out of the US, while widening the corporate tax base and lowering the statutory corporate rate in a revenue-neutral fashion.[562] Further, a worldwide system could drastically simplify the code and assure that domestic companies and MNCs paid their fair shares, as they maintained their competitiveness in the global economy.

The EU and US country examples as discussed above and until appropriate tax reforms, such as suggested are designed, a twentieth century international tax regime could still very much be relied upon to govern a twenty-first century global economy. This raised questions, as to whether this could work, and if not, what and how to

558. R. Clemons & M.R. Kinney. 2013. 'U.S. corporate tax reform: Why is a worldwide tax system absent from the debate?', *Tax Notes International 16/9/13*: 1093-1099.
559. M. Sullivan. 2013. 'Designing anti-base erosion rules', *Tax Notes International 29/4/13*: 375.
560. S.C. Morse. 2017. 'Taxing the US$2.5 trillion', *Tax Notes*, Vol. 154(2): 247-249.
561. R. Clemons & M.R. Kinney. 2013. 'U.S. corporate tax reform: Why is a worldwide tax system absent from the debate?', *Tax Notes International 16/9/13*: 1093-1099.
562. *Supra* note [561]. Clemons & Kinney. 2013.

replace it with. It is tough to make predictions about the future, even with the BEPS in place. Still, a dozen of observations was bravely made as follows:[563]

(i) BEPS would unlikely usher in a new era of international cooperation in international taxation, because nations would continue to compete for various reasons. Conventional R&D incentives would continue to be used, while new incentives for domestic businesses would emerge, as economies competed for investments, and so on.

(ii) Other than the US, nations would try to shift taxes onto someone else's MNCs, while anti-abuse laws would proliferate.

(iii) Corporate tax as a source of revenue would persist in most non-tax-haven countries, along with its political popularity, and so would BEPS-type efforts, with the OECD as the epicentre.

(iv) MNCs across the world would persist with complex tax planning to stay ahead of governments. This could generate more conflicts and opportunities for multiple taxation of the same income, requiring new dispute resolution mechanisms and enhance cooperation between tax administrators. Continued growth in EMEs, together with weak tax administrations could contribute more difficulties for MNCs.

(v) Likely shifts towards destination-based taxes, or at least in the form of minimum taxes would ease pressures on transfer pricing, but hardly going to be more rational, or certain, after BEPS. Formulas and ex post profit splits would become more significant over time. In large market economies, these would be based largely on sales, while for high export economies, on production.

(vi) BEPS initiative to link tax consequences to the location of 'real value enhancing activity' could cause greater distortions than that now exist into MNCs' decisions on where to locate such activities involving personnel and plant and equipment. Issues have arisen concerning corporate inversions for US MNCs.

(vii) Multiple avenues for tax reduction and complexities of tax arrangements would suggest that nations could be going to rely more on general anti-avoidance rules, or overriding economic substance requirements to challenge tax planning and transactions. Already in play in the US and elsewhere, the limits of the approach would be severely tested via litigations in the immediate future.

(viii) Increasing needs for revenues from destination-based consumption taxes like GSTs and VATs would suggest that more countries would emulate the New Zealand model with varying success. This could lead to further pressures on taxing international services that have already been saddled with problems. The EU would be slow to make changes because of treaty

563. M.J. Graetz. 2016. 'Bringing international tax policy into the 21st century', *Tax Notes International*, Vol. 83(2016): 315.

barriers, while UK's freedom from these barriers could be the advantage offered by Brexit.

(ix) Countries looking for tax revenues from location-specific activities, especially in relation to natural resources would need to exercise discipline to avoid overdoing this.

(x) Capital gains tax issue would attract more attention as concerns with inequality continue to surge.

(xi) To shore up the tax base, countries would search for new sources. Excise taxes could make a comeback, particularly on financial institutions on certain financial transactions, or perhaps on fossil fuel consumption.

(xii) Even with the context of the BEPS era, the market need for tax compliance and related services would persist.

International trade and investments have been galloping along nicely, albeit with occasional hiccups, due to drastically falling tariff and non-tariff barriers across the world because of binding global agreements, including the WTO agreements. These have led to the uplifting of living standards across the world, notably in China and other developing economies. But, inequality of income and wealth would persist within and between economies, despite several initiatives to narrow the gaps between the highly affluent and the poor. These have grown into global issues, as highlighted in the recent World Economic Forums,[564] and earlier by the works of Piketty[565] and others. Inequality has become a dominant big global issue. Reducing inequality has also become one of the UN SDGs.

The *LuxLeaks* and the leaks from the PP and PRP, as well as those others before them had suggested that senior politicians, highly affluent individuals, and many MNCs have been able to pay less tax by relying on tax evasion or tax avoidance schemes designed by highly skilled professionals and enabled by highly cooperative and secrecy-friendly offshore and inshore financial centres, otherwise known as tax havens. This had caused upsets across the world. The BEPS became the response from the G20 together with the OECD, but this focused on MNCs. As the world awaited whether the new tax arrangements and agreements could work to tame excessive tax evasion and tax avoidance, it would be worth mentioning that tax persisted as one of the last barriers to the integration of global capital markets, mainly because countries had refused to negotiate binding multilateral tax agreements. Investment decision-making on account of this would be sensitive to national tax differences. This above-said environment could induce several international tax policy challenges.[566]

First, the existing international tax regime permitted countries to maintain different tax rules thereby encouraging big businesses, and in particular MNCs to shift the locations of their investments and operations to countries that imposed lower, or zero tax burdens. Empirical studies have increasingly suggested that investment

564. B. Bucher. 2021. 'COVID-19 has shown us the true extent of inequality. In 2021, let's commit to ending it', *World Economic Forum (WEF) 25/1/21*.
565. T. Piketty. 2014. *Capital in the twenty-first century*, Boston: Harvard College.
566. A.J. Cockfield. 2011. 'International tax competition: The last battleground of globalization', *Tax Notes International*, Vol. 63(12): 867-870.

decisions could be impacted by tax considerations.[567] This implied loss of employment and tax revenues for the impacted economies. It has been also claimed that the different national tax regimes distorted cross-border investment decision-making, but not in an economically efficient manner, as assets were deployed strictly for tax reasons, and not out of pertinent economic rationale. In theory, the process reduced national and global welfare, as assets were not being applied in the most productive manner.

Second, when MNCs, particularly those from the US, shifted more paper profits via sophisticated tax-planning schemes to investments in jurisdictions that imposed relatively lower or zero taxes, this inevitably reduced taxes collected in relatively high-tax countries. Over the years, governments had reformed their tax systems to exempt from tax, all foreign-source active business incomes. This drove policy attention to tax rules that permitted interest deductions to fund foreign investments and operations that were exempted from residence-country tax.

Such interest deductions for exempt foreign-source incomes were said to have provided one of the biggest leakages in the global fiscal web, as they reduced taxable profits and revenues in jurisdictions that maintained relatively high taxes. Nevertheless, the residence-based taxation of foreign-source active business was equally exposed to taxpayers' manipulations. The practice of achieving zero or negative tax on foreign-source incomes had come to be known as self-help territoriality. This was because US residents via this were able to structure their activities to transform the ostensible US worldwide tax system into an exemption (or territorial) tax system.[568]

Third, it became increasingly more difficult to determine which country should assess the appropriate tax liability, together with the resulting tax revenues on globally integrated products and services derived through cross-border investments. The difficulty was greater where highly mobile intangibles were concerned. A connected concern was the fair sharing of tax revenues among governments from taxing these globally integrated products and services. Owing to the difficulties in identifying the jurisdictions where taxable value-adding activities have been occurring, resistance to solutions involving collective actions could also harm economically vulnerable jurisdictions with insufficient resources to audit and tax complex cross-border transactions involving highly mobile factors of production. International tax reforms became therefore one of the last policy debates of globalization.

So far, conventional or traditional international law principles have not been able to effectively shape international tax policies. Many of these key challenges and options were being addressed by the OECD BEPS project, where many jurisdictions, including those from the developing domains and others have signed up to cooperate in resolving cross-border and related tax issues.

567. S. Djankov, T. Ganser, C. McLiesh, R. Ramalho & A. Shleifer. 2010. 'The effect of corporate taxes on investment and entrepreneurship', *American Economic Journal: Macroeconomics*, Vol. 2(2010): 31-64.

568. US Treasury. 2007. *Approaches to improve the competitiveness of the U.S. business tax system for the 21st century*, Washington, DC: US Treasury.

However, because of the politically charged nature and slow pace of international tax reforms, it could be helpful to integrate current thinking about economic theory with the wider appreciation of the broader political, social, historical, and other realities that could decide whether tax reform measures would succeed. The main policy challenge for this perspective could be the development of effective international tax rules and processes within essentially non-cooperative government settings. Governments in general could potentially deploy their tax systems to advance perceived national welfare interests, including tax-friendly reforms to attract foreign investments in conjunctions with the promotion of the competitiveness of their multinational firms.[569]

Meanwhile, it could be helpful to draw attention to the Tax Cuts and Jobs Act (TCJA) of 2017.[570] The idea behind this was to motivate US multinationals in particular to bring home to the US profits they stored in lower-tax foreign jurisdictions; and in particular, for OFCs and tax havens to migrate to a territorial tax regime, where such corporations would be taxed only on their US revenues and not their global revenues. These measures were intended to stimulate business expansion and consumer spending and thereby expanding the tax base sufficiently to recoup the revenue loss caused by the tax cuts and incentives. Prior to the passing of the 2017 legislation, the One-Page White House Handout from the US Treasury Secretary and Director of the National Economic Council was however short on details, and without specific proposals for raising revenue elsewhere to finance the tax cuts.[571]

The skeletal plan created the impression that increased government borrowings would be relied on to finance the revenue gap to lead to crowding out of private investments and capital formation. There were concerns that the expansion of economic activity and business formation, as a consequence of the tax breaks would fall short of the plan's expectation. Other worries included the net impact on individual taxes upon the proposed elimination of deductions and the regrouping of income thresholds under fewer categories, as well as the impact on small and medium enterprises (SMEs).[572] While details were being awaited at the time, responses from other economies and in particular US major trading partners were also anxiously being awaited, as the world had already been edging towards the focus on national interests. This could have significant implications for the sustainability of OFCs and tax havens.

The TCJA turned out to be the largest overhaul of the tax codes in three decades. It created a single corporate tax rate of 21%.[573] The legislation has made it cheaper to bring back earnings from abroad, while also keeping corporations from perpetually avoiding taxes on those profits by 'deeming' them repatriated.[574] It imposed a 15.5%

569. *Supra* note [566]. Cockfield. 2011.
570. J. Sahadi. 2017. 'Trump calls for dramatic tax cuts for individuals and businesses', *CNN Money 26/4/17*.
571. T. Anderson. 2017. 'How Trump's new tax reforms proposal may impact every income bracket', *CNBC 27/4/17*.
572. *Supra* note [570]. Sahadi. 2017.
573. D. Floyd. 2021. 'Explaining the Trump tax reform plan', *Investopedia* 1/2/21.
574. L. O'Neal. 2021. 'The Trump tax cuts: Promises made, promises kept?', *Bloomberg Tax 26/1/21*.

tax on cash and other liquid assets stored in MNCs' offshore structures, and an 8% rate on other assets held overseas.[575] Hitherto, those profits would be subject to the then corporate tax rate of 35% when brought back to the US. The impact on US corporations' investments was clear, with repatriated dividends starting to spike in 2018.[576]

Tax experts suggested that in recent years there had not been many notable inversions in which US-based companies restructure so that they became owned by a foreign parent. However, corporations could still be taxed on international profits below the 21% rate, with the law not creating the fully territorial regime that policymakers were aiming for. Indeed, the law and IRS rules for parts of the international provisions also provided some competing incentives, both discouraging and encouraging the accumulation of assets overseas.[577]

Professor Reuven Avi-Yonah argued that this could be a badly structured case, if the incentive was to move assets back to the US or to create jobs as against just moving cash back.[578] The level of US MNCs' income shifted to seven major tax havens, and flattened out in 2018 and 2019, instead of dropping according to Professor Kimberly Clausing at Reed College. He further added that the law was really making the problem better with one hand while making it worse with another, with the two sides cancelling each other out.[579]

Public Law 115-97 or the TCJA 2017 moved US tax system away from ideal tax policy principles. First, the legislation finances tax cuts with deficits which might not be always bad, but the increasing deficits and debt under the TCJA could risk displacing other urgent fiscal priorities.[580] Second, at a time of worsening inequality, the TCJA provided far larger tax cuts for those at the top of the distribution than others, both relative to incomes and in absolute terms.[581] Third, the legislation could exacerbate the under-taxation of capital in the US tax system arising from the dramatic tax cuts for capital income, including corporate income, pass-through business income, and estates.[582] Fourth, the TCJA made limited progress on the substantial problems of profit shifting and corporate tax base erosion, and importantly the post-TCJA tax system tilted the playing field in favour of earning foreign income and making foreign real investments.[583] Fifth, modest simplification gains on the individual side of the legislation were more than offset by increased complexity on the business side, as both the new pass-through deduction and the new international provisions were hugely complex.[584] Also, the planned expiration of many provisions in TCJA, including the

575. *Supra* note [574]. O'Neal. 2021.
576. *Supra* note [574]. O'Neal. 2021.
577. *Supra* note [574]. O'Neal. 2021.
578. R.S. Avi-Yonah. 2018. 'The international provisions of the TCJA: Results after six months', *Law & Economics Working Papers 158, University of Michigan Law School.*
579. K. Clausing. 2020. 'Fixing five flaws of the Tax Cuts and Jobs Act', *Columbia Journal of Tax Law*, Vol. 11(2): 31-75.
580. *Supra* note [579]. Clausing. 2020.
581. *Supra* note [579]. Clausing. 2020.
582. *Supra* note [579]. Clausing. 2020.
583. *Supra* note [579]. Clausing. 2020.
584. *Supra* note [579]. Clausing. 2020.

planned changes in tax rates, R&D amortization, and other provisions could enhance uncertainty, complexity, and budget costs of TCJA where provisions are extended.

The TCJA though could be rendered more progressive by keeping tax cuts benefiting the lower-end of the income distribution, reinstating the enforcement of the individual mandate, and expanding the now larger child tax credit to be fully refundable and to be applicable to more low-income taxpayers.[585] These proposed changes could be reinforced with changes that eliminate tax cuts for those at that top, repealing the pass-through deduction, corporate tax rate hikes, and toughening the minimum tax.

This menu of incremental changes would eliminate the additional deficits generated by the legislations, while making the US tax code substantially more progressive than hitherto before the TCJA. Such said changes could also address profit shifting, as the minimum taxes on international income under TCJA could be a useful reference point that could be strengthened to operate better.[586] Additionally, to counter under-taxation of capital income, stronger business taxation would be essential, as some 70% of US equity income had been untaxed by the US at the individual level.

Back at the global level, Angel Gurria, the Secretary-General of the OECD claimed that the BEPS Inclusive Framework since its formal inception in 2016 had driven a sea change in international tax policies, especially with regard to the four BEPS minimum standards that countries and jurisdictions had been implementing on equal footings.[587] These minimum standards were further claimed to have established coherence, realigned substance with taxation, and enhanced transparency thereby essentially eliminating prevalent widespread harmful tax practices.[588]

For instance, since 2016, over 285 regimes were reviewed to ensuring that there was substance associated with the activities they were intended to attract, culminating with the amendments or abolishment of virtually all harmful preferential regimes.[589] Countries opted to implement the BEPS 4 Minimum Standards because of prestige, political incentives, and chance and necessity.[590] These said standards comprised AEI across borders, public registers of beneficial ownership of financial assets, CbC reporting, and unitary tax with formula appointment.

Also, the Multilateral Instrument that the BEPS framework created for resolving a range of BEPS challenges embedded in bilateral tax treaty networks presently covered 95 jurisdictions, with sixty-one of these having ratified the Instrument that impacted over 1,700 tax treaties.[591] Additionally, more than 2,600 bilateral exchange relationships had been established to exchange CbC Reporting thereby providing tax administrations with aggregate data on the global allocation of income, profit, taxes paid, and

585. *Supra* note [579]. Clausing. 2020.
586. *Supra* note [579]. Clausing. 2020.
587. A. Gurria. 2021. 'Remarks by Angel Gurria, Secretary-General, OECD', *11th Meeting of the Inclusive Framework on BEPS 27/1/21*.
588. I. Johanna & M. Valderrama. 2020. 'Policy Note: The study of the BEPS 4 minimum standards as a legal transplant: A methodological framework', *Intertax*, Vol. 48(8/9): 719-732.
589. *Supra* note [587]. Gurria. 2021.
590. *Supra* note [588]. Johanna & Valderrama. 2020.
591. *Supra* note [587]. Gurria. 2021.

other valuable data of global MNCs.[592] The breath and reach of this OECD initiative could be reflected in the commitments to implement these said minimum standards by 138 countries and jurisdictions.

Currently, some sixty-eight members of the BEPS Framework are developing countries, and their efforts over and above the BEPS minimum standards had yielded handsome outcomes. The OECD-UNDP Tax Inspectors Without Borders initiative ushered in experts to collaborate with developing economy national tax authorities on real-time basis and had helped to raise USD 775 million in additional tax revenues in 2020.[593]

Going forward, the BEPS Framework would be working on delivering a multilateral, consensus-based solution to the tax challenges arising from the digitalization of the economy based on Pillar 1 envisaged to providing a new taxing right to allocate a percentage of residual profits of MNCs to market jurisdictions; and Pillar 2 envisaged to providing for a global minimum tax to ensuring that multinational profits incur a minimum level of taxation, no matter how much tax planning is deployed.[594] The digitalization of the economy left unchecked, together with exacerbations brought about by the COVID-19 pandemic, could entrench longstanding imbalances and unilateral actions that could aggravate existing tax-related trade tensions.

Where OECD fails to deliver the promised solutions by mid-2021, some over forty economies could move ahead with a Digital Services Tax (DST).[595] While this could be reflective of pressures from citizens to take actions, most governments would agree that a multilateral, consensus-based solution would be preferable and had accordingly indicated that DSTs would be removed once agreement could be successfully brokered by the BEPS Framework. The OECD and indeed the world has been reassured by the newly appointed US Treasury Secretary that the US is committed to the cooperative multilateral effort to address BEPS via the OECD/G20 process and collaborating to resolve the digital taxation disputes in that context.[596] The OECD, apart from this, would also be formulating guidance or solutions for the carbon pricing challenges, as well as rising inequality matters.

Members of the Independent Commission for the Reform of International Corporate Taxation (ICRICT) that included some Nobel Laurates have jointly petitioned the current US President drawing attention to his promise to lead initiatives internationally to bring transparency to the global financial system, go after illicit tax havens, seize stolen assets, and making it harder for leaders who pillaged from their economies to hide behind anonymous front companies.[597] The ICRICT members claimed that the MNCs by shifting their profits to tax havens had deprived governments worldwide annually at least USD 240 billion in fiscal revenues. This impacted not only the US, where some 50% of overseas profits made by US MNCs were transferred to tax havens

592. *Supra* note [587]. Gurria. 2021.
593. *Supra* note [587]. Gurria. 2021.
594. *Supra* note [587]. Gurria. 2021.
595. *Supra* note [587]. Gurria. 2021.
596. *Supra* note [587]. Gurria. 2021.
597. J.A. Ocampo, J.E. Stiglitz & J. Ghosh. 2021. 'An open letter to Joe Biden on international corporate taxation', *Project Syndicate 26/2/21*.

annually, but also, the Global South, where revenue sources were more constrained, and ergo reliance on corporate tax receipts to fund public services was greater.[598]

The ICRICT members called upon the US to engage actively in ongoing efforts to overhaul the international tax system to ensure fair taxation of MNCs. This was presently discussed within the G20-mandated OECD process, but has not gone on well, as governments of leading Member States had negotiated under the misplaced assumption that their national interests would be best served by protecting those MNCs headquartered within their borders. Discussions on the reform of international taxation had thus therefore sacrificed common ambition to the lowest common denominator.[599] In the meantime, MNCs continue to avoid taxes that could have been employed to fund public expenditures to support post-COVID-19 pandemic recovery.

Nevertheless, agreement has been reached that MNCs would be treated as unitary businesses, meaning that their worldwide profits would be taxed in line with their real activities in each jurisdiction.[600] However, the present proposal would apply this allocation criterion to only a small share of a firm's global profits, especially those of highly digitalized MNCs, that were mainly US-based. As e-commerce grew by a third during the 2020 pandemic, it would be critical that not only digital MNCs but also all MNCs digital business operations paid their fair share of taxes. This means that an ambitious and comprehensive reform should therefore be adopted replicating the US system at international level, without differentiating digital and non-digital businesses.[601] This kind of rule could help to establish a more level playing field, reduce distortions, limit opportunities for tax avoidance, and provide certainty to MNCs and investors.

This approach should be reinforced by a global minimum tax on MNCs, thereby ending harmful tax competition between economies, and reducing the incentive for MNCs to shift profits to tax havens. However, the 12.5% minimum rate being discussed at the OECD and elsewhere could become the global ceiling, whereby the laudable mission to oblige MNCs to bear their fair share of taxes could end up doing the opposite. The US campaigned promise of raising the US minimum tax on US corporations' foreign earnings known as GILTI would not only increase the fiscal resources of the US but could also provide the political support for other countries' policymakers to follow suit. The fight against tax avoidance could be decisive where G20 economies, for instance, could agree to impose a 25% minimum corporate tax on the global incomes of their multinational entities, more than 90% of worldwide profits would automatically be taxed at no less than 25%.[602]

It would be though essential that this kind of tax be designed to allocate taxing rights fairly between firms' home and host economies.[603] The newly appointed US Treasury Secretary has mentioned that the US would work with other economies to try to stop what had been a destructive global race to the bottom on corporate taxation. In

598. *Supra* note [597]. Ocampo, Stiglitz & Ghosh. 2021.
599. *Supra* note [597]. Ocampo, Stiglitz & Ghosh. 2021.
600. *Supra* note [597]. Ocampo, Stiglitz & Ghosh. 2021.
601. *Supra* note [597]. Ocampo, Stiglitz & Ghosh. 2021.
602. *Supra* note [597]. Ocampo, Stiglitz & Ghosh. 2021.
603. *Supra* note [597]. Ocampo, Stiglitz & Ghosh. 2021.

this respect, it merits mentioning that there was no evidence that the recent trend towards lower corporate tax rates have stimulated productive investment and growth, and in fact the 2017 US rate cut primarily ended up funding dividend payments and stock buybacks.[604]

The ICRICT members further contended that, until equitable reforms are adopted, trade sanctions against countries that have opted to tax digital businesses, where many of whom were developing economies desperately seeking additional review, would be counterproductive. As such, the idea of reengaging with the multilateral system, while accepting a weak international compromise on taxation of MNCs would not work, but would instead further erode, not restore, trust in the system.[605]

In the meantime, the OECD had proposed to grant taxing rights over a part of MNC firms' profits where consumers reside. Those would be assessed irrespective of the companies' physical presence. The tech entities' digital profits would be allocated based on a formula, with around USD 100 billion in global tax revenue targeted to be distributed more evenly across economies.[606] The previous US administration had resisted solely approving a new digital tax, with the issue remaining as a major impediment to a wider deal. The new US administration appeared more opened to this change, when the newly appointed Treasury Secretary Yellen declared to the G20 that the US would no longer insist on a safe harbour allowing tech entities to escape from the new digital tax.[607] The country's concession on digital taxation could help pave the way for reaching agreement on a separate major part of the OECD tax agreement that was primarily about enacting a floor on international corporate tax rates.

Under this constituent of the plan, the OECD would set up a global minimum tax rate, probably around 12% of profits, although the final rates remained unsettled.[608] Low-tax economies would face pressures to increase their rates to align with this new minimum, because when they fail to comply, other economies would be empowered to levy additional taxes on the overseas earnings of their firms. Some sceptics have warned that this approach would be accompanied by separate sets of trade-offs and significant procedural and administrative hurdles, while others cautioned this would be inadequate to slow the decline in corporate taxes. Yet others further cautioned that the OECD's blueprint offered little more than a tax haven lite framework where tax havens could keep the majority of profits they siphon from across the world as long as they share some of those profits with the richer economies. Still, it has been argued that the cost of inaction would remain a less attractive alternative.

As MNCs, celebrities, politicians, and highly affluent continued to store their wealth in tax havens, as alluded to earlier, there is still no generally accepted definition for them. A derogatory version has defined it as escaping from rules to elsewhere more

604. *Supra* note [597]. Ocampo, Stiglitz & Ghosh. 2021.
605. *Supra* note [597]. Ocampo, Stiglitz & Ghosh. 2021.
606. J. Stein. 2021. 'Yellen pushes global minimum tax as White House eyes new spending plan: The Biden administration seeks to reverse decade-long "race to the bottom" in corporate taxation-but obstacles loom large', *The Washington Post 15/3/21*.
607. *Supra* note [606]. Stein. 2021.
608. *Supra* note [606]. Stein. 2021.

accommodating, usually offshore, and across borders.[609] These destinations could exert impact far more than tax, offering escape routes from financial regulations, disclosures, criminal liabilities, and more. As the main users and beneficiaries were likely to be big MNCs and large financial institutions, the system tilted the playing filed against SMEs, thereby boosting monopolization.

There would also be considerable political damage, as tax haven offer hiding enclaves for the illicit activities of elites using them at the expense of the less powerful majority. While tax havens justified their roles as tax neutral conduits assisting international finance and coordinating investment flows smoothly, the benefits for the private participants were self-evident; but the same for the world as a whole would not hold. It had become increasingly recognized that, in addition to tax losses, enabling capital to flow freely across borders generated risks, including the danger of financial instability in EMEs.[610]

Generally, the wealthier and bigger MNCs and the more affluent individuals tend to deploy more complicated structures and entities with hundreds of subsidiaries offshore, and ergo more deeply embedded in the offshore system that they had come to vigorously defend. Other stakeholders, included powerful governments, as some major tax havens are also located in advanced economies, contrary to the more popular perception that they were usually found in far-off far-flung islands. Indeed, the TJN's Corporate Tax Haven Index[611] has ranked the BVI, Bermuda, and the Cayman Islands, all British Overseas Territories, as the top three; while the FSI[612] ranked Switzerland, the US, and the Cayman Islands as the top three destinations for private wealth. These would constitute sound evidence that offshore capital was more likely to drain from poor economies to rich ones. In particular, pertaining to US MNCs, corporate profits shifting into tax havens rose from an estimated 5%-10% of gross profits in the 1990s to around 25%-30% currently.[613]

A deeper and more relevant question involved asking and knowing whether the financial flows attracted by tax havens helped the receiving economies. Financialization literature from the IMF, the BIS, and others have argued that financial sector growth could be beneficial up to an optimal point, where after which it would begin to harm economic growth. Most advanced economies, including the US, the UK, and other major tax havens had passed that point a while ago; and as such for them shrinking the financial sector to remove harmful financial activities could boost prosperity.[614] In conjunction with this, there is the notion of a financial curse afflicting jurisdictions with oversized financial sectors.

609. N. Shaxson. 2019. 'Tackling tax havens', *Finance & Development September 2019*: 7-10.
610. *Supra* note [609]. Shaxson. 2019.
611. Tax Justice Network (TJN). 2019. 'Corporate Tax Haven Index'.
612. TJN. 2020. 'Financial Secrecy Index 2020 reports progress on global transparency- but backsliding from US, Cayman and UK prompts call for sanctions', *TJN 18/2/20*.
613. A. Cobham & P. Jansky. 2017. 'Measuring misalignment: The location of US multinationals' economic activity versus the location of their profits', *Development Policy Review*, Vol. 37(1): 91-110.
614. R. Sahay, M. Cihak, P. N'Diaye, A. Barajas, R. Bi, D. Ayala, Y. Gao, A. Kyobe, L. Nguyen, C. Saborowski, K. Svirdzenka & S.R. Yoousefi. 2015. 'Rethinking financial deepening' *IMF Staff Discussion Note 15/08*, Washington, DC: IMF.

This paradox of poverty in the midst of plenty was argued to have multiple causes, such as a brain drain of skilled people from government, industry and civil society into the high-paying dominant sector; rising and growth-sapping inequality between the dominant and the other sectors; increase in local prices making other tradable, less competitive with imports; recurrent booms and busts in prices of commodities and financial assets; and increases in rent-seeking and loss of entrepreneurship at the cost of productive, wealth-creating activities as easy money sept in.[615] Financialization would therefore represent a shift from wealth-creating activities into more predatory, wealth-extracting activities, like monopolization, TBTF banking, and the deployments of tax havens.

It has been further contended that financial flows questing for secrecy or fleeing from corporate taxes would appear likely to be precisely the kind that would aggravate the finance curse, worsening inequality, enhancing vulnerability to crises, and unleashing unquantifiable political damage, as secrecy-shrouded capital seeped into Western political systems.[616] It would also appear that, for many economies hosting OFCs it could be a lose-lose strategy, as it would transmit harm not only outward to other economies but also inward towards the hosts.[617] Those economies acknowledging this could act unilaterally to rein their OFCs by simply staying away from the race to the bottom and curbing tax haven activities, while also striving to improve their domestic population's economic welfare.[618]

Meanwhile, most recently, the US startled the global taxation system again, when it led the G7 economies to reach consensus in strongly supporting the initiatives underway to address tax challenges flowing from globalization and the digitalization of the economy and to adopt a global minimum tax. The G7 in this regard commit to reach an equitable solution on the allocation of taxing rights, with market economies awarded taxing rights on at least 20% of profit exceeding a 10% margin for the largest and most profitable MNCs.[619] Further, the G7 would provide for appropriate coordination between the application of the new international tax rules and the removal of all Digital Services Tax, and other equivalent measures, on all corporations. The G7 additionally commit to a global minimum tax of at least 15% on a country-by-country basis; and agreeing on the importance of progressing agreement on both Pillars, besides looking forward to achieving agreement at the forthcoming July meeting of the G20 Finance Ministers and Central Bank Governors representing 139 countries.

A further matter of interest to those expanding the use of digital currencies in tax havens pertains to the increasing interest of central bank digital currencies (CBDCs) is the G7's intension to work towards common principles and publishing conclusions on CBDCs in the later part of 2021.[620] For now, the G7 notes that any CBDCs as a form of

615. J. Christensen, N. Shaxson & D. Wigan. 2016. 'The finance curse: Britain and the world economy', *The British Journal of Politics and International Relations*.
616. *Supra* note [609]. Shaxson. 2019.
617. *Supra* note [609]. Shaxson. 2019.
618. *Supra* note [609]. Shaxson. 2019.
619. G7. 2021. 'G7 finance ministers & central bank governors communique', *G7 London 5 June 2021*.
620. *Supra* note [619]. G7. 2021.

central bank money could act as a liquid safe settlement asset, and as an anchor for the payments system. G7's objective is to ensure that CBDCs are grounded in long-standing public sector commitments to transparency, rule of law and sound economic governance. For the G7, this necessarily implies that CBDCs should be resilient and energy-efficient; support innovation, competition, inclusion, enhancing cross-border payments; while operating within appropriate privacy frameworks, and minimizing spillovers.

The US and the OECD on the other hand have said that a final sign-off would have to wait until a subsequent G20 meeting in October 2021, as the US positions may not be finalized by July as a domestic tax package would need to wind its way through Congress. Still, should finalization take place, as hopefully anticipated by the G7, this G20 sign-off would confirm that the world's largest economies would implement it, implying that its reach would be effectively worldwide. This though is unlikely to end the main activities of various tax havens, but it would likely make them far less attractive for many companies seeking to bring down their tax obligations, and those investors focusing on environment, social and governance (ESG) matters.

The whole purpose of the global minimum tax is that it provides countries with rights to add a top-up tax on company profits in economies with tax rates lower than the global minimum. The G7 is seeking also to ensure that the minimum rate be applied on a country-by-country (CbC) basis, rather than an average across the countries a corporation operates. This approach when adopted would carry tougher implications for tax havens.[621] A US MNC, for instance, could book profit in the British Virgin Islands, where there is no corporate tax, but US tax authorities could apply a 15% tax on those profits, assuming that is the global minimum figure finally agreed upon. This is major focus for the US domestic agenda of retrieving more revenues from taxes on US MNCs reportedly using offshore tax havens to bring down their tax obligations.[622] The US sees the global minimum tax as potentially ending the race-to-the-bottom in corporate taxation thereby ensuring fairness for the middle and working people not only in the US but for most others across the world. It also sees the deal as representing the revival of multilateral cooperation after years of strain under the Trump administration.

A separate part of the international tax agreement focuses on tax companies based on were they operate, and not just the location of their headquarters. This is of priority to big European economies which have sparked trade tensions through the imposition of special digital taxes on US tech giants. This implies grappling with how to divide up governments' rights to tax excess, or non-routine, profit of the largest MNCs, among them major digital platforms, like Google and Apple. The G7 reached consensus that governments should have the right to tax at least 20% of the profit

621. L. Thomas. 2021. 'What now for the G7 tax deal on multinationals', *Reuters 8 June 2021*.
622. Associated Press. 2021. 'Explainer: Curing tax avoidance by multinational companies: The Biden administration is pushing for agreement on a global minimum tax', *Associated Press 11 June 2021*.

earned in their country by a MNC over a 10% margin, and all indications are that the excess profit would also be subject to the global minimum.[623]

This implies the US giving up some taxing rights on overseas profits of US-based tech giants. The deal though not explicitly naming tech MNCs appears to be a nod to the push by European countries to levy taxes on the operations in their economies of MNCs, like Amazon and Apple with headquarters in the US but reaping enormous revenues from abroad. The Europeans have been insisting unfairness for the digitalized giant platforms accumulating revenues in their respective countries without paying more in taxes. The matter was resolved with both the US and the Europeans agreeing not to singling out tech companies but to apply the change to a wider set of MNCs that the tech firms would in any case fall under by any definition.[624]

This said, a lot of matters and priorities would still need to be calibrated and resolved, meaning there is still room and time for MNCs and others to get their views across. Past experiences on international agreements have shown that they are likely to have unintended loopholes, and this present one is unlikely to be the exception. Countries involved in the negotiating the global tax regime are likely to exempt some sectors. Extractive industries, for instance, are likely to be carved out as corporations usually pay royalties upfront to the governments where the oilfields and mines are sited. There are also rumours of potential carve-outs for particular financial services, and flexibility on tax breaks for research and development. Those other developing and emerging economies relying on low-tax economic zones to attract investments would likely seek for these to be protected.[625] Even some advanced economies using relatively low-tax regimes to compete for investments despite global pressures would because of more pressing domestic agenda could stay firm on their respective positions.[626]

Even before the flashing out of details in the later stages, notable objections are emerging from respectable quarters. The first concern, pertaining to the G7 deal, is that the proposed minimum tax rate of 15% is low, close to the rates in tax havens like, Ireland and Switzerland.[627] This suggests a preference by several G7 economies to protect their own MNCs, instead of following the lead of the US, which had earlier advocated for a global minimum of 21%. Also, under the present proposal, the majority of the additional tax revenues would go MNCs' home countries, not the source countries where these MNCs generate their profits. G24 member nations unsurprisingly want source countries to have priority in applying the minimum tax, especially pertaining to payment of services and capital gains, so as to protect their tax base.

As such, the giving of priority to MNCs' home countries would reinforce rather than alleviate the unfairness already built into the existing international tax system.

623. *Supra* note [621]. Thomas. 2021.
624. J. Stein & A.N. Farzan. 2021. 'G7 countries reach agreement on 15 percent minimum global tax rate: The accord announced by finance ministers could reshape tax obligations of multinational corporations', *The Washington Post 6 June 2021.*
625. *Supra* note [621]. Thomas. 2021.
626. *Supra* note [621]. Thomas. 2021.
627. J.A. Ocampo & T. Faccio. 2021. 'A global tax deal for the rich, not the poor', *Project Syndicate 11 June 2021.*

The EU Tax Observatory[628] has earlier estimated that a 21% minimum rate would yield an additional USD 220 billion (EUR 100 billion) of corporate income tax revenues in 2021 for the twenty-seven EU countries; whereas a 15% rate would generate half those amounts. This is even more striking for developing countries. South Africa and Brazil, for example, with a 15% rate would respectively gain an additional EUR 600 million and EUR 900 million, compared to EUR 2 billion and EUR 3.4 billion at a 21% rate. With most African countries having corporate rates of 25%-35%, a global rate of 15% would thus be simply too low and unlikely to lead to a significant reduction in profit-shifting from the region. As such, the G7 and G20 economies have been urged to show good global leadership by unilaterally committing to introducing a much higher minimum rate than whatever is finally agreed upon, preferably in the 21%-25% range.

The second prong of the G7 deal introduces a formula to apportion MNC's global profits for tax purposes, but with caveat that this is applicable only to the largest businesses with global profit margins beyond 10%, and where at least 20% of their residual profit exceeding this threshold would be subject to tax in the economies where it is generated. While this new rule would impact US tech MNCs, it could end up being applied to only a tiny fraction of the global profits of some 100 or so of the largest MNCs. The measure as such would likely generate little additional revenue, something like less than USD 10 billion a year, globally.[629] In the face of this likely scenario, the G24 has insisted a bigger reallocation of global profits, something ranging from 30% up to 50% for the most profitable enterprises. The African Tax Administration Forum (ATAF) has likewise called for the rules to apply to all MNCs with annual revenues above EUR 250 million, somewhat much lower than the G7 proposed threshold of USD 10 billion, with further calls that a percentage of all global profits, whether routine or residual, should be apportioned to countries where these enterprises do business.[630] In practice, it is not easy to differentiate between the routine and residual profits of a MNC, as all profits are essentially the outcome of the enterprise's global activities.

A far more practical answer would involve the allocation of global profits among economies on a formulaic basis, in tandem with the key factors generating the profit, like sales, assets, and employment.[631] This approach would help in setting up a more level playing field, bring down distortions, constrained opportunities for tax avoidance, apart from providing certainty to MNCs and investors. By comparison, the G7 proposed differentiation, between routine and residual profit would reflect a political agreement seeking to avoid a far-reaching global reallocation of taxation and revenues.

The global tax negotiations thus far appear to draw parallel with the ongoing COVID-19 vaccine discussions at the World Trade Organization (WTO), where EU leaders are blocking the temporary exception to intellectual-property rights insisted by developing economies with US support. The challenge for advanced economies is to go

628. M. Barake, T. Neef, PE, Chouc & G. Zucman. 2021. 'Collecting the tax deficit of multinational companies: Simulations for the European Union', *EU Tax Observatory June 2021*; D. Meyer. 2021. 'A 21% global tax floor would mean $140 billion more for Europe and U.K., think tanks claim', *Fortune 1 June 2021*.
629. *Supra* note [627]. Ocampo & Faccio. 2021.
630. *Supra* note [627]. Ocampo & Faccio. 2021.
631. *Supra* note [627]. Ocampo & Faccio. 2021.

beyond domestic agenda to ensure fairness to poorer nations. For economies operating as tax havens, with focus merely in shifting paper profits, without bringing in new capital, they have little to complain about, as they have doing MNCs a great service by facilitating tax avoidance at immense costs to other countries' treasuries. The G7 global tax rules as being proposed though not perfect are fully justified to prevent these hitherto blatant beggar-thy-neighbour actions, and ergo an important step in the right direction.[632].

632. D. Rodrik. 2021. 'The G7 tax clampdown and the end of hyper-globalization', *Project Syndicate 7 June 2012.*

CHAPTER 7

Concluding Remarks

Free trade, or at least freer trade, has been the mantra for the world, for a long while already. This was reinforced by the notion of globalization, where economies the world over were being integrated through economic activities for the benefit of all. Financialization next made the scene, but which somehow helped to lead further the condemnation of globalization for all the wrongs wrought to economies, societies, and the environment.

The new global economy is now getting more used to the idea and practices of financialization. This is a seemingly simple term to refer to the growing stature of finance in daily activities from local to global, but gets complicated and complex when made in reference to the expanding scale and profitability of the finance sector over the rest of the economy facilitated by massive deregulations, as witnessed in particular during the Clinton Presidency from 1993 to 2001, and the Bush Presidency from 2001 to 2009.

The UK perhaps due to its special relationship with the US not only shared this idea of finance but also actually contributed many of the financial innovations that eventually came to swamp the rest of the world. Compared to the past when the financial sector's main purpose was to serve the capital and related needs of businesses and even governments, it had grown by leaps and bounds to even overwhelm the rest of most economies.

The fate of the financial sector, whether in terms of success or failure, had serious repercussions to the rest of the economy, nationally and globally. The quest of financialization was supposedly financial innovation, generating greater efficiency and productivity to support economic development, and hence global market efficiency. Since the 1980s the world economy, as led by the US, saw the finance industry placing more emphasis on the achievements of short-term financial returns, at the expense of longer-term considerations, meaning further technological developments and investments for even higher productivity and sustainability. The general impact, because of this, was the dramatic and disproportionate rise of finance relative to the role of labour, as shown by the phenomenal rise of profits in the capital markets, from less than 10%

in the early 1980s, to around 40% by early 2000s. Indeed, labour's share of income, or the amount of GDP paid out in wages, salaries, and benefits had been slowing since the 1980s in various economies, notably the US and UK, relative to that achieved by capital.[633]

It became unsurprising therefore to witness the hollowing out of manufacturing, especially in the US, UK, EU, and many other advanced economies, as the finance industry proudly demonstrated how more profit could be made by making money from money, or in the new financial lexicon, from financially engineered products. With greater returns from wizardry financial instruments and software, less and less attention was paid to the manufacturing sector. This was followed by less and less attention for upskilling and research funding in the sector because these were considered relatively less important towards the making of short-term profits, the efficiency barometer in the capital and financial markets across the world. Back in the 1980s and early 1990s, for instance, the corporate raider approach was brought into play by the more aggressive members of the affluent and professional communities to achieve quick financial returns by dismembering businesses, laying off personnel, and doing fire-sales of assets.

The lavish lifestyle for those in the financial sector was the envy of many others who were apparently less savvy. In particular, hedge funds managers and other financiers donated millions and acquired fabulous properties. More and more of young and old alike in advanced economies took to finance as the source of their financial wealth or powers. Banks and other financial service providers fund their lifestyles with flows of easy credits, or easy credit cards with high interest rate, and higher fees for the less bankable. This went on to include even subprime mortgages for those with no incomes, no jobs, no assets (NINJAs). These kinds of predatory lending practices preyed on the poor to make them poorer became fashionable financial practices. Back in the old days, banks do not touch them. As it turned out in the 2000s many did as they relentlessly sought higher and higher profits. Banks and financial institutions became more able to do this because of greater use of securitization.

Recall securitization and off-balance sheet financing drove once upon Wall Street darlings to their dramatic fall from grace in 2000. These included the Enron and WorldCom debacles and others. Enron's founder shortly before his death in a yacht explosion had claimed that securitization would be the next big thing in finance. Securitization was where issuers created financial instruments by combining other financial assets to market different tiers of the repackaged instruments to investor to promote liquidity in the marketplace. Liquidity was created by facilitating smaller investors to purchase shares in larger asset pools.

Hence, retail investors could not have been able to buy into large pool of mortgages, if not for the securitization of mortgages. Creditors on the other hand were provided by instruments that lowered risks, via the division of ownership of the debt obligations. This meant investors effectively assumed the lenders' position when they bought into the security. The process enabled creditors to remove the associated assets

633. J. Manyika, J. Mischke, J. Bughin, J. Woetzel, M. Krishnan & S. Cudre. 2019. 'A new look at the declining labour share of income', *McKinsey Global Institute (MGI) Discussion Paper May 2019.*

from their balance sheets. Investors earned returns in these financial vehicles backed by tangible assets that could be liquidated for recovery purposes.

In practice because of the relentless drive for more and more profits, discipline and cautions broke down, when massive credit was created from off-balance sheet, netted out and moved to special investment vehicles, or even offshore into secrecy tax havens. Enron did that in the late 1990s, and banks and other financial institutions did that massively in the 1980s, and more so into the 2000s to compete for profits through vast opportunities provided by securitization and off-balance sheet mechanisms. Debts could now be hidden, other than to the very meticulous.

Initially, good securities were offered for securitization, but in later stages when these became less and less available, junk loans were repackaged into toxic securities for sale throughout the world. When the subprime mortgage bubble burst in late 2007 triggered by the collapse of Lehman, the US, UK and EU economies were among the first to go into recessions. Soon the effects radiated to other economies plunging the world into an unprecedented global recession larger in impact than the great recession in the late 1920s.

It needs to be said that the US had emerged successfully from the tech bubble of 2000 via very serious regulatory reforms to curb some of the excesses of financialization, and lots of loose money popularly known as QE.[634] Anglo-Saxon economies and other developed economies enjoyed good economic growths till late 2007. Instead of market efficiency and the like as promised by financial innovation, it became a world awash with massive credit creations, huge leaps in finance in terms of speed, scale, and spatial dimensions.

Above all, the financial sector became the master in charge, rather than hitherto as a service provider. It was not just about the US sneezing, with the rest catching cold. It was just about almost every economy in the world becoming of some importance as economies became more and more interconnected and integrated. Indices became available to demonstrate the degree of integration. This implied that the fortunes of economies or regions could impact one another, and no longer just confined to the US. China, for instance, despite being a middle-income economy in per capita terms impacted much of the rest of the world, when its capital market took some beatings in 2016.

The simultaneous fall of Ponzi schemes in the likes of Madoff in 2008 accentuated matters, as in the end investors lost some USD 50 billion. Importantly, the dubious actions of credit ratings agencies (CRAs), banks, and others did not result in senior executives being penalized, but instead gave handsome rewards for their departures. The widespread rewards for failures and corporate fines for flawed CG practices led to massive public angst. As if to aggravate matters, shareholders paid the government fines, while taxpayers' money was used to bail out many of these failed banks and big corporations. These were justified on the basis of too big to fail (TBTF), in the sense

634. A. Rebucci, J.S. Hartley & D. Jimenez. 2021. 'An event study of COVID-19 central bank quantitative easing in advanced and emerging economies', *NBER Working Paper 27339 February 2021.*

that they could not be let to go down, as they were envisaged to have extensive contagion impacts, such as seen in the Lehman debacle.

Public angst was assuaged through massive regulatory interventions. In 2002, to contain corporate excessive risk-taking and flawed financial reporting, the 2002 Sarbanes-Oxley (SOX) was enacted in the US. The subsequent time around, on the belief of the inadequacy of SOX, a very massive legislation running into thousands of pages was enacted in the form of the 2010 Dodd-Frank Act (DFA). The legislation was designed to ensure that such massive financial failures should not recur, as entire financial system, inclusive of shadow banks were overhauled with tighter legislations.

These new rules were accompanied by more financialization to curb the excesses of financialization. This involved further use of QE.[635] This further inflating of debt could only be sustained by lower interest rates. However, under such conditions, pensions and insurance funds were bound to suffer, as their incomes were being drastically brought down. Since then, there has been growing beliefs, that instead of increasing the quantity of liability, the better option could have involved increasing the quality of equity accompanied by structural reforms.

The focus on financialization, particularly from the late 1990s onwards in the US, UK, and many other developed economies help to drive manufacturing to developing economies in both East and West. Soon, much of the manufactured goods for much of the world came from these lesser-developed economies, whether from Eastern Europe, Africa, or Asia. In turn, as these economies progressed with their new roles as the factories of the world they too eventually got caught up with the wonders of finance, as they too leveraged heftily with debts to finance their own growth dreams.

This debt-excess way of doing things soon became unsustainable, as shown by the dramatic and sudden onset of the 1997 AFC and other crises in other parts of the world equally damned by excessive debts. Upon recovering, Asian and other impacted economies appreciated the risks of financial leveraging and got down to serious reformulations of their economic strategies. Many realized the risks of capital flights and began to pay more attention on savings and building of financial buffers or financial reserves to ward off potential waves of capital flights. Global finance that led to the so-called finance curse disease arising from the use of excessive debts were not confined to developing economies, but some advanced economies as well, as exposed through the world of tax havens, monopolist, megabanks, private equity firms, Eurobond traders, lobbyists, and a motley host of scandals quietly financializing entire societies, harming both businesses and individuals.[636]

Still, financialization, or the accelerating roles of financial motive, financial markets, financial actors, and financial entities in the operation of local and international economies has persisted with its upward trajectory. China, the largest emerging economy to have benefited from its development has begun feeling the impacts of the excessive use of debts in its shadow banking system where financial service providers

635. K. Amadeo & M.J. Boyle. 2021. 'Explaining quantitative easing (QE: It allows central banks to create massive amounts of money)', *The Balance 21 May 2021*.
636. N. Shaxson. 2020. *The finance curse: How global finance is making us all poorer*, New York: Grove Press.

were subjected to minimal regulatory oversight, as well as in many of the country's provincial authorities' disproportionate reliance on debts. Measures have since been taken to curb these, including even the imposition of stricter regulations on some of the country's globally known financial technology entities, popularly referred to as *Fintechs*.[637]

The advanced economies of the US and the UK continued to favour providing economic incentives for promoting or discouraging particular behaviours. This was best exemplified by the cap-and-trade scheme to disincentivize pollution. This market-based solution involved the sale of the rights to pollute. This could alternatively be read as the onset of an example of financialization of nature. This approach extended from the trading of carbon emission, trading of water quality, to the trading of the right to fish. From a more positive note, this could also be read as the creations of more novel or innovative ways for the financial sector to earn higher profits. The process in the end had more to do with speculating on nature, rather than using proven methods to curb pollution. Hence, instead of advancing the expansion, integration, and financialization of carbon/water markets it might be better to implement and enforce regulations to protect and preserve essential resources.[638]

Meanwhile, the bailed out big global banks and big global corporations had more than recouped their pre-crisis profitability and capitalizations. They simply became become bigger thereby elevating further the financialization of national and global economies. Global TBTF mega banks benefiting from state help have not shrunken, but instead amassed even greater financial power and influence,[639] while global big tech platforms were not far behind with their massive trillion dollars market capitalization and counting,[640] even as IFFs persisted,[641] inequality issues became more serious,[642] CG practices dithered,[643] and the environment exposed to greater climate change risks despite rebooted financing approaches.[644]

Most of these market participants continued to have significant activities in various onshore and offshore tax havens, not necessarily implying financial shadiness, but definitely varying levels of opaqueness.[645] Unsurprising though, these financial

637. R. Zhong. 2020. 'In halting Ant's I.P.O., China sends a warning to business', *New York Times 24/12/20.*
638. S. Fawzy, A.I. Osman, J. Doran & D.W. Rooney. 2020. 'Strategies for mitigation of climate change: A review', *Environmental Chemistry Letters*, Vol. 18(2020): 2069-2094.
639. S. Loannou, D. Wojcik & G. Dymski. 2019. 'Too-big-to-fail: Why megabanks have not become smaller since the global financial crisis?', *Review of Political Economy*, Vol. 31(3): 356-381.
640. D. Copolla. 2020. 'Market capitalization of U.S. tech and internet companies 2020', *Statista 27/11/20.*
641. A. Aziani. 2018. *Illicit financial flows*, New York: Springer.
642. V. Romei. 2020. 'How the pandemic is worsening inequality', *Financial Times 31/12/20.*
643. R.J. Gilson & C.J. Milhaupt. 2020. 'Shifting influences on corporate governance: Capital market completeness and policy channeling', *European Corporate Governance Institute (ECGI) Law Working Paper No. 546/2020.*
644. M. Ferridun & H. Gungor. 2020. 'Climate-related prudential risks in the banking sector: A review of the emerging regulatory and supervisory practices', *Sustainability*, Vol. 12(2020): 5325-5344.
645. P. Jansky, M. Meinzer & M. Palansky. 2021. 'Is Panama really your tax haven? Secrecy jurisdictions and the countries they harm', *Regulation & Governance 15/1/21.*

enclaves prided themselves as reliable guardians for individuals and businesses and others seeking confidentiality or secrecy.

The main concern of the financial sector, having achieved its profitability goal, would be tax avoidance. This helped to explain the geography of financial centres, as money migrated to spaces that enabled it to escape from the hands of fiscal authorities. The ability of OFCs and tax havens to mobilize capital and money in the interests of their owners and to direct these away from tax authorities had not gone unnoticed. The OECD estimates that in 2007 some USD 5 trillion and USD 7 trillion were funnelled into such centres. This rose to between USD 21 trillion and USD 32 trillion by 2012, while the TJN found that three out of four Fortune 500 firms were active in countries known for their low or no-tax policies, and an Action Aid study found that just two of the companies listed in UK's FTSE 100 have no subsidiaries in tax havens.[646]

The phenomenon of offshore finance is arguably indispensable to the understanding of financialization, generally interpreted and referred to earlier as the growing dominance of finance over society at large. Rather than merely being a fringe phenomenon, offshore finance is very much the nerve centre of contemporary capitalism, as the world's dominant capital stocks and flows are presently habitually routed and deposited offshore, with global corporations and elite wealth thoroughly interlaced with the onshore world, for reasons of secrecy, tax and related missions to boost asset protection and financial returns.[647] Offshore finance, among others, is a pivotal driver of mounting inequality, the breaking-up of social contracts underlying welfare states, ecological disasters, financial crises, and growing authoritarianism.

Datasets from the Panama and Paradise Papers revelations showed various legal innovations, in particular, anonymous shell companies are instrumental to the rise of the global offshore system, besides underscoring the weight of offshore capital sock and flows shaping financialized capitalism that in turn reveal a core geography of OFCs underlying global finance. Despite individual OFCs being formally cultivated by governments and sovereign lawmakers, offshore finance as an integrated system, is effectively maintained by a small cluster of global banks, law and accountancy firms.[648] In the context of financialization, the world needs to come to terms with the sweeping powers of offshore finance, that systematically accumulates and assumes, and effectively enjoys and exerts, slivers of state sovereignty anchoring the planetary rule of capital. In this sense, if financialization indeed refers to the growing dominance of finance over society at large, then offshore finance could quite literally represent the very crown upon this space.[649]

Experienced professional financial experts have cautioned policymakers not to merely unwisely hope for the best, wherein a strong and quick economic recovery redeems the humongous run-up in debts, leverage, and asset valuations. Instead, the

646. M. Bennedsen. 2015. 'Using tax havens secretly is bad for shareholders', *Knowledge INSEAD 23/6/15*.
647. R. Fernandez & R. Hendrikse. 2020. 'Offshore finance' in P. Mader, D. Mertens & N. van der Zwan (eds), *The Routledge International Handbook of Financialization*, Abingdon: Routledge.
648. *Supra* note [647]. Fernandez & Hendrikse. 2020.
649. *Supra* note [647]. Fernandez & Hendrikse. 2020.

need for action is now for moderating the financial sector's excessive risk-taking.[650] This should further include containing and reducing margin debt; the enforcing of stronger suitability criteria on broker dealers; enhancing assessment, supervision, and regulation of non-banking institutions; and reducing the tax advantages of currently favoured investment gains,[651] as well as those found in tax havens.

While corporate boards might have sound reasoning behind their strategy of setting up networks of companies away from their home countries, this could also be a sign that the management might have the ulterior motive to avoiding monitoring of their activities to potentially engage in dubious activities that could harm shareholders' interests. The alluded to tax leakages at the country level could also help to explain why tax increases to reduce budget deficits had not been able to produce the intended effects. These in consequence also exacerbated the income/wealth inequality within and between economies. For these and other reasons, the UN High Level Panel on International Financial Accountability, Transparency and Integrity, known as the FACTI panel, was launched in March 2020 with the aim of evaluating the impact of tax abuse, money laundering, and annual IFFs of USD 427 billion on the ability of states to fulfil the UN's SDGs by 2030.[652]

OFCs and tax havens might not be synonymous. OFCs generally comprised usually an expatriate community of offshoots of global banks, other global financial institutions, and professional service providers like accountants and solicitors, and so on. They would be transient communities generating disproportionate high value financial services, relative to the economy of the jurisdictions where they operated, and could be footloose, as they habitually followed the flows of capital and investments. They would be 'offshore' from a different sense, meaning financial transactions could be recorded in one location, usually a tax haven, but originated from another place, usually the home countries from where the substantial economic activities took place.

This would suggest a divergence between the form and substance of transactions, with the obvious intentions of locating substantial economic activities in low or no-tax havens, and dormancy in high-tax jurisdictions. This could explain the 'offshore' element, or the entities and individuals who would be elsewhere in their respective home countries, with their apparent substantial economic activities undertaken in low-tax regime jurisdictions. Hence, tax havens would not all be necessarily OFCs, but could likely transform to one. This could be attributed to the high value financial activities usually taking place in OFCs. Indeed, those few tax havens that failed to do so, remained as islands in the sun, or mere recreational destinations, while those others plying the secrecy business could cost sovereign governments, billions.[653]

For those tax havens that were able to do so, they enjoyed higher levels of financial activities that grew to be disproportionate to the local domestic economy. They grew to become attractive to the world at large, because of any combination of

650. M.A. El-Erian. 2021. 'The return of the finance threat', *Project Syndicate 9 June 2021*.
651. *Supra* note [650]. El-Erian. 2021.
652. A. Cobham. 2021. 'The global struggle for tax justice', *Tax Justice Network 25/2/21*.
653. L. Wier. 2020. 'Tax havens cost governments $200 billion a year. It's time to change the way global tax works', *World Economic Forum (WEF) 27/2/20*.

distinctive features. These usually had to do with bank secrecy, ownership secrecy, and artificial obstacles to exchange of financial and related information between jurisdictions. In general, these tax havens were empowered to enact legislations with features undermining the harsher rules and procedures found in other jurisdictions.

It was such appealing differentiating features that acted as magnets for capital flows from residents elsewhere across the world. Tax havens became particularly enticing when they were able to provide bank secrecy, beneficial ownership secrecy, general inertia to exchange financial data with other jurisdictions, competitive tax rates, and generally stable socio-economic-political conditions.[654] Usually, they were also able to attract the presence of global accounting firms and global tax advisors that could lend further appeals and confidence about the stature and global reputation of these tax havens in question.

However, when stretched to disproportionate levels, they could come under the scrutiny of policymakers, especially in times when many economies were looking to strengthen their financial coffers. This was aptly demonstrated in large tracts of Europe and the UK. In the UK, Her Majesty's Revenue and Customs (HMRC) in its 2013-2014 Annual Report estimated that the annual tax gap consisting of tax arrears, evasion, and avoidance at some GBP 5 billion.

The more startling revelation was that this estimated amount persisted for nearly a decade, including tax evasions of some GBP 4.1 billion and avoidance of some GBP 3.1 billion.[655] In response, the UK House of Commons Committee of the Public Accounts (PAC) generated six reports substantially related to organized tax avoidance and the tax avoidance industry. The latter dominated by the Big Four accounting firms were alleged to have designed, marketed, and implemented these schemes.[656] They were further said to have sold tax advice to multinationals, involving the constructions of artificial tax structures or arrangements serving only to avoid UK taxes.

Interestingly, the PAC reports argued that the UK, a highly respectable jurisdiction, has a well-established tax avoidance industry that eroded the tax base of the country as they were the ones providing the affluent with expensive professional advice to avoid taxes.[657] The absence of any legal compulsions for the examination of crucial witnesses, or the subpoena of crucial documents meant that crucial evidence was lacking to pursue further measures. The PAC though did make some major recommendations, including the need to end self-regulation for the tax advisory industry. Not unsurprisingly, the firms concerned opposed suggestions for reforms, or the ending of self-regulation back then.

The government for its part claimed that the HMRC was already undertaking robust actions against tax avoidance.[658] It also rejected the necessity for statutory code of conduct for the industry, as it felt that the existing voluntary code of ethics was sufficient for the purpose, even though this had no statutory underpinning, and was

654. G. Tobin & K. Walsh. 2013. 'What makes a country a tax haven?', *The Economic and Social Review*, Vol. 44(3): 401-424.
655. P. Sikka. 2015. 'No accounting for tax avoidance', *The Political Quarterly*, Vol. 86(3): 427-433.
656. *Supra* note [655]. Sikka. 2015.
657. *Supra* note [655]. Sikka. 2015.
658. *Supra* note [655]. Sikka. 2015.

not applicable to non-accountants, like the legal profession. Though PAC recommended barring tax avoiders and their advisors from receiving public contracts, as far as is known, no individuals or entities engaged in tax avoidance had been excluded from getting taxpayer-funded contracts. It has been further said that no follow-up actions by the UK Treasury and Department of Justice (DOJ) took place.

It was telling that three British Overseas Territories of the BVI, Cayman Islands, and Bermuda headed the Corporate Tax Haven Index 2021's list of top ten greatest enablers of corporate tax abuse risks. To put in context, OECD countries and their dependencies accounted for something like up to 68% of the world's global tax breaks estimated at about USD 176 billion annually. The Index claimed that the lion's share of responsibility for enabling corporate tax abuse belonged to the UK and its overseas Territories and Crown Dependencies, where the UK enjoyed full powers to veto law-making and implement key appointments, and which accounted for some 31% of the world's corporate abuse risks.[659] The Index ranked each jurisdiction based on how intensely the jurisdiction's tax and financial systems enabled MNCs to shift profit out of locations where they do business and consequently pay less tax than they should have.

US Special Committee hearings differed somewhat from UK Select Committee Hearings. Senate Committee hearings in the US were usually followed-up by the department of justice (DOJ) leading to fines for the firms and prison sentences for senior professionals involved.[660] It has been further argued that based on past developments without major shifts in UK government policies on the regulation of the tax avoidance industry, there would be little prospects of curbing the massive leakage of tax revenues.[661] Flaws in the professional accounting and related services of this nature continue to persist within a background of weak governance practices and ineffective regulatory supervision.[662] This on other hand could imply better prospects for tax havens providing the convenience for the housing in particular of tax avoidance structures that could be essentially legal. It was also of no great surprise that these service providers were generally present in OFCs and tax havens associated with the highly valued secrecy feature.[663]

Tax havens while appearing to be understood by almost everybody did not appear to have a universal definition. Some even claimed that tax havens could be identified or recognized as such, by sight. Tax havens had been referred to differently, even in the legal community. They had also been referred to diplomatically, as tax shelters in a foreign country preferred over other countries because of their better educated labour force, modern economic systems, use of advanced technologies, good

659. S. White. 2021. 'British Virgin Islands top tax haven ranking', *Accountancy Today 10/3/21*.
660. *Supra* note [655]. Sikka. 2015.
661. *Supra* note [655]. Sikka. 2015.
662. A. Katsomitros. 2021. 'Trouble is starting to brew at the top for the "big four"', *World Finance 22/2/21*.
663. M. West. 2016. 'Tax havens and the "big four"', *Independent Australia 12/7/16*; L. Holmes & A. Hawkes. 2011. 'Big four auditors "embedded in the tax haven world"', *This Is Money 29/1/11*.

transportation, and good climate.[664] Or, they could be referred to more bluntly, as any jurisdictions with tax features that would attract the attention of tax planners.[665] This could then include countries, where little, or no taxes were imposed on profits generated from transactions undertaken in those countries.[666] Others went further to differentiate on policies towards taxation.[667] On this basis, tax havens were grouped as so-called classical tax havens or no-tax havens, tax havens with no tax on income from foreign sources, tax havens with special tax regimes, and treaty tax havens.

Wider perception of tax havens could refer to tax practice of a jurisdiction relating to the establishment of businesses for the purpose of a more privileged tax regime relative to other jurisdictions.[668] From a political perspective, tax havens back in the 1950s referred positively to escape from the harsh tax regimes of developed economies,[669] but this gradually metamorphosed to the negative situation of erosion of tax bases of nations and unfair tax competition, as well as by the implications of money laundering and facilitation for terrorism financing.[670]

The significance growth of tax haven practices in world economy in the twentieth century could therefore be attributed to the increasing globalization of the world economy, paralleled by improvements in infrastructures, and transportation and communications that lowered significantly the transaction costs of using different tax-planning schemes. Motivated individuals and big businesses then contemplated on the application of foreign jurisdictions to shelter from taxation their incomes from domestic and foreign transactions. Tax havens emerged then to cater to such needs that also expanded further when globalization prompted overall increase in foreign investments, where taxation was consistently of prime consideration.[671]

Second, classical tax havens emerged in response to harsher tax policies in developed economies to answer the demand for tax planning, tax avoidance, and tax evasion strategies. Third, such tax haven practices were facilitated by the accelerated coming into being of an elaborate network of double taxation conventions in the second half of the twentieth century. These and other developments led to the boom in switching to tax haven practices in the 1960s through to the 1980s, such as seen in the Cayman Island, the Bahamas, Bermuda, the BVI, and Hong Kong. This, however, slowed down in the 1990s because of a change in public attitudes to tax havens and increasing attention on the legality and morality of tax havens and their practices. More important, however, was the general liberalization of national tax regimes and

664. G.W. Beyer & K.R. Redden. 2008. *Modern dictionary for the legal profession*, 4th edition, New York: William Hein & Co.
665. M.J. Ellis. 1980. 'Some reason for the use of tax havens and the legal schemes adopted for their use', in *Recourse to Tax Havens-Use and Abuse*, Seminar Proceedings of the 34th Congress of the International Fiscal Association, Paris.
666. B.A. Garner. 2014. *Black's law dictionary*, 10th edition, Eagan: Thomson West.
667. D.A. Kleinfeld & E.J. Smith. 2016. *Langer on practical international tax planning*, 4th edition, New York: Practicing Law Institute.
668. G. Kurtz. 1993. *218 tax havens*, Berlin: Gerhard Kurtz.
669. G.S.A. Wheatcroft. 'The general principles of tax planning', *British Tax Review*, January/February 1963: 1-20.
670. M. Orlov. 2004. 'The concept of tax haven: A legal analysis', *International Tax Review*, Vol. 32(2): 95-111.
671. *Supra* note [670]. Orlov. 2004.

regulatory practices in the 1980s and 1990s making the employment of tax havens less attractive to taxpayers of high-tax jurisdictions.[672]

Various countries employed tax haven practices to enjoy competitive edge over other competing economies, as in the UK and the US, and to complement their hitherto high-tax systems. Others, like those in the Caribbean and Pacific islands never bothered to introduce new taxes, as their collection would require more resources than the expected revenue. The Turks and Caicos, on the other hand, are said to have been 'persuaded' by the UK Foreign and Commonwealth Office to adopt legislations that could assist them in deriving revenue from tax planning and financial services operations.[673]

Much though remained to be done in many economies to build effective tax administrations.[674] Improving tax compliance required sustained efforts and coherent strategies. Policymakers were increasingly becoming more aware that priorities for developing these capabilities differ across countries. It has been said that the tax haven stage could boost national economies, which when skilfully leveraged could lead to significant economic growth, as exemplified by the Republic of Ireland's case. It appeared that some jurisdictions were prepared to forgo a part of the tax revenues, so as to attract foreign investments and thus filling their national coffers less directly via sales taxes or estate duties.[675] Recent research suggested that tax performance could be positively and strongly associated with the operational strength of tax administration.

Emerging and low-income economies at the top 25% in terms of operational strength also collected substantially larger tax revenues by some 3.25% GDP than countries at the lowest 25%, other conditions being equal.[676] It has been further found that key administrative tax practices, like compliance risk management and employment of third-party data, was associated with stronger tax collections.[677] Such findings were of important policy implications, especially during the current ongoing COVID-19 global pandemic.

Tax havens could also be grouped via public international law, spatial distribution, and by aims.[678] Tax havens under public international law could be represented by supranational bodies, like the EU, because of common tax policies and single passport regulation; by sovereign states; by quasi-sovereign dependent territories, like the US-affiliated territories in the Caribbean; or those affiliated with Denmark, such as Greenland. They could also be represented by autonomous bodies enjoying limited

672. G. Graham & R. Wright. 1998. 'Winds of change in treasury islands', *Financial Times, 24/1/98*, p. 9.
673. R.E. Moore. 1980. 'Attitudes of tax haven countries with regard to the tax haven problem', in *Recourse to tax havens-use and abuse*, Proceedings of 34th Congress of the International Fiscal Association (IFA), Paris: IFA.
674. IMF. 2015. *Current challenges in revenue mobilization: Improving tax compliance*, Washington, DC: IMF.
675. H.W.T. Pepper.1977. 'From tax haven to tax paradise', *Bulletin for International Taxation*, IBFD: 33-36.
676. E.S. Chang, E. Gavin, N. Gueroguiev & J. Honda. 2020. 'Raising tax revenues: How to get more from tax administrations', *IMF Working Paper WP/20/142 July 2020.*
677. A. Chooi. 2020. 'Improving tax compliance: Establishing a risk management framework', *Asian Development Bank (ADB) The Governance Brief Issue 39 2020.*
678. *Supra* note [721]. Orlov. 2004.

sovereignty, like autonomous regions within countries as exemplified by Hong Kong; by regions of a country, like Campione in Italy; and by localities, like the free economic zones found in Shannon Airport in Ireland.

This therefore revealed the importance of understanding what kinds of bodies of public international law could be involved, and on which levels the decisions concerning tax practices were being adopted. These could refer to the supranational, national, or local levels. Simultaneously, it would be important to recognize very often major powers in their respective regions, like Australia in the Pacific, that could influence the orientations of small economies' tax havens on specific issues.

As far as the spatial dimension was concerned, tax havens were represented on all the continents, including offshore territories. This reflected historical patterns, and the point that tax havens could be ubiquitous. The classical tax havens over more than ten decades comprised largely small states, such as inland enclave states, like Lichtenstein and Luxembourg; coastal enclaves, like Monaco and Hong Kong; and island kinds, like the Cayman Islands and the BVI. Despite globalization, classical tax havens because of their historical links with particular developed countries still maintained their regional specializations.

Thus, European taxpayers favoured the Channel Islands, Monaco, Luxembourg, and Lichtenstein; while US taxpayers preferred the Caribbean or Latin American tax havens; the Asian taxpayers liked Hong Kong; while Australian taxpayers were fond of using Vanuatu and Nauru. This was also prompted by geographical proximity to particular global financial and trade centres. This pattern, nevertheless, was not followed by the transnationals using tax havens, as they habitually used tax havens across different parts of the world. This has been attributed to advancements in transportation and communication and the wider geographical spread of businesses.

As such, the choice of tax havens would increasingly be ascertained by their tax specialization, and their adjacency to particular target markets, instead of nearness to taxpayers. Beyond classical tax havens, tax haven practices were also employed in many other jurisdictions, including developed states. There did not appear to be clear distribution patterns here, but usually tax haven practices followed certain economic specialization of the states that often arose from their geographical location. For instance, the UK and the Netherlands located in the major trade routes to and from Europe have historically developed as financial centres, and their tax have practices directed at the financial sectors had served to complement this specialization.

Going by the targeted kinds of taxation, tax havens could be categorized into income tax havens providing complete or partial shelter from income taxation. This could further be divided in accordance with the kinds of income tax relieved, the means employed to grant this relief, and the extent to which the relief is granted. The latter were exemplified as import duties (excise) tax havens, estate tax havens, and tax havens with privileged regimes for the taxation of particular forms of activities, like 'flags of convenience,' or tax havens for captive insurance companies. Tax haven practices could also target several kinds of taxation. Panama, for instance, was well recognized as a flag of convenience state, low tax haven in terms of corporate income tax, and as host for the Colon free trade zone.[679]

Drawing from a different perspective, tax havens could also be further differentiated in terms of the taxpayers using them, like havens for individuals, havens for companies and banks, or havens for trusts. Or they could be differentiated by particular activities that were targeted by tax havens, like OFCs, free economic zones, flags of convenience, and so on.

Aside from tax relief granted, tax havens could be marked out by high standards of financial administration, including banking and commercial secrecy, no or liberal currency control, developed infrastructure, availability and accessibility to world-class service providers, and lower financial regulatory standards. These features were often reinforced by stable governments, equitable treatments of foreigners, existence of free trade zones, investment incentives, or self-promotions as tax havens.[680]

Economic and political realities further contributed to the split of tax haven jurisdictions in terms of the businesses and activities they targeted.[681] The first group comprised quality tax havens because of their leading discreet policies, both with regard to banking supervision and corporate laws. These covered reputable jurisdictions like Switzerland, Monaco, UK, Luxembourg, Bermuda, or Hong Kong. The second covered tax havens that did not have all the advantageous of quality tax havens that could allow them to compete effectively with the first group. These tend to deploy lower taxation and legal standards and have been said to have attracted less prudent companies and murky deals, like Liberia, Vanuatu, or Nauru.

This did not necessarily imply that shady deals did not occur in the first group, as shown by what happened in the *LuxLeaks*,[682] as alluded to earlier. Here, the main contentions were the official attitude and the general conduciveness of the regulatory regimes towards such inclinations. Nations have not been shy of competing for FDIs and so on, by having different range of attitudes, and by having well-drafted regulations and well-timed innovations, as exemplified by the case of the BVI in the mid-1980s.[683]

Analysis of competition between tax havens generated insights on future development of tax haven practices and therefore the potentials for the designing of effective mechanisms against the employment of tax havens for tax abuses and criminal activities. These tax haven practices, while harder to achieve are argued to be easier to defend than those using practices at the bottom end of the generally perceived list of tax havens.[684]

679. R. Hausmann, J. Obach & M.A. Santos. 2017. 'Special Economic Zones in Panama', *Center for International Development at Harvard University May 2017.*
680. B.J. Arnold. 1986. *Taxation of controlled foreign corporations: An International comparison (No. 78),* Toronto: Canadian Tax Foundation.
681. *Supra* note [721]. Orlov. 2004.
682. P.J. Baruch, M. Ferrer & M.V. et Anne Michel. 2021. 'OpenLux: The secrets of Luxembourg, a tax haven at the heart of Europe', *Lemonde February 2021.*
683. *Supra* note [721]. Orlov. 2004.
684. *Supra* note [721]. Orlov. 2004.

The OECD, the TJN, and the EU over the years have provided their views on tax havens. The 1998 OECD study[685] found tax competition disruptive and harmful as it eroded national tax base of non-haven economies and shifted revenue-raising burden to property and labour. It also accentuated inequality in income and wealth and curtailed the employment of progressive taxation. The OECD then viewed tax havens as those jurisdictions characterized by no or only nominal taxes, absence of effective exchange of information, and the general lack of transparency in the operation of the legislative, legal, or administrative provisions.

The OECD in June 2000 provided its tax haven criteria.[686] These included no or nominal tax on relevant income, lack of effective exchange of information, lack of transparency, and absence of substantial activities. The controversies following this led to revision of the criteria and changes in the categorizations. These revisions led to reclassifications of jurisdictions, as those getting largely compliant letter from the OECD's Global Forum; jurisdictions committing to the adoption of OECD's Common Reporting Standard (CRS); jurisdictions having signed the Multilateral Convention on Mutual Administrative Assistance in Tax Matters (MCMAA); or those having sufficiently broad exchange network providing for EOIR or through AEI.

Countries needed only to satisfy only two of the criteria cited. This could mean they might not be blacklisted, even though they shunned the common reporting standard (CRS) project. This helped to explain why the OECD's listing of tax haven criteria had been interpreted as a politically drawn tax haven list, especially when widely perceived tax havens in several advanced economies have been able to get off the list. Further, committing to participate in the CRS could lead to artificial delays and excuses by certain economies. The TJN criticized this major weakness, as well as major exceptions that have excluded powerful advanced economies.[687] The EU was firmed on the fulfilment of all three major criteria, as well as the ratification requirement.

The EU's tax haven screening criteria grew stricter than that of the OECD, as it included assessment of preferential harmful tax regimes, implementation of BEPS reforms, and potential zero corporate tax rates.[688] However, to ensure consistency with the OECD's Global Forum, including the use of the BEPS Inclusive Framework, the EU implemented four minimum BEPS reforms. These included preferential tax regimes (PTRs), tax coordination centres, risk reserves for international group financing, and international trading companies and foreign sales corporations. The EU was also involved in the drawing up of an economic substance test to facilitate offshore structures or arrangements aimed at attracting profits that did not reflect real economic activities. The EU's economic substance rules came into effect on 1 January 2019.[689]

685. OECD. 1998. 'Harmful tax competition: An emerging global issue'.
686. OECD. 2000. '2000 progress report: Towards global tax cooperation: Progress in identifying and eliminating harmful tax practices'.
687. Tax Justice Network (TJN). 2016. 'Will the OECD tax haven blacklist be another whitewash', *TJN 20/7/16*.
688. J. Kurwin. 2016. 'EU identifies 28 tax regimes that could make blacklist', *Bloomberg BNA 5/12/16*.
689. Deloitte. 2019. 'New economic substance rules introduced by "tax havens" brought into force from 1 January 2019', *Deloitte February 2019*.

The EU targeted twenty-eight jurisdictions considered to have harmful tax regimes, meaning economies that could face scrutiny in early 2017 as part of the process to define its tax haven blacklist.[690] The EU Code of Conduct Group for Business Taxation is said to include a range of Pacific and Caribbean nations with OFCs. Among them were Belize, Grenada, Cook Islands, Montserrat, Cabo Verde, Dominica, Saint Kitts and Nevis, Macao, Saint Lucia and Samoa, Anguilla, the Bahamas, Bermuda, the BVI, the Cayman Islands, Guernsey, the Isle of Man and Jersey. These were then all cited for potential screening in 2017, on account of their zero tax rates. Thirteen of the twenty-eight were categorized as particularly problematic, because of their failures to commit to the OECD's Inclusive Framework for implementing the minimum BEPS reforms. The EU list was updated on 26 February 2021.[691] The updated list, now containing twelve jurisdictions, saw the removal of Barbados and the addition of Dominica. Also, a large number of jurisdictions that had committed to agreeing necessary changes to their tax system with the EU, remained on a second grey list, including Turkey, which was given more time to comply with EU transparency requirements.

Back in 2016, the TJN, in response, had proposed the use of its financial secrecy index (FSI) as the better option to the politically drawn tax haven list.[692] The FSI was argued to be an objective evaluation, as every ranking and assessment could be tracked down to its legal sources and explanation. The FSI was also claimed to be the only global analysis on tax havens that provided searching questions on the OECD countries' secrecy provisions. The TJN argued further that, even if the OECD ignored the FSI, its second and third criteria could be enhanced by requiring ratification and signing of the Multilateral Competent Authority Agreements (MCAAs). The MCAA was the other requisite to have the CRS in place. It implements the OECD's Standard for Automatic Exchange of Financial Information, while the linked common reporting standards (CRS) requires jurisdictions to obtain information from their financial institutions and automatically exchange that information with other jurisdictions on an annual basis. The 2020 FSI ranked 133 jurisdictions, of which the top ranked included the Cayman Islands, Hong Kong, Luxembourg, the Netherlands, the United Arab Emirates, the BVI.[693]

The brief excursion on tax haven definitions has drawn out several observations.[694] First, the tax haven phenomenon was very diverse and defied clear-cut universal definition. Even classical tax havens and treaty tax havens were not homogeneous, and at best provided limited guidance. They could share particular common features, like low taxation, but differed considerably in bank secrecy, or supervision of financial institutions. Remedial response measures would thus need to

---

690. Council of the EU. 2016. 'Report by the Code of Conduct Group (Business Taxation) to ECOFIN', *ECOFIN 992 13924/16, 3 November 2016.*
691. 742 Council of the EU. 2021. 'Council conclusions on the revised EU list of non-cooperative jurisdictions for tax purposes', *Official Journal (OJ) of the EU, 26 February 2021.*
692. M. Meinzer. 2016. 'Financial Secrecy Index: Shedding light on global financial secrecy', *TJN 29 September 2016.*
693. TJN. 2020. 'FSI 2020'.
694. *Supra* note [721]. Orlov. 2004.

take into account historical developments, current practices, and respective revenue and policy goals of the jurisdictions involved. Measures targeting tax havens would have also to address the relationships between them and their national tax systems, as these were bound to impact both international trade and the national tax systems of individual states.

In dealing with the harmful impacts of tax havens, the US and Canada used the transactional approach that required tax haven definition, but had instead singled out particular transactions, usually involving passive capital. The UK, Japan, and France used a defined jurisdiction approach that identified tax havens by relying on comparative tax rates. Both approaches suggested several limitations pertaining to the application of the notion of tax havens. This situation in part helped to explain why the OECD responded as they did, but in the end also had to improve on its 1998 version that was weakened by the lack of level playing fields, lack of policy justification, and lack of adequate criteria for identifying transgressing tax havens.[695]

As mentioned earlier, the current initiatives to address these limitations were not being universally accepted, but for public international law, it would be important to have consensus as to the groundwork concepts. The OECD and other experiences over more than a decade have suggested that the abuse of tax haven practices could be better addressed by targeting particular abuses, and the underlying weaknesses or flaws in various legal frameworks, rather than relying primarily on the concept of tax havens.[696] This was what the OECD, EU, and TJN recent initiatives were trying to improve on. The OECD now uses four basic criteria for identifying tax havens, namely no or low tax burden; ineffective exchange of information; absence of transparency; and investment primarily on the basis of tax incentives and savings without real economic activity. To this end, the OECD publishes black and grey lists that are often updated.

This further meant the need to understand the motivations for using tax havens or tax haven practices. They varied, but in most cases, it was about paying less tax legally, although there could be those instances bordering tax evasion, and hence an economic crime in most economies. The UK, for instance, is now seeking consultation whether in some circumstance where the commission of an offence by a corporate body was attributable to the neglect of one or more directors, a failure to prevent, targeted at the individual director or equivalent officers might be appropriate.[697] For most economies, taxes were design and implemented for revenue generation, bridging inequality between the poor and the rich, for inducing particular behaviours, or for stimulating concerns over the use of public funds.

Affluent individuals, like celebrities, politicians, and so on used tax havens obviously for tax avoidance, while those engaging in nefarious activities for tax evasions, money-laundering objectives, and terrorism financing purposes. The list of personalities leaked in the 2016 Panama and PRP, however, thus far showed names of

695. *Supra* note [721]. Orlov. 2004.
696. *Supra* note [721]. Orlov. 2004.
697. Law Commission. 2021. 'Corporate criminal liability: A discussion paper', *Law Commission 8 June 2021*.

celebrities and political leaders, but have not shown criminal figures. This probably helped to explain why, thus far, there had been little prosecutions although national tax regulators and other prosecutors have warned of possible criminal prosecutions where these involved tax evasions.

As for big businesses and MNCs, shareholders expected them to maximize shareholder value in general, and this could imply minimal taxation paid to enhance shareholder value. Although in more recent times, there had been more and more cases of them seeking other considerations, like good corporate citizenship. This could mean asking corporate directors and managers to avoid excessive aggressive tax-planning behaviours that risked tarnishing the MNCs' brand reputation. This came on the back of several high-profile tax litigations, where the MNCs concerned were said to have employed unfair untenable tax practices that went against particular norms and rules.[698]

Media attention of late focused on global MNCs making use of transfer pricing and so on to engage in very aggressive forms of tax planning. This helped to explain why the OECD saw fit to launch its BEPS project that has since witnessed the participation of many economies, including the developing economies that MNCs have been leveraging on. The general idea was to curb such abusive tax practices by MNCs, and by others in jurisdictions generally known for their harmful tax haven practices. It is to the credit of the OECD, the EU, and the TJN, that most jurisdictions had since fought shy of being associated as one by either of them. Tax havens connote bad reputation, not only for the jurisdiction concerned but also for its residents. Thus, both Panama and Luxembourg learned the hard way why this was the case because of tax leaks in their respective jurisdictions.

Their experiences provided good guidance for other offshore, onshore and midshore financial centres. OFCs basically offer preferential tax options, including in some destinations, beneficial privacy, and financial terms. Onshore financial centres (ONFCs) do not usually offer preferential tax options and are usually located in advanced economies with superior financial infrastructures, but tend to follow closely international regulatory rules, and in particular those to do with corporate transparency and corporate governance (CG). Midshore financial centres could be cross-breeds of OFCs and ONFCs offering the benefits of more favourable tax rates that usually abide by international tax laws and standards, as exemplified by Ireland, Hong Kong, Singapore, Labuan, and Malta.[699]

Midshore financial centres, such as the Labuan International Business Financial Centre (Labuan IBFC), generally tend do the right things, meaning their activities adhere to domestic and international laws, standards, and best practices. In the case of the Labuan IBFC, it involved committing to tough OECD's rules and standards for OFCs. It also meant having world-class regulatory and financial regulations that

698. H. Lenz. 2020. 'Aggressive tax avoidance by managers of multinational companies as a violation of their moral duty to obey the law: A Kantian rationale', *Journal of Business Ethics*, Vol. 165(2020): 681-697.

699. TBF Finance. 2021. 'What is the difference between offshore, onshore, and mid-shore companies?'; Signature Trust. 2020. 'An Offshore, Onshore or a Midshore jurisdiction', *Signature Trust 20/5/20*.

Labuan IBFC could claim to possess. Labuan IBFC ergo opted to compete internationally for FDIs and global financial services participation on the basis of its world-class physical infrastructure, world-class information communication technology (ICT) facilities, world-class networking system, world-class business support ecosystem, world-class centre of Islamic financial products, and above all world-class living conditions reinforced by socio-economic-political stability. All these were further complemented by a comparable competitive corporate tax regime.[700] This, indeed, helped to explain its stellar reputation as a midshore IBFC.

As more and more nations strived to avoid excessive or disproportionate tax haven practices, it would be important to appreciate the compelling reasons for this. This had a lot to do with IFFs, especially from developing economies. The World Bank considered IFFs as money illegally earned or used that crossed borders. The IFFs concept emerged in the 1990s and was linked initially with capital flight, but had grown to be gradually employed to refer to cross-border movements of capital connected with nefarious activities. In other words, money illegal earned, transferred, or used that crossed borders. IFFs could be categorized under three domains. They could be illegal acts, like corruption and tax evasion; they could be the outcomes of illegal acts, like smuggling and trafficking; or money applied for illegal purposes, like the funding of organized crimes and terrorism. Such illegally transferred funds would be of particular importance to the economy of developing and poor countries.

IFFs reduced domestic resources and tax revenues required for funding poverty-eradication initiatives and necessary infrastructures in developing economies. As such, IFFs have been receiving increasing global attention, especially by global CSOs, like TJNs, and multilateral developmental institutions, like the IMF, World Bank, and the Asian Development Bank (ADB). While IFFs reduced the revenue base for developmental purposes, they could be said to be symptomatic of other matters that disrupted poverty reduction and shared prosperity initiatives, like vested rent-seeking interests; weak transparency; flawed governance and accountability; and above all erosion of trust. Nevertheless, there had yet to be consensus as to whether tax avoidance should be considered as part of IFFs. This implied that interpretations of estimates of IFFs would have to take account of this point.

Estimates on IFFs were inherently difficult to do, given that these originated from illegal activities, but there seemed to be general consensus on their rising levels. Global Financial Integrity (GFI) estimated that between 2003 to 2012, developing and emerging economies lost USD 6.6 trillion in IFFs, with illicit flows increasing at a staggering average of 9.4% annually, about twice as fast as global gross domestic product (GDP).[701] GFI, however, cautioned that its estimate was highly conservative, as it did not account for movements of bulk cash, mispricing of services, and many kinds of money laundering. The GFI IFFs estimates have been used in most forums, as there

700. P. Goncalves. 2019. 'Feature: Labuan IBFC- The gateway to Asia-Pacific', *International Investment 2/9/19*.
701. D. Kar & J. Spanjers. 2014. 'Illicit financial flows from developing countries: 2003-2012', *GFI 16 December 2014*.

were no comparable data with reasonable stature. Its estimates have been criticized for not paying proportionate attention on the channels employed.[702]

Nevertheless, other advocacy groups drew on its findings, the UN Office on Drugs and Crime, and the IMF to similarly reach the general conclusion that developing economies lost at least USD 1 trillion, and potentially much more annually to illicit activity that could have been used for funding various urgent development activities in these economies.[703] The insights generated were backed up by five policy proposals designed to promote greater transparency to the global financial system. These included calls requiring companies to publicly disclose their beneficial owners, publishing company payments to governments for natural resource extraction projects, automatically exchanging financial information between countries for exposing tax evaders, requiring multinationals to publicly report financial information on a CbC basis, and ensuring that government data was published in open, easily accessible formats to empower citizens and civil society to hold ether leaders accountable.[704]

Research had been suggesting that four distinctive groups contributed to IFFs with individuals participating in more than one of such activities. They included MNCs, corrupt officials, tax evaders, and criminal entrepreneurs.[705] There were multiple incentives for moving around illegally generated money internationally, rather than holding it domestically. For individuals, they were undertaken for portfolio diversification purposes; for better risk management; for hiding financial assets from national authorities; and for navigating around currency controls. For MNCs, it was about arbitraging on tax rates differentials, foreign exchange restrictions, and political risk managing. Recent scandals revealed by the EC have suggested the massive powers of global MNCs to manipulate the tax systems of both developing and developed economies with the help of global service providers, or global tax consultants.

The magnitudes of IFFs would continue to depend on crude estimates because of its inherent nature. The notion had been notably poorly defined, and accordingly has no single agreed definition.[706] This could be attributed in large part to the breath of the term 'illicit', defined by the Oxford Dictionary as 'forbidden by law, rules or custom' and ergo conveniently used interchangeably with 'illegal' by many. However, financial flows forbidden by rules or customs might not necessarily be illegal as these could incorporate those that could be socially and/or morally unacceptable, but not necessarily legally so. This perspective would align with developments in criminology that have increasingly criticized the limitations of the crime-led approach.

Among which, was the view that crime could be a social construct based on value judgments that varied across time and geography thereby undermining it as a

702. Reuter. 2017. 'Illicit financial flows and governance: The importance of disaggregation', *World Development Report 1/1/17*.
703. D. McNair, J. Kraus, K. McKiernan & S. McKay. 2014. 'The trillion-dollar scandal', *One Organization Report 2014*; GFI. 2014. 'GFI welcomes ONE Campaign's report on the "Trillion-Dollar-Scandal" of illicit financial flows', *GFI 2/9/14*.
704. *Supra* note [703]. GFI. 2014.
705. P. Reuter. 2017. 'Illicit financial flows and governance: The importance of disaggregation'. Background Paper for World Development Report 2017.
706. A. Cobham & P. Jansky. 2020. *Estimating illicit financial flows: A critical guide to the data, methodologies, and findings*, Oxford: Oxford University Press.

consistent basis for comparison, and the further contention that crime as a category excluded other serious harms, like poverty and pollution. By way of example, commercial tax evasions impacting low-income economies, where tax authorities with limited administrative capacity would unlikely uncover or effectively challenged the miscreants in court, compared with the equivalent behaviours in high-income economies with relatively better empowered authorities. This would therefore result in systematically and wrongly understating the scale of the problem in lower-income and lower-capacity countries, when a strictly legal definition of IFF is applied. The phenomenon for which the world has been grappling with pertained to hidden, cross-border flows, where either the illicit origin of capital, or the illicit nature of transactions engaged in was deliberately obscured.

Going by the above contentions, three components for IFFs had been suggested, namely grand corruption accounting for just a few percent; laundering of the proceeds of crime between a quarter and a third; and 'commercial tax evasions' via the manipulation of trade practices, the largest by far accounting for about two-thirds of the problem.[707] When distinguished by motivations, four components could be identified. These referred to market regulatory abuse, tax abuse, power abuse, and proceeds of crime.[708] This categorization in turn identified three major actors in IFFs, namely private actors, public officeholders, and criminal groups.

As different kinds of IFFs deployed multiple channels, clean or unpolluted estimates of individual IFF types would be hard to come by. Worth mentioning here though is that IFFs are not capital flights that had been portfolio investment responses to capital controls and problems typically found in lower-income economies. Nevertheless, there had been occasions of overlap for the two flows in some measurement approaches. Increasing attention has gravitated to the nature of companies' tax abuses and the extent of their inclusions in the definitions of IFFs. These have expanded from the two categories of illegal tax evasions and legal avoidance to three, namely, illegal evasion, unlawful avoidance, and lawful or successful avoidance, and possibly grey areas between each.[709]

The wider definition for IFFs as alluded to above reflected harm rather than strict illegality found also in UN documents that preceded the global, political agreement on the SDGs, and in particular MNC tax avoidance, as stressed in the United Nations Economic Commission in Africa Conference (UNECA) High Level Panel Report on IFFs from Africa, and subsequently in the report of the High Level Panel of Eminent Persons to the UN Secretary-General. This much simpler outline of IFFs into legal, unlawful, and criminal categories helped to show behaviour types, extending from tax compliance to lawful tax avoidance, unlawful tax avoidance, market/regulatory abuse, illicitly transferred, tax evasion, proceed of corruption, and proceeds of thefts to profits of illegal markets to culminate in licit or illicit flows when transferred abroad.[710]

707. R.W. Baker. 2005. *Capitalism's Achilles heel: Dirty money and how to renew the free-market system*, New Jersey: Wiley.
708. A. Cobham. 2014. 'Benefits and costs of the IFF targets for the post-2015 development agenda'.
709. S. Picciotto. 2018. 'Why tax avoidance is illicit', *International Centre for Tax and Development (ICTD)*.
710. A. Cobham & P. Jansky. 2017. 'Illicit financial flows: An overview'.

The controversial inclusions of aggressive tax avoidance schemes contributed to further controversies. Little has been known about the relative importance of component sources, or of the channels that were applied to move funds overseas, and which would vary over time and across economies.[711] Exchange of insights on the probable impacts of different control measures had been likened to the exchange of impressions, rather than the outcome of any systematic analysis. This state of affairs was not necessarily the consequence of patchy research insights, but showed more the lack of any sustained research agenda. Meanwhile, the world would depend extensively on the efforts and contributions of the GFI, the TJN, and various research outputs from dedicated individual researchers and those of the OECD and the World Bank Group.

But, importantly, IFFs could end up in financial institutions in developed economies, like the US and the UK, including in tax havens like Switzerland, the BVI, Lichtenstein, and Luxembourg. GFI had further suggested that around 45% of IFFs ended up in OFCs, and the rest in developed economies. It further claimed that these had not been chance happenings. These had been enabled or facilitated by both developing and developed economies and their institutions and global financial service providers that enjoyed enormous profits as active participants of such massive thefts of money from developing economies.

The general idea has been to make tax policies more transparent, including public disclosures of all tax holidays, as well as names of officials making such decisions. These could reduce the risks of corruption and the opportunities for businesses to abuse tax holiday provisions that could drive IFFs further. International initiatives to curb the proceeds of crimes had already been undertaken for more than twenty years by the Global Forum on Taxation, the Financial Services Task Force (FSTF), and the UN Convention against Drugs, Transnational Organized Crime and Corruption. These have produced mixed outcomes suggesting more and better initiatives would be needed. Coordinated efforts would also be required from all market participants, including governments, multilateral institutions, CSOs, global financial institutions, shadow banking institutions, and so on. Actions could involve combating illegal activities and identifying and sanctioning serious and substantial illegal tax evasions.

GFI suggested detections and deterrence of cross-border tax evasions, eliminations of the use of anonymous shell companies, strengthening AML laws and practices, curtailing trade mispricing, and enhancing transparency of MNCs via OECD's BEPS project. Incidentally, Goal 16 of the 2015 UN SDGs in this connection contained particular commitments to reduce IFFs. Equivalent commitments could also be found in declarations from the G7 and G20 economies. This aside, the World Bank Group as a global development institution would have the technical expertise, knowledge, and convening power to bring together developed and developing economies, international business organizations, CSOs like Oxfam and TJN, and standards-setting bodies like the IOSCO to collaborate on reducing IFFs and returning illegal assets. All these parties could collaborate to coordinate global activities and country work and to help shape global standards.

711. *Supra* note [705]. Reuter. 2017.

Indeed, it was the release of the PP in April 2016 that provided the global spotlight on the IFFs phenomenon. Hitherto, interests on this were confined largely to global developmental agencies, the OECD, the EU, CSOs, academic researchers, and policymakers. The PP were said to be relatively bigger than the 2010 WikiLeaks and Snowden's NSA leak in 2013 combined. They comprised 2.6 terabytes of data from the Panamanian law firm Mossack Fonseca. The data suggested links of about 140 world leaders from more than 50 economies to secret offshore accounts in 21 different tax havens. The PRP that followed shortly thereafter leaked around 13.4 million confidential documents from Appleby, Estera, and Asiaciti Trust again to the ICIJs, just like the PP. It revealed the setting up of companies and bank accounts in low-tax jurisdictions, with the list of names dominated by US companies and individuals, Fortune 500 companies, financial institutions, high-net-worth individuals, including politically exposed persons (PEPs) from various countries.

While offshore accounts and investments were generally common, US laws required reporting and recordkeeping. These included know-your-customer (KYC) obligations under money-laundering regulations and revised Customer Due Diligence (CDD) rules for financial institutions, hedge funds, private equity firms, and trust companies; Foreign Account Tax Compliant Act (FATCA) and the OECD Common Reporting Standard (CRS) for foreign financial institutions; disclosure requirements for all-cash real estate purchases over particular locations for domestic title entities; internal revenue service (IRS) disclosure requirements for foreign beneficial owners of US limited liability companies; reporting non-US transactions by entities and trusts; and reporting of foreign assets and accounts by US persons. The leaked information from both the PP and PRP could lead to investigations into money laundering, tax evasion, breach of the Foreign Corrupt Practices Act, and other charges, including investigations in the US of tax evasion in other economies. Those impacted might well be advised to resolve any past non-compliance, or engage in voluntary disclosure initiatives where needed.

The use and abuse in the employment of offshore accounts had been controversial. It involved individuals and businesses holding financial assets in low-tax jurisdictions like the Panama and elsewhere to achieve privacy and avoid or evade taxation. Though tax avoidance schemes were largely legal, especially those designed by global tax consultants, shell companies were generally perceived to be linked to illegal activities and much of what went on in the underground economy. The major revelations of both the PP and PRP were in the details provided as evidence of the dealings of powerful political personalities and financial elites.

The impact of the revelations would likely be felt in gradual phases as the detailed analysis flowed over time, irrespective of whether significant global tax and related changes taking place as a consequence. The three major effects included: first, the lost creditability of some major political figures, some household name MNCs, and some prominent financial elites; second, that corruptions had been more widespread than generally thought, involving governments, political leaders, private individuals, and many kinds of businesses; and third, in response, governments and regulators committed to the launching of investigations, with political leaders and policymakers promising to enact legislations to curb such practices. Pressures, since then, have mounted for tax reforms, crackdowns on tax evasions, and international collaborations to tame the illicit activities expanded. However, these planned actions might have to be tampered with caution, to distinguish legal from illegal financial activities.

The PP lend support to earlier research efforts. Financial service providers, such as Mossack collaborated with more than 14,000 banks, other law firms, company incorporators, and other financial enablers to set up elaborately designed special-purpose vehicles (SPVs), shell companies, foundations, and trusts to house both legal and nefarious activities. Some 8% of global financial wealth of households was estimated to be held in tax havens, with three-quarters of which go unreported in official statistics. There appeared to be wide variations between economies, with estimates for US at 4%, Europe some 10%, Latin America some 20%, Africa some 30%, and in Russia some 50%.[712]

Further, some 40% of the world's FDIs flowed through tax havens amounting to USD 15 trillion passed through empty corporate shells, with no real business activities, and more than 85% of those USD 15 trillion phantom investments hosted by them.[713] These flows grew about half over the five years to 2017, rising to 38% of total FDI from about 31% in 2010.[714] Phantom capital in 2017 alone was equivalent of the combined GDP of China and Germany, while Luxembourg's estimated USD 4 trillion in phantom FDI inflows alone was equivalent to annual direct investment in the US.[715]

Thus, OFCs with enormous inward and outward investment positions blurred macro statistics on FDIs. Foreigners held foreign securities around USD 2 trillion via Switzerland bank deposits and portfolios. These were equivalent to China's foreign exchange reserves.[716] Moreover, in 2008, only one-third of all foreign securities in Swiss banks belonged to Swiss savers. The US Council of Economic Advisors according to media report estimated that US-controlled corporations domiciled in Cayman Islands and BVI appeared to have generated profits higher than the GDPs of these islands, like 1,578% of Bermuda's GDP, 1,430% of Cayman Islands' GDP, and 1,009% of the GDP of the BVI.[717]

Offshore tax schemes were claimed to be responsible for about two-thirds of the decline in effective tax rates since 1998 in the US alone. This represented an estimated

712. G. Zucman. 2015. *The hidden health of nations: The scourge of tax havens.* Chicago: The University of Chicago Press; G. Zucman. 2013. 'The missing wealth of nations, are Europe and the U.S. net debtors or net creditors?, *Quarterly Journal of Economics*, Vol. 128(3): 1321-1364.
713. J. Damgaard, T. Elkjaer & N. Johannesen. 2017. 'The rise of phantom investments: Empty corporate shells in tax havens undermine tax collection in advanced, emerging, and developing economies', *Finance & Development September 2019*: 11-13; D. Jannick, T. Elkjaer & N. Johannesen. 2019. 'What is real and what is not in the global FDI network', *IMF Working Paper WP/19/274 December 2019*; P.R. Lane & G.M. Milesi-Ferretti. 2018. 'The external wealth of nation revisited: International financial integration in the aftermath of the global financial crisis', *IMF Economic Review*, Vol. 66(1): 189-222; P. Goncalves. 2019. 'Tax avoidance drives nearly 40% of global FDI: IMF', *International Investment 11/9/19*.
714. *Supra* note [713]. Jannick, Elkjaer & Johannesen. 2019; Lane & Milesi-Ferretti. 2018; Damgaard, Elkjaer & Johannesen. 2017.
715. *Supra* note [713]. Jannick, Elkjaer & Johannesen. 2019; Lane & Milesi-Ferretti. 2018; Damgaard, Elkjaer & Johannesen. 2017.
716. *Supra* note [712]. Zucman. 2015; 2013.
717. *Supra* note [712]. Zucman. 2015; 2013.

loss of over USD 100 billion for the US Treasury in 2013, while the EC in turn estimated that tax avoidance in EU economies amounted some EUR 50-70 billion annually in lost tax revenues. Indeed, further research revealed that tax haven use was strongly correlated with developed-country MNCs owning subsidiaries in developing countries, frequently marked by significant market imperfections and weak institutions.[718] This relationship also held for developed-country MNCs owning subsidiaries in locations marked by significant capital flight. Such market imperfections had significant impacts on the developing world, as it removed wealth and income which could have been deployed to finance public expenditure targeted at the poor.[719]

The above-said revelations generated various serious policy implications. Foremost, developing economies need to strengthen their rules pertaining to beneficial ownership of companies, trusts, partnerships, and foundations. Enhanced understanding of who ultimately owned or had legal control within their borders could enable greater oversight by the public aside from providing incentive to representatives to hold these corporations and their owners to better account.[720] This could also enable better oversight and monitoring compliance thereby enabling these economies to pass legislations to mitigate the degree of profit shifting to lower revenue losses.

Domestic policy though might not be adequate to curb the profit shifting and wealth extraction out of developing economies, suggesting strongly that the international system of corporate taxation based on the arms-length principle would need to be reformed quickly as the rules were designed at a time when the role of MNCs were much less significant than today. Also, the pervasiveness of digital MNCs and their ability to transact goods and services in markets without needing a physical presence meant that profit shifting was becoming more pervasive. Research has also shown further evidence for this trend with revelations that MNCs in more digital industries had less conventional FDI than less digitally oriented MNCs and instead had higher incentives to invest in subsidiaries with fiscal and financial motivations.[721]

For its part, the OECD's BEPS project achieved some success with respect to recognizing these challenges, and had accordingly stressed much greater transparency pertaining to CbC reporting; but it would be crucial for the global community to collaborate in the reforming of international taxation, especially with regard to data and methodological matters when implementing BEPS.[722] The pace of reforms though could be delayed by the departure of the US and the EU from the OECD/G20 Inclusive Framework on BEPS that had put significant stress on trying to ensure that profit were taxed where economic activity and value creation took place. The idea has been that

718. A. Ahmed, C. Jones & Y. Temouri. 2020. 'The relationship between MNE tax haven use and FDI into developing economies characterized by capital flight', *Transnational Corporations*, Vol. 27(2): 1-30.
719. *Supra* note [718]. Ahmed, Jones & Temouri. 2020.
720. *Supra* note [718]. Ahmed, Jones & Temouri. 2020.
721. B. Casella & L. Formenti. 2018. 'FDI in the digital economy: A shift to asset-light international footprints', *Transnational Corporations*, Vol. 25(1): 101-130.
722. D. Bradbury, T. Hanappi & A. Moore. 2018. 'Estimating the fiscal effects of base erosion and profit shifting: Data availability and analytical issues', *Transnational Corporations*, Vol. 25(2): 91-106.

this would eventually lead to a system of unitary taxation and formulary apportionment that could go a long way towards curbing profit shifting and mitigating the impact of tax havens.

The OECD had on 12 October 2020 released over 900 pages of documents pertaining to its ongoing initiative to resolve the challenges of taxing the digital economy. This work started with the OECD recognizing that current tax systems did not sufficiently address the ability of enterprises to participate in an economy independent of physical presence. This led the OECD to work towards a new global tax system via two pillars. Pillar 1 would involve introducing a new tax right on consumer facing businesses and certain highly digitized businesses for jurisdictions wherein users or consumers reside, even when taxpayers have no physical presence in the jurisdiction. Pillar 2 would involve a global minimum tax applicable to all large multinational groups, irrespective of industry. The use of digital sales taxes, enacted unilaterally by various economies, like France and the UK, could undermine the multilateral framework, and with developing economies being also marginalized from the process.[723]

The OECD October 2020 Blueprint already deliberated in various public forums told a tale of many unanswered questions, with the 137 members of the Inclusive Framework yet to reach accord on a specific implementation plan. This signalled a delay in the timeline for global agreement till mid-2021; and could be indicative of the challenges encountered by the OECD in achieving political consensus on issues that would see a reallocation of global taxing rights between territories under Pillar 1, as well as a potential impact on jurisdictional tax sovereignty under Pillar 2.[724] As alluded to earlier, the OECD blueprint appeared to be a relatively better option than letting the cost of inaction persist, even though sceptics have warned about this being accompanied by separate set of trade-offs and significant procedural and administrative hurdles, as well as the risk of the new US concessions not being ratified by the US Congress.

There could likely be two important outcomes for businesses.[725] Countries would first push forward with unilateral tax measures focused on remote activities, like digital services tax (DST), and changes to indirect tax regimes. This would lead to a complex compliance environment for MNCs, given the varying scope and focus of these different measures around the world. Second, a new wave of tax disputes focusing on value creation would emerge as many jurisdictions were of the view that the current global tax framework did not provide a sustainable basis for the allocation of value around parts of a multinational group. This signalled harder work and difficult negotiations ahead in the reforming of the global system of corporate taxation and the elimination of harmful tax practices impacting developing economies.

The PP and PRP, together with past research insights, such as those alluded to earlier, catalysed governments in more than 70 economies to launch over 150 investigations, inquiries, audits, and probes into the financial affairs of thousands of

723. *Supra* note [718]. Ahmed, Jones & Temouri. 2020.
724. R. Robertson & P. Daly. 2021. 'Taxation of the digital economy and pushing fiscal boundaries'; R. Robertson. 2020. 'The OECD and the ticking clock-What a delay in global agreement may mean', *Bloomberg Tax 3/11/20*.
725. *Supra* note [724]. Robertson & Daly. 2021; Robertson. 2020.

people and corporations inked to the revelations. Many governments acted, but lesser democracies appeared to ward off the implications as Western propaganda to undermine their political leaderships. For its part, the PP investigation had been awarded the Pulitzer Prize for explanatory reporting.[726]

Tax evasion, tax avoidance, and avoidance of regulatory oversights were of different implications. All these were featured in OFCs in varying combinations in different tax havens or jurisdictions. This implied OFCs could broadly be tax havens, secrecy havens, regulation-lite havens, or any combinations of these three. Tax havens and their variants have been shown to be linked to both legal and illegal activities undertaken by individuals and businesses. Curbing both tax evasion and tax avoidance required the use of appropriate laws and reporting rules and norms.

The abusive use of special purpose entities (SPEs) or structured investment vehicles (SIVs) conduits, and other off-balance sheet devices by Wall Street corporations have led to the kind of problems seen earlier in the 2000 Enron and WorldCom debacles. That led to regulatory responses like the 2002 SOX Act in the US, the 2006 corporate law reforms in the UK, and so on. The 2007 GFC saw more significantly much larger examples of the abusive use of securitization and structured financial products. The 2010 Dodd-Frank legislation in the US and updated CG codes in the UK targeted the misuse and abusive use of such financial products. The PP revelations suggested that more would have to be done to curb these abusive practices facilitated by tax and regulatory havens. The OECD's BEPS project would be a step in the right direction, but further revisions would be needed to make the measures more effective.

This is because various very large US MNCs in particular are alleged to have collaborated with various EU Member States. Cases revealed by the ICIJ, included: Apple in Ireland having to pay only 12.5% tax; Amazon in the UK reporting minimal revenue as the UK online store revenues flowed through a Luxembourg branch that reimbursed the British for the cost of distributing goods; Starbucks in the Netherlands not having to pay any taxes for four years; Fiat in Luxembourg being able to reduce its tax liability by EUR 20-30 million since 2012; and McDonald's in Luxembourg not having to pay corporate tax on its European and Russian subsidiaries for more than eight years.[727] The European Commission (EC) has earlier in October 2015 assessed these practices as unlawful state aid, but the General Court annulled these state decisions in September 2019.[728] The PRP revealed that the number of Slovak companies moving their registered offices to jurisdictions in tax havens had increased considerably from 1,510 in 2005 to 4,362 in 2014, showing an increase of some 189%.[729] The most used tax havens by them included 1,154 in the Netherlands, 1,028 in the US, 750 in Cyprus, 393 in Luxembourg, 205 in Seychelles, and 155 in the Isla of Man; and where the most common motives for their use of these tax havens were tax savings, arising likely from tax evasion.

726. L. Harding. 2017. 'Panama Papers investigation wins Pulitzer prize', *The Guardian 11/4/17*.
727. G. Lenartova. 2020. 'The economic and social consequences of tax havens in the world', *SHS Web Conferences*, Vol. 83(2020): 1-8.
728. Deloitte. 2019. 'EU General Court rules in state aid cases on transfer pricing rulings', *Tax at Hand 25 September 2019*.
729. *Supra* note [727]. Lenartova. 2020.

The above illustrations imply that the numerous initiatives and measures taken by the OECD and other international institutions have not been generally effective, and further suggesting that the fight against tax havens need to be more vigorous, stronger and more effective for all component professionals, and politicians, nationally and globally.[730] Also, tackling tax havens would not be comprehensive enough. Initiatives are needed in other clusters of global finance, other directions, as well as other relevant laws and regulations.

This is why the recent June 2021 Finance Ministers' agreement of the ambitious two Pillar global solution to address the tax challenges flowing from an increasingly globalized and digital global economic is historic and in the right direction. Via Pillar 1, the largest and most profitable MNCs would be required to pay tax in the countries where they operate, and not just where they have their headquarters. The rule is applicable to global enterprises with at least a 10% profit margin. This would see 20% of any profit above the 10% margin reallocated and then subjected to tax in the countries where they operate. Via Pillar 2, the G7 agreed to the principle of at least 15% global minimum corporation tax operated on a country-by-country (CbC) basis thereby creating a more level playing field, as well as cracking down hard on tax avoidance. These measures are not perfect and indeed have already been criticized by tax experts and other tax advocates as being not really good enough for developing and emerging economies, as highlighted in the previous chapter.[731] Still, compromises are needed to provide the initial steps.

Given the expanding development needs of all economies, their tax base needs strengthening. This applied particularly to developing and EMEs. Images and narratives of political leaders, financial elites, and MNCs making use of different rules to game the global financial system need to be responded, not by mere rhetoric, but also by concrete globally coordinated concrete actions targeting the source of the problems, as highlighted here. This required attending to flawed business reporting standards, and abusive tax and secrecy haven practices. Only then perhaps could large proportions of the global population be convinced that everybody from individuals to political leaders and MNCs all play by the same rules, with no exceptions. This might sound idealistic, but worth fighting for, especially when linked with the 2015 UN SDGs.

As the world heads towards the post-COVID-19 global pandemic in the immediate coming years, global attention would be drawn to the onward march of the OECD DSTs and other gross revenue taxes, dissatisfactions of less developed economies, ongoing transatlantic tax tensions, the relentless pressures for tax transparencies, the COVID-19 ongoing crisis and tax implications, and the search for safe harbours or shelter for the potential economic and financial storms, particular preparations could be made. These could include giving continuing support for tax multilateralism, finding answers on how to equitably tax the profits of businesses able to operate remotely without physical presence, promoting greater tax transparency, and joint consultations

730. *Supra* note [727]. Lenartova. 2020.

731. J. Ghosh. 2021. 'The G7's tax reform could entrench global inequality', *International Politics and Society (IPS) 11 June 2021*.

between businesses, CSOs, and policymakers about how taxes could rise in the least damaging way.[732]

To be sure, even before the onset of COVID-19, conversations on taxes had always been fractious. Rising fiscal concerns have not helped with discussions and seemed stalled at both national and international levels. Recent leading business dialogues suggested that business leaders were more concerned about uncertainties in the global tax systems, than tax rates.[733] Certainty though could be achieved when businesses engaged or collaborated more with policymakers, who also needed to work with one another to harmonize national and international agendas. Taxes at play and in negotiations could generate disproportionate media and political attention compared to the revenues they raise, which means achieving compromise here could increase the capacity of negotiators and others to focus more strategic areas with greater potentials for increasing revenues.

Nationalistic short-term policies, while popular with domestic audience, could end up doing more harm than good in a hypermobile and highly linked world. The aligning of tax systems internationally had been ongoing for many decades, but now with the economic damages wrought by COVID-19, there would be more than ample justifications in compromise to improve trust and certainty for individuals and corporate taxpayers, especially by looking at national tax policies from a more international perspective, and a strong bias for the fairness agenda. Still, it could be more feasible economically, and politically more acceptable at both national and international levels to compromise and end the patchwork of isolated actions leading to tit-for-tat tax wars that hurt people more than businesses, besides slowing the rate of progress.[734]

Most economies aspired to have some kind of international financial centre that could help to link their domestic economies to those parts pf the world that matter to their economic survival and prosperity. As discussed in this book, these could be onshore, midshore, or offshore that could best serve their economic agendas. Strong evidences of IFFs in some of these OFCs have given warnings of potential more serious damages occurring if no focus is given to the curbing of such and related nefarious activities. But these require strong and consistent collaborations between powerful economically advanced economies, multilateral development institutions, the global banking and shadow banking systems, impacted developing and EMEs, as well as multinationals of all stripes to reach consensus on new global tax rules that could make global and offshore finance stronger, inclusive, and fairer, by relying more on transparency, and less on secrecy such as now peddled by some tax havens.

732. W. Morris. 2020. 'The gathering storm? The other side of the COVID portal', *Bloomberg Tax 2/11/20*.
733. C. Stubbings. 2021. 'Taxing times require a new era of compromise', *PwC 1/2/21*.
734. *Supra* note [733]. Stubbings. 2021.